IN DEFENSE OF CHILDHOOD

IN DEFENSE OF
CHILDHOOD

Protecting Kids' Inner Wildness

CHRIS MERCOGLIANO

Beacon Press

BOSTON

BEACON PRESS
25 Beacon Street
Boston, Massachusetts 02108-2892
www.beacon.org

Beacon Press books
are published under the auspices of
the Unitarian Universalist Association of Congregations.

10 09 08 07   8 7 6 5 4 3 2 1

This book is printed on acid-free paper that meets the uncoated paper ANSI/NISO
specifications for permanence as revised in 1992.

Text design and composition by Yvonne Tsang
at Wilsted & Taylor Publishing Services

Library of Congress Control Number: 2007924360
ISBN 978-0-8070-3286-2

I dedicate this book to
SAINT ANTHONY OF PADUA,
the patron saint of lost things.

CONTENTS

INTRODUCTION

Who would envy Huck's battered childhood? Yet he
enjoyed something too many children are denied and
which adults can provide: opportunities to undertake
odysseys of self-discovery outside the goal-driven,
overstructured realities of contemporary childhood.
—Stephen Mintz, *Huck's Raft: A History of American Childhood*

CHILDHOOD IS IN TROUBLE. The relentless forces of modernity are pressing in from all sides, slowly but surely squeezing out the novelty, the independence, the adventure, the wonder, the innocence, the physicality, the solitude—the juice, if you will—from the lives of today's children.

This book is not the first commentary on the dizzying technological, sociocultural, and educational changes of the past century. In the pages to come I will touch on a great many of them, but my mission here is to go deeper: to sound an alarm about the impact of those changes on the luminescent spark that animates the young, serves as the source of their uniqueness and creativity, and supplies the energy and the impetus for them to become who they are intended to become. I have chosen to call this spark "inner wildness."

Why "inner wildness"? "Inner" denotes its approximate location, which is deep beneath the human surface, out of reach of the conscious mind. "Wildness" defies description by these linear symbols we call words but attempts to depict an elusive essence that strives mightily to resist the control of others. The term also invokes the urgent and parallel importance of preserving the earth's outer wildness, the wildlife and wild places without which existence would become a barren exercise.

The idea for this book emerged while I was in the middle of writing another, about how the unusual school where I have worked since 1973 assists students with behavioral and cognitive difficulties without resorting to the use of biopsychiatric labels or drugs. I had been researching the question of why there was a sudden epidemic of children—primarily boys—whom mainstream scientists and medical professionals claim to be suffering from a chemical imbalance in their brains, most likely genetic in origin. In evolutionary terms, how could as many as ten million kids have come down with a neurological disease virtually overnight? The idea defied reason. After I'd carefully sifted through the voluminous literature on attention deficit hyperactivity disorder, it made even less sense to me.

A clue arrived in the mail when a dear friend, who has spent the better part of her forty-year career as a special-education teacher on Native American reservations in Minnesota and New Mexico, sent me an essay she had come across in the *New York Times*. Rosalie is equally dubious about the idea that kids who can't sit still in class and concentrate on academic tasks, or who refuse to do as they are told, have a medical disorder.

The article, "A Strange Malady Called Boyhood," written by Pulitzer Prize–winning science writer Natalie Angier, suggested that there has been a subtle but relentless shift in our culture's definition of what constitutes a "normal" boy. The nineteenth-century Tom Sawyer / Huck Finn archetype—brash, willful, naughty, rambunctious, aggressive, and always dirty—is no longer acceptable. Today, parents, teachers, psychologists, and pediatricians alike increasingly view the temperamental and behavioral distance between such boys and an ever narrower definition of normality as evidence of pathology. Such boys, they feel, are sick enough to require medication. And the powerful psychotropic drugs with which they then "treat" them enforce society's new definition all the way down to the biochemical level.[1]

Angier's ideas resonated with my experience at the Albany Free School, a noncoercive, democratic, inner-city school for sixty-five students ages two through fourteen, where we permit Sawyeresque behavior in children as long as it doesn't violate the rights and sensibilities of others. Here, we eschew assigning labels to kids who don't fit in or measure up. We say that a child who is constantly on the move is *highly* active, which is a descriptive term, not *hyperac-* tive, which is a prescriptive one. Since the school is always buzzing with noise and activity, highly active kids don't really stand out and are not considered to have or to be a problem. Moreover, we've noticed that when highly active children can run, jump, climb, yell, dance, dig holes in the sandbox, and hammer ten-penny nails into two-by-fours in the wood shop to their hearts' content, they gradually settle down and develop the ability to modulate their energy level. The trouble begins when you suppress their need to move and do.

Similarly, we say that kids with minds like hummingbirds, who aren't yet inclined to spend long stretches of time reading, writing, and figuring, are flighty or easily distracted, not that they have attention deficit disorder. The interesting thing about these children is that given the chance to pay attention to what *they* want to pay attention to, they will often spend hours at a time working on a drawing, or a birdhouse, or a new skateboard move. When it is *their* choice, they will devour good books and stories and keep asking for more. But if you try to force them when the desire and excitement are missing, that is when the trouble begins.

Meanwhile, the redefinition of childhood norms urged me to reflect back on my own boyhood, which straddled the second half of the 1950s and the first half of the '60s. I began making comparisons between my youth and that of my father and grandfather on one hand and that of today's children on the other, now two generations hence. I noted the striking changes in the fundamental nature of play, of school, of work, of electronic media and their impact on childhood, and finally of adolescence—changes that affect girls just as much as boys, though sometimes in different ways.

Across this broad spectrum, one change in particular began to stand out as a sort of common denominator: today, virtually every arena of a child's life is subject to some form of adult mediation, supervision, or control. Kids go from before-school programs to school, from school to after-school programs, and from there to a host of extracurricular lessons and organized sports. Even the youth peer culture into which young people retreat to gain a sense of independence has become a commercial product created and promoted by adults—profit-hungry professionals interested only in exploiting an increasingly lucrative market, not in the inner well-being of the younger generation. As the CEO of MTV put it when asked how he regarded the huge influence his television empire has on children: "We don't just influence them—we own them."[2]

Suddenly it occurred to me that we are witnessing not only the taming of Mark Twain's wild boys but the systematic domestication of childhood itself.

Here is my argument in a nutshell: a pattern of domestication is established even as we draw our first breath, and it repeats itself at every stage throughout childhood. The problem begins at birth. In the name of risk management, current obstetrical practices have turned what was once a natural—you might say "wild"—process into a carefully scripted medical procedure. The technological interventions that are part and parcel of the modern hospital birth often cause serious breaks in the all-important mother-infant bond, which nature intends to occur immediately following the child's emergence from the womb. Recent neurological research shows that the skin and eye contact that takes place between mother and newborn when the baby is held at the left breast, close to the mother's heartbeat, is essential to the complete awakening of the brain centers that will accomplish the rapid-fire developmental steps that lie ahead.[3]

At the same time, according to child-development expert and author Joseph Chilton Pearce, the uninterrupted connection between mother and newborn activates a corresponding set of "birth intelligences" inside the mother. This instinctive form of knowing, which cannot be taught, enables her to communicate intuitively with the baby and respond confidently to his or her signals.[4]

In today's typical birth, however, the baby is immediately taken away from the mother and attended to by the delivery-room nurse, with numerous additional separations soon to follow over the course of the hospital stay. To make matters worse, more than 85 percent of American women are anesthetized during labor, and nearly 25 percent deliver by Caesarian section, a figure that is still rising.[5] Research indicates that infants are depressed for as much as a week after birth by maternal birth drugs and that the coming in of the mother's milk is delayed by twenty-four to thirty-six hours.[6] The result of this domestication is that the overwhelming majority of today's babies are being denied the instinctive, developmentally active beginning that was once their birthright, effectively sowing seeds of passivity that can last throughout their childhood.

Meanwhile, the same kind of cautious overmanagement that

governs childbirth has steadily crept into contemporary child rearing. Hyperconcern for their children's safety and development is causing mothers and fathers to monitor their kids' activities and whereabouts far more stringently than my mom ever did. Fearful that their children will be left behind once they start school, many parents also focus on formal learning at ever earlier stages of growth. Or parent substitutes—nannies, day-care providers, preschool teachers—do so in their stead. Oftentimes both occur.

As children grow older, there is the aforementioned proliferation of extracurricular programs and lessons. Solitude and reflection are lost in the constant shuffle from place to place and from structured activity to structured activity. The evolution of play reveals a similar trend.

A vivid example, which I think serves as a metaphor for what is happening to all areas of childhood leisure and recreation, is the change that has taken place in swimming. In my grandfather's day, children swam—usually unsupervised—in lakes, rivers, creeks, and old abandoned quarries. When my father was a child, public pools began to appear, providing children with two options: they could walk to the nearby pool, or, given the time and a serviceable bicycle, they could choose the wilder of the two venues. Fast-forward to my childhood: a high fence has been built around the quarry to keep out youthful swimmers. "No Swimming" signs have been posted along the riverbanks because the current is sometimes strong enough to endanger the inexperienced. But all is not lost. The pool has two diving boards, one a scary height above the water, which is deep enough to make it an exhilarating challenge to swim all the way down and touch the bottom. Yes, lifeguards are on hand to make certain that no one drowns; however, there remains at least a measure of daring and adventure. Now let's examine today's swimming pools. Diving boards have disappeared from a great many of them, and the majority of newly constructed pools no longer have deep ends—they are a uniform three and a half feet in depth, with white lines to create individual swimming lanes. If children are lucky, a permissive lifeguard might still let them jump into the water.

Meanwhile, our compulsory, factory-style, standards-driven model of education has become perhaps the largest single agent of childhood domestication. As I have already noted, students who are too untamed—and very little is fast becoming too much—are quickly subdued and brought back into the herd by means of bio-psychiatric labels and drugs. An argument could be made that these "misfits" are American society's canaries in the coal mine, a human warning signal for what is in store for more and more children if we don't soon pump oxygen into the cultural air they are forced to breathe. The demands of high-stakes testing have forced schools to eliminate nearly every vestige of physicality, imagination, and creativity from the curriculum; more than ever, classrooms are becoming places where kids spend their days like cloned sheep, grazing passively in a pasture of uniform right answers.

And so it goes with children's access to meaningful work. When I was a child, even as young as five, there were numerous opportunities to earn money. My first attempts to establish a regular income involved pulling my wagon around the neighborhood in search of two-cent-deposit bottles. In a good week I brought in as much as five bucks, not a bad paycheck for a kindergartener in 1959. Most important, that money was entirely mine to save or spend as I saw fit.

On hot summer days my young pals and I would set up a lemonade stand on the corner, an easier and even more lucrative enterprise than bottle collecting. Then, as soon as I was strong enough to wield a garden spade or snow shovel, pull a leaf rake, and operate a lawn mower, I graduated to a set of seasonal businesses that kept me flush with cash year-round. By the time I was seven I had my own bank account, and I can still remember the delight of watching my personal capital increase from the tens to the hundreds of dollars as I approached my teenage years.

Today, only on rare occasions do I see little kids hawking lemonade. Likewise, seldom can young entrepreneurs be found cutting their neighbors' grass or raking their leaves anymore. With the base of our economy having morphed from industry to service, child workers have largely been displaced by adult-operated franchises that perform household and landscape tasks on a subscription basis. Schoolwork has become the primary, and for some the only, job of childhood, displacing even household chores. Almost all of the children I know depend on their parents for money, which very often comes with strings attached—yet another blow to the sense of autonomy that feeds a young person's emerging sense of self.

Then, of course, there is the proliferating variety of electronic media that profoundly dominate the life of every child in America, regardless of geography, race, or social class. Media ecologist Neil Postman has argued that electronic media, particularly television, are in the process of causing childhood to disappear altogether. Bombarded twenty-four hours a day, seven days a week, by TV's adult imagery and information, children, Postman predicted nearly three decades ago, will soon revert to their pre-Renaissance status as miniature adults.[7]

Finally we arrive in the shifting sands of adolescence, and it is here that we encounter perhaps the most glaring signs that the domestication of childhood is already beginning to weigh heavily on young people. A rapidly increasing number of adolescents, according to a recent study by the University of Pennsylvania's Network on Transitions to Adulthood, are experiencing significant delays and difficulties in becoming full-fledged adults. Researchers have discovered that the average age at which young people reach the traditional markers of adulthood—finding a career, achieving financial independence, forming their own household, and starting a family—has taken a sudden statistical leap upward, with many people not achieving them at all until well after age thirty.[8] Such a striking change has led Canadian sociologist James Côté to coin the term "arrested adulthood" to describe this extended period of transitional limbo, a state into which some individuals appear to be settling permanently.[9]

Part of the problem, according to Côté—and here he is joined by historian of childhood Stephen Mintz—is that young people struggling to gain their footing in modern adulthood face a multitude of contradictions. On the one hand they are more fully integrated into the consumer economy than ever before, but on the other hand they are more segregated in their peer culture than ever before, with very little contact with adults other than their parents, teachers, and coaches. There is more space inside their homes, but less space outside. Technological progress continues to make life easier; at the same time it removes many of the mental and physical challenges that stimulate children's ability to think at the complex levels needed to succeed in the adult world that awaits them. And the biggest change of all is that young people are maturing sexually and psychologically at an ever earlier age, with many of them facing adult choices much sooner than previous generations did—and yet our society isolates and infantilizes them, offering very few positive ways for them to express their hard-won maturity. We give them, in other words, a maddening double message: grow up fast, but you really don't need to grow up at all.[10]

Thankfully, agree Côté and Mintz, there is an upside to the radical social and cultural changes confronting today's children. Their lives will be longer, healthier, and in most cases more materially prosperous than those of their predecessors. They will be less tied to child rearing, a trend that established itself in the previous generation: one-third of American women born in the 1950s never had children, and among women with professional careers the figure increases to nearly half. Both of these trends are ongoing. Because of the relaxing of traditional religious, cultural, and social barriers and taboos that has taken place over the past fifty years—as well as the reduction in racial and gender inequity—a majority of the younger generation will enjoy far more personal freedom and face far fewer external restrictions than generations past. The playing field, so to speak, will be more level and more open than ever before in human history.[11]

But such unprecedented potential is available only to those prepared to utilize it—young people who are independent, resilient, and self-aware enough to develop the attitudes and skills that one day will enable them to step confidently into adulthood with clear vision and a reliable sense of direction. For, writes inspirational author Maxine Schnall,

> Positive freedom is possible only for the person who is neither exclusively inner-directed nor exclusively other-directed, but a combination of the two—the self-steerer, if you will, whose compass is a set of *freely chosen* internal personal standards shaped by both parents and peers. The magnetic north is the individual's own particular sense of purpose.[12]

And so, too, will I argue in the following pages that only those fortunate young people who are allowed to lead unscripted, authentic childhoods will find themselves ready to become the authors of their own experience and lead lives filled with satisfaction, excitement, and distinction.

• • •

The demise of childhood is anything but a foregone conclusion. There is plenty that those of us who choose to involve ourselves in the lives of children can do to preserve and enhance their uniqueness, spontaneity, and exuberance.

On the microcosmic level parents, grandparents, and teachers can resuscitate the tradition of literacy by turning off the tube and putting away the videos and DVDs, no matter how educational they may be, and instead telling or reading exciting, engaging stories to children. Fairy tales are an especially good source of nourishment for children's inner wildness. Embedded in fairy tales, according to child psychiatrist Bruno Bettelheim and Jungian analyst Marie-Louise von Franz, are rich, archetypal symbols and themes that enable children to integrate rather than suppress the turbulent dimensions of their personalities.

On the macrocosmic level, school districts can band together to resist the current onslaught of federally mandated testing, which is punishing teachers and administrators as well as students. As of this writing, ten states have already joined to file a lawsuit that, if successful, will free those states from having to implement the No Child Left Behind Act. The plaintiffs argue that the testing is excessive and will force the schools to cut other important programs in order to fund it. Also, concerned parents, teachers, and activists are contributing to a national explosion of educational alternatives reminiscent of the 1960s and '70s, resulting in hundreds of new innovative schools, both public and private, in the last decade alone. Some parents decide to teach their children themselves: current estimates have as many as two million households—and 7 percent more each year—opting not to turn their kids over to a monolithic educational system that often has little regard for their children's inner well-being.[13]

This diverse set of options reflects a wide array of approaches to teaching and learning, but taken as a whole they share a common commitment to fostering originality, individuality, and autonomy. They recognize that children need to be on their own often enough to become fluent in responsible decision making; at the same time children need nurturing relationships with adults who serve as mentors and role models, not taskmasters. They need real knowledge and experience and the chance to learn from their own mistakes, not constant immunization from risk. To quote Stephen Mintz, they need "challenging alternatives to the world of malls, music lessons, instant messages, and play dates," and real opportunities to explore where their place in the adult world might one day lie.[14]

And so, just as the efforts of conservationists and environmentalists over the past century have greatly improved the chances that there will always be enough unspoiled wilderness to nourish the human experience, there is still time for those who understand the parallel importance of an undomesticated childhood to come to its defense.

ONE

THE TAMING OF THE CHILD

It is easy to substitute our will for that of the child
by means of suggestion or coercion; but when we have
done this we have robbed him of his greatest right,
the right to construct his own personality.
—Maria Montessori, *The Absorbent Mind*

THE DOMESTICATION OF CHILDHOOD, and likewise of children's inner selves, did not happen overnight. It has been steadily gathering momentum for over a century, yet only recently have some of the warning signals of the potential demise of childhood risen to the radar of public awareness. Understanding the root causes of the domestication, and more importantly how we can begin to reverse them, first involves a look back in time.

The enormous transformation we are presently witnessing began fairly quietly, with a development that drew little notice at the time. There was a shift in the prevailing image of the child, which prior to the twentieth century had been that of a naturally sturdy being with inherently good instincts, who, unless felled by disease, was regarded as capable of learning from experience, surmounting obstacles, receiving the necessary guidance, and following a sure and steady path to adulthood.

According to historian Peter Stearns and others, a snowballing series of developments between 1900 and 1950 would steadily reverse that image into its polar opposite. The change began with a sharp decline in the birthrate: for the first time in history, having children became an intentional choice for many parents. Smaller families and conscious conception meant that children were felt to be far more precious than ever before.[1] At the same time, psychology was establishing itself as a legitimate science and soon included children within its scope. Behaviorism contributed the idea of rewarding good behavior and managing the environment to prevent bad behavior, and the depth psychology of Freud and others introduced the notion that unconscious forces could easily overwhelm children, and that the unresolved issues of their mothers and fathers had the potential to wound their vulnerable psyches. As poet and social critic Robert Bly has noted, "Millions of parents now knew that to raise children without damaging them is impossible."[2]

The marketplace wasted no time in seizing the golden opportunity before it. Self-appointed experts cranked out child-rearing manuals by the dozens, and monthly parenting magazines delivered the latest child-rearing tips into middle-class homes across the country. Advertisers bombarded parents with messages of impending disaster, and before long the market for medicines, protective devices, and special children's products likewise boomed. Observed historian Christopher Lasch: "By keeping parents in a state of chronic anxiety, psychiatry thus frustrates desires that advertising can then claim to satisfy. It lays the emotional foundation for the insistence of the advertising industry that the health and safety of the young, their daily nutritional requirements, their emotional and intellectual development, and their ability to compete with their peers for popularity and success all depend on the consumption of vitamins, band-aids, cavity-preventing toothpaste, cereals, mouthwashes, and laxatives."[3]

By midcentury, the hardy, self-sufficient youngster of the past had been entirely reconfigured as a delicate, dependent creature who at any moment might be struck down by germs, physical and psychological imperfections, or unforeseen circumstances. All of a sudden childhood was an accident waiting to happen, and, writes Stearns, "An American society normally hostile to government regulation became obsessed with safety, with warning signs, railings, and every conceivable intervention between children and danger."[4] The public-service announcement "Do you know where *your* children are?" was intoned like a mantra between evening TV programs, and as the twentieth century moved fearfully to a close, the parental imperative to keep kids close to home, confined to playgrounds and playrooms, had become nearly universal.[5]

All of this is not to romanticize pre-twentieth-century childhood. The life of the average youngster was hardly idyllic in Huck Finn's day, when, for instance, 25 percent of all Americans died before the age of one, and 50 percent died before the age of twenty-one.[6] If you were poor or of Native American or African descent and you managed somehow to survive your early circumstances, your chances of life, liberty, and the pursuit of happiness were ultimately virtually nil. Trace the history of childhood back into medieval and ancient times and the picture gets only grimmer. For the majority of kids it was a story of infanticide, slavery, abuse, abandonment, and economic and sexual exploitation. Mortality rates ran as high as two out of three, and the average life span hovered around thirty.[7]

Some would even argue that prior to the Renaissance, childhood as a distinct life phase with its own customs and rituals didn't exist at all. Children and adults, according to British historian J. H. Plumb, lived in the same premodern world, sharing the same games, the same toys, the same stories.[8]

The reasons for the advent of childhood are beyond the scope of this book, but suffice it to say that after 1600 or so, it slowly assumed the status of a separate phase of life. As at least the more fortunate children ceased to be treated as utilitarian objects, childhood became an increasingly longer period in which kids—to varying degrees depending on external factors such as race, gender, and socioeconomic status—were allotted the time and space to play unconditionally, and try out the mental and physical gifts with which they were born, before having to face the rigors and responsibilities of the adult world. Childhood at any juncture has been a bed of roses only for a privileged few, but the critical point is that until relatively recently it belonged to children themselves. It contained a certain privacy and sanctity, and compared with the current version it was an unstructured, unmediated, and unencumbered preserve within which the young could explore and map their inner and outer worlds largely on their own terms.

Thus it is a supreme irony that while we have eliminated much of the actual danger, deprivation, and abuse from the lives of today's children, the perceived danger is causing us to fence them in as never before. What sociologist Barry Glassner calls a "culture of fear" has enveloped this country and cast a pall of anxiety over contemporary childhood, one that is based almost entirely on unsubstantiated hype by news media hell-bent on sensational stories.

Glassner cites as a prime example the great Halloween-candy scare that sprang to life in the early 1970s and has likely forever dampened the way we celebrate what is arguably children's own holiday.[9] More than a decade passed before University of California researchers Joel Best and Gerald Horiuchi debunked the myth of October sadists victimizing children nationwide. Poring over national crime data going back to 1958, the two young sociologists found only seventy-six reports of any kind of treat tampering, most of which turned out to be mistaken or fraudulent. Out of these seventy-six, three child fatalities were alleged to be caused by tainted candy. When the researchers dug even deeper, they discovered that none of the deaths actually resulted from trick-or-treating at strangers' homes. In one case, the father of a Houston boy gave him candy laced with arsenic in order to collect on a large insurance claim. In the second, a boy stumbled upon his uncle's heroin stash, ingested some of it, and died. The boy's family tried to hide the facts by sprinkling the drug over some of his candy, but the family soon confessed to their cover-up. In the third case, a Los Angeles girl suffered a fatal seizure that was first blamed on poisoned candy but was later found to reveal a congenital heart condition.[10]

Even though Best and Horiuchi's exhaustive research showed an absolute lack of substance in the hysteria surrounding Halloween, the damage had been done. Thanks to news stories like the one the *New York Times* ran in 1970 that began, "Those Halloween goodies that children collect this weekend on their rounds of trick or treating may bring them more horror than happiness" and went on to give specific and frightening examples of potential tampering, most parents had already taken to heart the annual warning to scrutinize their children's treats, and many no longer allowed their kids to roam about freely after dark collecting sweets and reveling in their costumed personas.[11] Halloween was forced indoors, restricted to haunted houses and parties choreographed, as always, by adults.[12] Sadly, the domestication of Halloween serves as a sort of template for society's defensive reactions to the multiplicity of perceived threats to children.

To domesticate something means, quite simply, to tame it. When early humans first set out to domesticate plants and animals, it was a matter of learning to manage their growth and movements. The advantages are obvious: domesticated organisms are more predictable and less dangerous, which makes them easier to exploit as resources. Those early agriculturalists were motivated by powerful survival concerns. They wanted to ensure a steady food supply, and at the same time reduce their feelings of vulnerability by maintaining a buffer between themselves and an environment they increasingly saw as hostile. To quote the natural philosopher Paul Shepard, "In the ideology of farming, wild things are the enemy of the tame."[13]

In the case of children and childhood, the domestication process was triggered in part by the powerful feedback loop that formed between the new image of children as fragile and mounting parental anxiety over raising them right. The common denominators in both cases are fear and control, both of which now dominate the ways in which many parents bring up their kids. Apprehensions about children's future success have given rise to what psychologist David Elkind terms "hyper-parenting"—the overprogramming of students' free time with a myriad of extracurricular enrichment activities.[14] Forever worried about their kids' safety and well-being, a new generation of what fellow psychologist Foster Cline calls "helicopter parents" can be found hovering protectively over their offspring, ready to swoop in and rescue them at the first sign of trouble. Helicopter parents run interference for their children. They pave their way, fight their battles for them, and generally deny them free rein to succeed or fail on their own.[15] One statistic in particular tells the story: the amount of unstructured, unsupervised play outside the home by middle-class kids between the ages of three and eleven declined by a drastic 40 percent between the early 1980s and late 1990s.[16]

This is not an insidious development. Rather, according to social psychologist Wendy Grolnick, we are inherently invested in our kids' welfare due to certain "biological hooks." Mammalian bonding and an evolutionary instinct for family survival translate naturally into wanting what's best for our kids, which can then translate all too easily into fear and control.[17] Grolnick, a parent herself, has spent much of her career researching patterns of parental control, hoping to reach a compassionate understanding of both its causes and its effects. She points out that a parent's instinctive concern receives layer upon layer of reinforcement from our competitive, hierarchical social institutions. For instance, many of the conditions that prevail in our classrooms and workplaces appear to parents as a threat to their kids, and the resulting parental insecurity causes conscientious moms and dads to try to increase their influence over their children's circumstances.[18]

Both Grolnick and Elkind also cite basic stress as a culprit in the rise of a controlling parenting style. Sometimes parents control simply because they want conformity and obedience, but more often they are simply under too much pressure. Financial woes, job scenarios that don't take children into account, the demands of single parenting, and rampant busyness eat up the psychological resources mothers and fathers need in order to parent in ways that support their kids' autonomy. We all know how much time and patience it requires to allow children to learn to do things for themselves and figure out how to solve their own problems.

Furthermore, writes Elkind, stressed-out parents tend to see their children "in the shorthand of symbols." Kids become objects rather than subjects, which frees the parents from the energy-consuming task of knowing their children as whole people. They can then hurry them around from place to place and task to task without regard for their authentic needs and desires.

Mothers and fathers under stress also tend to become self-centered and eventually to see their kids as reflections of themselves. These parents feel that the way their children dress or perform in school will affect how they are judged as caregivers. They push their kids in order to relieve their own inner pressure and boost their own self-esteem, and thereby turn their children into status symbols.[19] This kind of parenting becomes yet another project based entirely on an adult's agenda, leaving little room for kids to just be kids.

Stress, as Grolnick points out, also frequently leads to irritability, which in turn leads to a reflexive exertion of control. Here Grolnick cites her study of families on welfare, which revealed a strong correlation between financial hardship and punitive parenting. Another study of rural families showed that the greater the number of stressors in the environment—poverty, large number of children, low education, single parenting—the less supportive mothers were of their children and the more they made derogatory statements about them, threatened them, and controlled them both physically and emotionally.[20]

To discover the effects of controlling parenting on children, Grolnick conducted a series of studies that focused on interactions between mothers and their infants. In one experiment, researchers gave a group of moms two toys to play with on the floor with their one-year-olds. The instructions were intentionally ambiguous: "Sit next to your child while he/she plays with the toy." A hidden camera then videotaped the pairs for three minutes. It soon became evident that some of the moms took the instructions to mean they must make sure their children played with the toy *properly*. They became serious and critical and repeatedly intervened to show the child how to use the toy. Other mothers interpreted the instructions to mean that they should be a resource for their kids: they let them explore and problem-solve on their own, but were available if their child became too frustrated. Grolnick rated the mothers according to how controlling or "autonomy supportive" they were. Autonomy-supportive mothers followed the child's lead, provided encouragement, and gave just enough assistance to get the child back on track when he or she got stuck. Controlling mothers tended to lead the interaction and repeatedly tell the child what to do, consistently helping more than was needed.

The researchers then separated the infants from their mothers and gave the infants a challenging task in order to measure their persistence. The children of the controlling moms tended to give up easily, whereas the children of the autonomy-supportive moms persisted in trying to solve the problems presented to them. Grolnick's conclusion: the managerial, pressuring behavior of the controlling mothers tended to undermine their children's natural ability and motivation.[21]

Grolnick's ideas were heavily influenced by the earlier work of Diana Baumrind, head of the Family Socialization and Developmental Competence Project at the University of California at Berkeley and best known for her formulation of three basic parenting styles: authoritarian, permissive, and authoritative. What sets the three types apart are the degree of nurturance in parent-child interactions and the amount of control parents exercise over their kids' activities and behavior.

First, Baumrind contrasted the two extremes. Authoritarian parents tend to be low in nurturance and high in control compared with other parents. They set absolute standards of behavior that are not to be questioned or negotiated; they favor forceful, punitive discipline; and they demand strict obedience. The authoritarian type believes in keeping children in a subordinate role and restricting their independence and individuality.

Permissive parents, on the other hand, tend to be moderate to high in nurturance but low in parental control. They are overly tolerant of their children's impulses and hesitant to curb them. They impose few demands and habitually excuse misbehavior.

Baumrind called the happy medium *authoritative*. Authoritative parents set firm, consistent limits when their children's behavior is out of bounds but don't hem them in with restrictions. They maintain an adult perspective while at the same time respecting the child's point of view, and they encourage verbal give and take. As their children grow older and more responsible, they grant them increasing levels of independence and share more of the power within the family.[22]

Baumrind conducted a series of landmark longitudinal studies to explore the outcomes of the various parenting styles. Each research project reached the same conclusion: the children of authoritative parents are the most likely to end up as mature, competent, and self-directed individuals.

The issue of parental control is complex and sensitive. Every family has its own heritage and set of internal dynamics. Baumrind was careful to point out that her types are just that: artificial constructs designed to make certain generalizations about different styles of child rearing. There is, she added emphatically, no one right way to do it.

Moreover, it goes without saying that children do at times need protection, guidance, and direction. In psychological parlance, they need to be socialized, meaning that they need to learn to bring their impulses into line with social mores. It is generally acceptable in American society for children to express anger, for instance, but it is not acceptable for them to repeatedly settle their differences with sticks and fists. Sex play among young children is likely to meet with mild disapproval at worst, while sibling incest is universally taboo. And so on.

For the purposes of our present discussion, the key questions are: how much parental control is enough, and how much is too much? At what point does socialization become domestication, with a parent's approach to child rearing only reinforcing the threats to childhood that come from the culture at large?

Wendy Grolnick takes an interesting semantic stab at an answer. She differentiates between a mother or father being "in control" and being "controlling." Being in control means establishing age-appropriate limits, while at the same time supporting children's growing sense of autonomy by allowing them to make choices and learn from their own mistakes. Parents who are in control apply minimal pressure to get their kids to behave in a certain way and allow them to feel that they are initiating their actions rather than being manipulated or coerced. They provide reasons for parental decisions, and these become increasingly negotiable as their children mature. Controlling, on the other hand, means placing a high value on obedience, shepherding children toward specified outcomes, and discouraging verbal give and take. It also means applying strong influence to conform through punishment, evaluation, deadlines, and guilt inducement, all of which undermine children's feeling that they are initiating their own experience.[23]

Here Grolnick is drawing from the work of Edward Deci and Richard Ryan, two professors of psychology at the University of Rochester who together have spent the last thirty years developing a model of human development based on the premise that children are born with an innate drive to understand and master their worlds. Observe any unfettered, well-nurtured infant, they say, and you will see how curious he or she is, how eager to actively explore the surrounding environment. This is not something we teach babies; it is in their nature to pursue what interests them because they are fascinated by novelty and "persistent in their attempts to make it familiar."[24]

Deci and Ryan named their model Self-Determination Theory because the term *self-determination* means acting out of personal choice, not out of coercion or a sense of obligation. It also implies that learning and growth are a natural outcome of the basic human need for autonomy and competence because children are "intrinsically motivated."[25] Intrinsic motivation is an urge to do something that comes from within and has its own rewards. It is the natural inclination toward spontaneous interest, exploration, assimilation, and mastery. It fuels play, exploration, and problem solving, and therefore it is essential to cognitive and social development. And most important, according to Deci and Ryan, intrinsic motivation propels the developmental process because it is "the energy source that is central to the active nature of the organism."[26]

Although children are born with an ample supply of intrinsic motivation, it can be readily disrupted by hostile conditions. According to Grolnick, "Allowing children the freedom to pursue their interests without outside interference is paramount for intrinsic motivation." Kids can exercise it, she says, only when they experience their actions as self-determined. Any kind of extrinsic reinforcer—threats, bribes, deadlines, directives, imposed goals, and even praise and rewards—tends to undermine it.[27] Deci demonstrated this crucial point with a pioneering 1971 study in which two groups of college students were given a set of highly interesting spatial-relations puzzles and asked to solve them in three separate one-hour sessions. Both the experimental and the control groups showed high levels of intrinsic motivation in the first session. In the second session, the experimental group was paid a dollar for each puzzle it solved while the control group continued to work for the fun of it. Then the levels of intrinsic motivation of the two groups in the third session were compared, and the results showed a marked decrease in that of the experimental group.

James Garbarino, codirector of the Family Life Development Center at Cornell University, conducted a study with younger children that similarly showed the negative effects of rewards. Researchers asked a group of fifth- and sixth-grade girls to serve as tutors to first- and second-grade girls. The tutors were instructed to teach their students the same task in separate one-on-one sessions, but half of them were promised a free movie ticket if they succeeded, while the other half were not offered any reward. The results were striking: observers noted that the rewarded tutors were often tense and hostile and held sessions that were high-pressured and businesslike. They made more demands and gave more negative evaluations, and there was less laughter and a much lower success rate among their students.[28]

The bottom line for Grolnick is that the archenemy of intrinsic motivation is control, even in its most subtle forms, such as parents giving children unsolicited help with their homework. She cites a more recent study by Eva Pomerantz and Missa Eaton in which 231 second- through fifth-graders from a predominantly middle-class elementary school were asked how they felt about their parents' assisting them with their homework without their having requested it. More than three out of four students felt that their parents' intentions were positive, but they also felt they were receiving a double message. They took their parents' attempts to control their homework performance as a sign of their incompetence, and their self-esteem suffered as a result. This effect increased as the subjects got older.[29]

Praise is a mixed bag because it can be controlling or informational, depending on the intention behind it. Controlling praise carries a pressure to achieve, as well as the unspoken agenda of manipulating the child into further performance. Controlling praise often takes the form of praising the child rather than praising the specific behavior: "You're such a good girl for doing all your homework." This kind of praise teaches kids that approval and self-worth are based primarily on meeting the praiser's standards, and thus it undermines intrinsic motivation.[30]

If, on the other hand, the praiser simply gives honest feedback and encouragement, praise will have a positive effect on children's motivation and performance. To test this point, Grolnick gave a group of children a series of problems to solve. After they finished, the entire group was told, "Wow, you did very well on those problems. You got x number right." Then she split the group and told subgroup A, "You kids are really smart," while she said to subgroup B, "You must have worked hard at those problems." The whole group was then given another set of problems on which they did not do as well as the first time. When the children were done, Grolnick asked them how much they had enjoyed the task. She gave them a choice between doing another set of easier problems or a set of harder problems that "you'll learn a lot from even if you don't look so smart." The subgroup that had been praised for their intelligence tended to say they didn't enjoy the task and then to choose easy problems that made them look good. Moreover, they were more likely to say that the reason they didn't do well the second time was that they just weren't good enough. The kids who had been praised for their effort tended to enjoy the problems more and to pick the harder problems that would teach them new skills.[31]

But what if children's intrinsic motivation steers them toward behavior that is potentially unsafe or socially inappropriate, thereby setting them in opposition to the outside world? Much has been written about the inevitable struggle between our instinctive selves and the rules and values of the culture into which we are born. This thread of the story, too, is beyond my scope, but many observers have tended to view it as a Bambi-meets-Godzilla encounter, with Bambi, of course, representing the instinctive self and Godzilla the surrounding culture.

This is not necessarily the case. Self-Determination Theory argues that it is entirely possible for children willingly to transform outer regulations into inner ones without sacrificing their curiosity or suppressing their hunger for novelty and excitement. The psychological term for the process is *internalization,* and Deci and Ryan write that it operates according to the same principle as intrinsic motivation: the child, of his or her own accord, seeks "to develop internal structures that allow for greater competence and self-determination."[32] In laymen's terms, children will gradually and naturally take responsibility for regulating their own behavior because they take pride in being more capable and covet the independence that their increasing self-control affords them. Thus internalization, like intrinsic motivation, is built into the developmental scheme.

However, the same extrinsic reinforcers that tend to undermine intrinsic motivation have a similarly disruptive effect on internalization—which brings us back to the process of socialization, whereby parents and other caregivers are called upon to "extrinsically motivate" their kids to behave in socially acceptable ways. To show how parents can socialize their children without damaging their inner wildness, Deci and Ryan provide the hypothetical example of a young boy who likes to throw his bouncy red ball around in the house. At first, the situation constitutes a conflict between Johnny's intrinsic desire to do it because it's fun and the prohibition of his parents, who have told him not to do it again.

Consider the following two scenarios. In scenario A, Johnny's father responds to him in a nonthreatening, nonjudgmental, *informational* manner: "I don't want you to play ball indoors because I'm worried you might knock over a lamp or something." He takes care to acknowledge Johnny's needs and feelings: "I know your ball is an exciting toy and that it makes you mad when you can't play with it in the house, but it is so bouncy that you will have to play with it outside." In addition, he gives Johnny a soft, spongy alternative that is safe to play with indoors.

In scenario B, Johnny's dad becomes angry and threatening: "Give me that damn ball! And if I ever catch you playing with it inside again, you're gonna get a good spanking."

In both scenarios, Johnny's initial motivation to stop is extrinsic, supplied by parental authority. In the second scenario, two possible outcomes are likely: he won't play ball indoors because he doesn't want to make his dad angry and be punished, or he will become defiant and do it anyway. If the way his dad reacted reflects the typical way in which his parents set limits, Johnny's appropriate behavior will continue to depend on adult monitoring and restrictions; whereas if his parents in scenario A are in the habit of consistently explaining the reasons for the limits they set, then as Johnny matures he will increasingly base his behavior on a self-regulating choice: "I'm not going to throw the ball in the house because I might break something, and I don't want to do that." Or alternatively, he might still decide to play with the ball indoors based on an assessment that he could do it safely, along with a willingness to accept responsibility for the damage if he was wrong.[33]

Again, there are always times when children's natural impulses and inclinations are at odds with parental standards. But if parents can remember that children are born with the intrinsic motivation to regulate themselves, then their kids will ultimately become self-determining based on values and consequences they have taken on as their own because those values and consequences make sense to them on their own terms.

My personal experience both as a parent and as a school director working closely with a great diversity of families confirms Deci and Ryan's model. When we nurture children unconditionally; set limits that are consistent, firm, and yet as nonrestrictive as possible; trust them to make responsible choices based on information rather than bribes or threats; and generally respect their deep-seated desire to be autonomous beings, they are indeed capable of self-determination, often at a surprisingly young age.

However, this very experience underscores how difficult it is for many parents to locate the balance between being sufficiently "in control," to return to Grolnick's terminology, and giving children the latitude they need to become self-determining individuals. The mistake made by a large number of parents in my generation, my wife and me included, was to overreact against the authoritarian parenting we received as children in the 1940s and '50s. We were too reluctant to set limits, too eager to share power with our kids before they were mature enough to handle it. While our intention was to set them free to develop into their own authentic persons, by abdicating too much authority we were actually giving them a false sense of self. Instead of helping our kids to sharpen their inner sense of direction, we unwittingly were encouraging them to focus outwardly on the power dynamics between parent and child. This is because, as David Elkind observed in 1981, "if children are not called on to control themselves, they use their behavior to control adults."[34] We didn't realize that having power over adults is frightening to young children, and it actually discourages them from gaining the firm footing in the world that we want them to have. Rather than pursue their own interests, they tend to remain within their parents' orbits, circling around and around trying to find new and better ways to manipulate them.

My sense is that this pattern of overcompensation is ongoing. Many of the young parents I encounter today are so anxious to be liked by their kids that they have a hard time saying no to them. These mothers and fathers have a tendency to avoid areas of conflict such as bedtime and chores, a pattern that ultimately allows children to be governed by their raw, often conflicting impulses rather than their true wants and needs.

Some of these parents have also adopted a new approach to child rearing known as "attachment parenting," made popular by pediatrician William Sears and his wife, Martha. The emphasis here is on doing everything possible to strengthen the bond between infant and parents. Under this approach, typically the mother will nurse the baby on demand for at least the first year. She will "wear" the baby during the day in some form of sling, and at night she, the father, and the baby will share the same "family bed."[35]

Attachment parenting is based on the earlier work of British child psychologist John Bowlby, who, heavily influenced by Konrad Lorenz's study of mammalian bonding, theorized that there are three possible "patterns of attachment" between children and their parents, and that these patterns profoundly influence a child's psychological development. The first two patterns of attachment—"anxious resistant," when parents are inconsistently available and use threats of abandonment as a means of control, and "anxious avoidant," when they tend to rebuff rather than nurture their kids when they seek comfort or protection—are forms of insecure attachment. Both patterns leave a child lacking in self-esteem and prone to separation anxiety. It is only those children who are "securely attached"—confident that their parents will be readily available and sensitive to their signals when they seek protection, comfort, or assistance—who will feel "bold in their explorations of the world and also competent in dealing with it."

Parents who discourage their kids' desire for autonomy, according to Bowlby, were often themselves insecurely attached as children. As a result, they unconsciously tend to invert the parent-child relationship by turning their children into their own attachment figures. This creates a vicious cycle wherein whiny and anxious or angry and aggressive children elicit negative responses from their mothers, resulting in the persistence of poor attachment.[36]

In theory, attachment parenting makes absolute sense as a way to safeguard and support children's inner wildness. In practice, however, at least in my observation, some attachment parents carry the whole enterprise too far. Maintaining too little separation between themselves and their kids, they risk becoming "helicopter parents," whom I described at the beginning of the chapter.

I have chosen to focus on the dynamics between parent and child in such depth because it is within this intimate, intricate, and sometimes confounding dance that inner wildness faces some of its earliest tests of survival. The extent to which we as parents can, early on, find ways to support our children's quest for self-determination goes a long way in determining how well they will stand up later to the forces that seek to tame them by denying their instinctive knowledge, as well as the experiences that will allow them to test that knowledge and gradually put it into practice.

As we have seen, the intrinsic motivation that urges the developmental process forward cannot survive on its own. Quoting Deci and Ryan one final time, "This motivation, though strong and persistent, is also vulnerable to the continued encroachment of environmental forces that are perhaps all too common and often socially sanctioned."[37] It is to these socially sanctioned sources of domestication beyond home and family, which are burying parents and children alike beneath a mountain of fear, competition, material excess, and the endless drive to conform and succeed, that we now turn.

TWO

INTO THE CORRAL

It is, in fact, nothing short of a miracle that modern methods
of instruction have not yet entirely strangled the holy curiosity
of inquiry. For this delicate little plan, aside from stimulation,
stands mainly in need of freedom.

—Albert Einstein, journal

INSTITUTIONALIZED EDUCATION, with all of its regimens and
routines, extrinsic rewards and punishments, prepackaging and
standardization, has always contributed to the domestication of
childhood. It is over the course of my lifetime, however, that schooling has become its single largest purveyor.

The reasons are both quantitative and qualitative. For example,
when I attended kindergarten in 1959, it was in session only from
12:30 to 3:00. Moreover, this had been my first experience with
school. I had spent the previous five years at our suburban Washington, D.C., home with either my mother or a housekeeper, my
days spent mostly outdoors playing with the children next door. Together we tramped in the small creek that meandered between our
houses, collected caterpillars, raided birds' nests, raced wagons, sled-
ded down a nearby hill in winter, and did all of the other things
little kids do when they are left largely to their own devices. When
the school day was over—and this would continue to be the case
throughout the elementary grades—I would quickly walk home
and resume tramping in the creek, collecting caterpillars, raiding
birds' nests, and so on. School, in other words, was a manageable
interruption.

When I was seven we moved to the city, where I also attended
public school and where my lifestyle remained essentially the same
except that now the nearest creek was fifteen minutes away by bicycle, and, because of sewage leaking from the National Zoo, the wa-

ter was not nearly as fresh as the stream that ran through my old backyard. But we were undeterred by such details.

Contrast my experience with that of contemporary youngsters. Full-day kindergarten has become nearly universal, and preschool isn't far behind. When you add after-school programs for the majority of children whose parent or parents work until five o'clock, before-school programs for those whose parent or parents have to go to work early, extracurricular lessons and enrichment activities, and then, of course, homework, you find the shoe squarely on the other foot: unstructured activity that isn't aimed at specific learning goals is considered an interruption in the schooling process.

Even within the confines of the school day, kids spend more and more time in the classroom. In my day we had morning *and* afternoon recess, and lunch hour was ours to do with as we pleased. We were free to leave school grounds if we chose, although, if the weather permitted, my friends and I usually inhaled our lunches and bolted out to the playground for a long, unsupervised game of one kind or another. Field trips were also a common occurrence. I can recall my fourth-grade teacher, an avid birdwatcher, taking us on frequent birding expeditions, binoculars in hand, sometimes in the school's surroundings and sometimes, when she could arrange transportation, to wilder locales. In the fifth and sixth grades we were able to attend, thanks to an arrangement with the Washington Symphony Orchestra, a series of four special concerts. Today's spiraling concern over standards has practically rendered recess and field trips a thing of the past. Fearing serious governmental sanction if too few students pass standardized exams at the end of the year, schools have been forced to eliminate nearly all of the so-called frills from the school day. "Time on task" has become the watchword in every classroom.

There has also been an enormous qualitative shift in the nature of schooling over the last two generations. The changes are too numerous to list, but perhaps the three with the most impact on inner wildness are the steadily increasing formality, the high degree to which the classroom routine is scripted from afar, and the skyrocketing pressure to produce quantifiable results.

It is important to pause here to remember that most urban middle-class children have been going to school since the 1830s. But it wasn't for another hundred years, when parental anxiety around education began to rise dramatically, that schools began to clamp down with attendance rules, age segregation, standardized tests, and report cards.[1] The demand for higher standards and greater accountability, based primarily on standardized tests as a measuring stick, took a quantum leap following the 1983 publication of a federally commissioned report card on education called *A Nation at Risk*. Citing falling scores and the increasing failure of U.S. schools to measure up to their overseas counterparts, the authors of the report wrote, "The educational foundations of our society are presently being eroded by a rising tide of mediocrity that threatens our very future as a nation and a people."[2]

The dark picture painted by *A Nation at Risk* unleashed a panic that is currently reaching the level of absurdity with the implementation of the No Child Left Behind Act. A local case in point: our superintendent of schools for Albany, New York, recently banned the tradition of bringing in cupcakes on birthdays. These little parties, he declared, represented too big a distraction from the work at hand. Another of his innovations aimed at raising district test scores: mandatory weekend homework for all elementary-school students.

All of this is not to say that concern over student achievement is entirely groundless. When I was in school, children were much more inclined to sit still and comply with classroom routines than they are today. The percentage of students who were unable or unwilling to fit in and keep up was exponentially lower. But the world I grew up in was a vastly different one. When thinking back to elementary school, I remember only one other classmate who was being raised by a single mother (I had lost my father to cancer, and Joey's parents had divorced when he was in the first grade). Most of my peers held an unquestioning respect for parental authority, which automatically carried over into the classroom. Television played a minor role in kids' lives because much of the time there was nothing on worth watching, and in any case there were many compelling alternatives. When I was nine or ten, our TV set broke; it was months before my mom could afford to have it repaired, and I scarcely missed it. I simply turned to the shelf of children's classics she had collected for my brother and sisters and me, books like *Hans Brinker and the Silver Skates*, *Toby Tyler*, and *The Prince and the Pauper*.

The list goes on: video games and personal computers had yet to be invented. Movies, television shows, and magazines had very little of what we now call "adult content." Families were more likely to stay in one place. (I lived in the same home from the age of seven until I went away to college, and I probably wouldn't have moved at all if my father hadn't died.) Information circulated more slowly. There was less grinding poverty and a smaller gap between the haves and have-nots. All of our cities were generally safer and more vibrant. Special-interest groups did not yet control the political process.

I'm not trying to portray the world of my childhood as any more ideal than Huckleberry Finn's. The point here is that the reasons for the apparent decline in learning and behavior in our schools are largely to be found in the massive social, cultural, economic, and technological changes of the last half-century. The so-called reform efforts of the last three decades have been little more than a series of misguided repairs that fail to address the root causes of the problem.

It is interesting to note that when schooling began to intensify in response to the gush of insecurity released by the Great Depression, there was a strident outcry concerning the unnaturalness of school, especially vis-à-vis younger children. The author of a 1935 article in *Parents* magazine—"What's Behind Naughtiness?"—wrote, "At the very same time when growing bodies demand movement and action, children enter school. . . . They want to run, to jump, to shout. They need such activity."[3] In the even earlier words of Swedish teacher, feminist, and author Ellen Key, from the education chapter of her 1909 international bestseller *The Century of the Child*:

> The modern school has succeeded in doing something which, according to the law of physics, is impossible: the annihilation of once existent matter. The desire for knowledge, the capacity for acting by oneself, the gift of observation, all qualities children bring with them to school, have, as a rule, at the close of the school period disappeared. They have not been transformed into actual knowledge or interests. This is the result of children spending almost the whole of their life from the sixth to the eighteenth year at the school

desk, hour by hour, month by month, term by term; taking doses of knowledge, first in teaspoonfuls, then in dessert-spoonfuls, and finally in tablespoonfuls, absorbing mixtures which the teacher often has compounded from fourth- or fifth-hand recipes. . . . When young people have escaped from this régime, their mental appetite and mental digestion are so destroyed that they forever lack capacity for taking real nourishment.[4]

Lest readers think Key was just some cranky Scandinavian, here is what Albert Einstein had to say when he finished his university studies: "One had to cram all of this stuff into one's mind, whether one liked it or not. This coercion had such a deterring effect that after I had passed the final examination I found the consideration of any scientific problem distasteful for an entire year."[5]

Such voices opposing the corralling of our children's bodies, minds, and spirits are rarely heard from the mainstream anymore. The illusion that things have always been this way and couldn't possibly be otherwise seems to be solidifying with each succeeding generation, which means that anyone with a dissenting point of view is seen as an "alternative" educator, unfit for mainstream consumption. It is precisely this conservative attitude that sounds the death knell for one successful innovation after another and that leaves our educational system so resistant to genuine reform.

Conventional schools wave a rhetorical baton at learning, but the overwhelming majority of them in this country are organized around a single fundamental principle: control. Students are told what to learn and when to learn it, and what to think and when to think it. Their physical movement is scrupulously managed. Their emotional selves are shuttered because feelings are by their very nature resistant to outside control, and so the entire focus of the educational process is on the mental life of the child.

The centrality of control is hardly incidental. It was carefully built into every facet by the model's designers, a claim I base first on the words of Edward Thorndike, recognized today as the father of educational psychology. "There can be no moral warrant for studying man's nature unless the study will enable us to control his acts," he wrote in 1911.[6] Heavily influenced by Darwin's theory of evolution, Thorndike experimented on caged cats and monkeys and proposed that learning is caused by the "selection of impulses." He believed that certain stimuli and responses become connected or dissociated from each other according to what he called the "law of effect": "When particular stimulus-response sequences are followed by pleasure, those responses tend to be 'stamped in'; while responses followed by pain tend to be 'stamped out.' "[7] Intelligence, then, is the ability to form connections, with humans being the most evolved animal because we form the most. Moreover, all learning is motivated by future rewards and punishments.

Thorndike's successor B. F. Skinner would later name the mechanism that supposedly underlies learning "operant conditioning." This school of psychological thought, known as behaviorism because it is founded on the belief that all behavior is exclusively the product of such conditioning, went on to become the "scientific" basis for the mainstream model of education. Given the growing body of research refuting the validity of behaviorist learning theory— a subject to which I will return in a moment—the questions beg to be asked: how is it that behaviorism still defines the educational process, and what is the secret to its staying power? Again we are faced with the central issue of control. Behaviorism's carrot-and-stick approach, though clearly it undermines true learning, remains a highly effective way of getting children to submit to classroom routine and unquestioningly absorb and regurgitate endless reams of information, much of which continues to be laced with moral, racial, and nationalistic bias. It is worth noting that another prominent behaviorist, John Watson, abruptly ended his research on behavioral conditioning in 1920 in order to take it into a field where he could apply it: advertising. By 1924 Watson was vice president at J. Walter Thompson, one of the largest ad agencies in the United States. Making masterly use of the findings of behaviorist research, advertising rapidly grew into a medium with tremendous influence over Americans' personal desires and choices.

While behaviorism continues to hold similar sway within the realm of education, it is hardly the sole explanation for the control-based model that continues to dominate mainstream schooling. There are deep cultural, political, and economic roots as well. The culture of colonial America, as educational historian Ron Miller reminds us in *What Are Schools For?* was overwhelmingly Calvinist.

While institutionalized education at that time had only a minor influence on the overall social fabric, what schools there were existed primarily to ensure the continuity of moral and religious values. Their methodology was heavily imbued with Protestantism's essentially pessimistic view of human nature, which held that humans are tainted at birth by original sin. Children come into the world depraved, or, as Reverend Benjamin Wadsworth said at the time, babies were "filthy, guilty, odious, abominable . . . both by nature and practice." Cotton Mather, another Puritan minister, wrote: "Are they young? Yet the devil has been with them already. . . . They go astray as soon as they are born."[8] And as historian Bernard Wishy put it, "A playful, energetic, pleasure-loving child would surely be on the road to perdition."[9]

The Calvinist colonizers also had a deep fear of nature, which they associated with the dangerous realms of passion and sensuality. Again, according to Paul Shepard, "Behind the proud self-consciousness and conscience of the Puritan is the despair of his own organism, fear of that involuntary and unconscious aspect of the self inaccessible to control. Nothing so clearly identifies the West as the distrust of the powers of the earth focused at last upon the un-domesticatable wildness within."[10] As a result, observed historian Lloyd deMause about Puritan upbringing in the Massachusetts colony: "Above all, whether they were raised by their natural parents, a relative, or a master, children were subjected to a regime designed to civilize and tame them, to restrain their natural tendency to 'run wild.' "[11] Puritan society placed great emphasis on proper child rearing and education, and believed that the entire community was responsible for these projects. In the end, it was the Puritans who published a majority of the early American works on child rearing and education.[12] According to Miller, this same ethos carried over into the often romanticized one-room schoolhouses of seventeenth- and eighteenth-century New England—which in reality were drab, uncomfortable places where discipline and order took precedence over children's interests and developmental needs—and then into the nation's first public-school system, established by Horace Mann in Massachusetts in the early 1850s.[13]

As with the one-room schoolhouse, there is a good deal of mythology surrounding Mann, widely regarded as American education's foremost father figure. Most of us were taught in school

that he was a great humanitarian who championed free public education in order to promote the Jeffersonian ideal of an enlightened
citizenry that would safeguard a democratic, egalitarian society.
Mann, who came from working-class stock, did see education as the
great equalizer, a way of establishing an open meritocracy instead
of a hereditary aristocracy; but that is only half the story. Mann's
lifetime spanned the height of the Industrial Revolution, and he
was deeply concerned about the effects of the explosive growth of
cities in New England and the rising ethnic diversity within them.
"As population increases, and especially as artificial wants multiply," he wrote in a letter in 1840, "the temptations increase, and
the guards and securities must increase also, or society will dete-
riorate." For Mann, schools should become those "guards and securities."[14] He expressed a similar sentiment in an 1849 issue of
Massachusetts Teacher: "Those whose minds and hearts have been
trained and disciplined by education, have control over their passions."[15]

Although Mann ultimately rejected his strict religious upbringing in favor of a more liberal Unitarianism, the Calvinist in
him is plainly visible in his work on education. After founding the
nation's first state-sponsored teachers' college, he wrote the following on the training of teachers: "Moral qualifications, and the ability to inculcate and enforce the Christian virtues, I consider to be of
even greater moment than literary attainments."[16] To strengthen
his case for the importance of a national system of education, Mann
visited Prussian schools during the summer of 1843. Prussia was the
first nation to take such a step, and the fact that it emerged as a world
power soon after had not escaped notice in the United States. The
connections between a compliant citizenry and military supremacy
have been explored elsewhere,[17] but suffice it to say that Mann was
so impressed by the efficiency and discipline of the Prussian system
that he returned and wrote the *Seventh Report to the Boston School
Committee*, in which he urged the committee to adopt the Prussian
ideas of a centralized education bureaucracy, standardized curriculum, and age-segregated, teacher-centered classrooms staffed by a
corps of specially trained professionals.

Mann's recommendations did not go unopposed. Religious leaders and other critics argued that education should be a community,
family, and personal endeavor, not an essentially political program

mandated by the state[18]—exactly why the townspeople of Beverly, Massachusetts, voted down a proposal for their first compulsory high school in 1838. The Association of the Masters of the Boston Public Schools, who resisted Mann's reforms for a mixed bag of reasons, published a 150-page rebuttal to his report in which it expressed outrage, claiming that the psychological result of the Prussian approach would be to break student potential "for forming the habit of independent and individual effort."[19]

Nonetheless, Mann emerged victorious. The Massachusetts school system became a model for the rest of the country, and modern American education coldly embraced control, obedience, and self-restraint as its central tenets.[20] One education journalist in the 1890s wrote, "The unkindly spirit of the teacher is strikingly apparent; the pupils, being completely subjugated to her will, are silent and motionless, the spiritual atmosphere of the classroom is damp and chilly."[21] In the words of William Bagley, editor in chief of the *Journal of the National Education Association* from 1920 to 1925 and author of *Classroom Management*, a standard teacher-training text reprinted over thirty times: "One who studies educational theory aright can see in the mechanical routine of the classroom the educative forces that are slowly transforming the child from a little savage into a creature of law and order, fit for the life of civilized society."[22]

Finally, observed British social philosopher Benjamin Kidd in 1918 about the first meeting of the Education Trust, which included policymakers from the schools of education at Harvard, Stanford, and the University of Chicago, not to mention the Rockefeller and Carnegie Foundations and the National Education Association: "The chief end was to impose on the young the ideal of subordination."[23]

The history of education in this country is a complex affair, and I have provided just enough of a glimpse to show that the overarching reason why the conventional education model is so steeped in control is that it was intended to do so from the very beginning. Historian Michael Katz was right when, after completing his exhaustive study of early-school reform in Massachusetts, he concluded that the way in which our education system started has had "permanent consequences." While the pendulum has repeatedly swung back and forth between more conservative and more liberal approaches to schooling children, writes Katz, the underlying ideology and social structure have remained the same.[24] "We have still to see a movement," he laments, "driven by a desire to bring joy and delight to the life of the individual, to enrich experience solely for the purpose of making life more full and lovely."[25]

As John Gatto, twice chosen New York State's teacher of the year, states categorically in *The Underground History of American Education*, "The secret of American schooling is that it doesn't teach the way children learn, and it isn't supposed to. School was engineered to serve a concealed command economy and an increasingly layered social order; it wasn't made for the benefit of kids and families as those people would define their own needs.... Initiating, creating, doing, reflecting, freely associating, enjoying privacy—these are precisely what the structures of schooling are set up to prevent."[26]

The supreme irony of it all is that while the generation that witnessed the creation of the conventional education model was aware of its Puritan, Prussian, and behaviorist roots, future generations would unquestioningly take to heart the influences that defined the model without realizing where they came from.

As we have seen, all of the various ways in which schools attempt to control children—the grades and other artificial incentives, the threats and punishments, the incessant testing, the virtual imprisonment in the classroom, and even the rewards and praise—are antithetical to the intrinsic motivation that guides the learning process. That is not all, however. The methods and structures of conventional education not only undermine a child's motivation but also fly in the face of the biological foundations of real learning.

Understanding this sad reality involves a look at recent neurological discoveries. For the last thirty years, Paul MacLean, a senior National Institute of Mental Health researcher in the Clinical Brain Disorders Branch, has been developing a model that he calls the "triune brain," meaning that it consists of three separate but interconnected layers, one enfolded around another.[27] According to MacLean, the tendency of all organisms is to hang on to old, outmoded structures as they evolve, adding to and improving them rather than casting them off altogether. This is exactly what happened with the human brain. Its innermost core, aptly named the reptilian brain or R-complex, is the original brain structure dating back to the days of the dinosaurs. Located at the base of the skull, it pilots the central nervous system, processes sensory information, and manages our vast array of survival instincts and behaviors. When we are generally at peace with our environment and ourselves, the reptilian brain plays only a supporting role, in deference to the higher two brain structures.

Next to evolve was the mammalian brain, or limbic system, which sits on top of and surrounds the reptilian brain. Here lies the source of our emotions and intuition, where crude reptilian instincts are transformed into true intelligence and applied to complex life situations. The limbic system also maintains the immune system and the body's capacity to heal itself.

Five times larger than its predecessors combined, the newest brain, or the neocortex, is the center of logic, memory, and cognition. Language and the imagination are also located here. Like a conductor, the neocortex takes the input from its older partners, searches for patterns, and harmonizes them into overall growth and survival strategies. Additionally, it has the uniquely human ability to be aware of itself.[28]

Again, when all is well, there is a general flow of energy and information from the lower two brains to the higher, with the lower structures working in support of the neocortex. When we feel threatened, however, the flow reverses direction, and suddenly all of the developmental powers of the higher two brains place themselves in the service of their reptilian core, fueling the individual's territoriality and other primitive drives and defenses. Watching ten minutes of world or local news on any given evening will confirm the reality of this basic biological survival mechanism.

Leslie Hart, author of *Human Brain and Human Learning*, calls this self-protective reflex "downshifting."[29] An advocate for what he terms "brain-compatible education," Hart's focus is on how the constant pressure and relentless pace of the conventional classroom make it virtually impossible for true learning to take place. For, as David Elkind observed, the "assembly line" style of education practiced by conventional schools is highly stressful. It is driven by the imperative to speed up production and increase the output. Efficiency is valued at all costs. Schools hurry children by the clock, from subject to subject, and lingering over favorite subjects is not allowed. "Management programs, accountability, and test scores are what schools are about today," he wrote in 1981.[30]

I cite the date of Elkind's already alarming remarks because conditions in our schools—for both students and teachers—have grown exponentially worse since that time. The conventional classroom now threatens children on myriad levels. To begin with, according to Hart, the reptilian brain dates back to a time when captivity meant almost certain death, and the confinement students increasingly experience during the school day is very likely to trigger this primitive fear that we still carry at the base of our skulls. There is a second, subliminal background threat as well: the primal insecurity caused by separating children from their families, especially their mothers. The younger the child, the more separation anxiety he or she will suffer, and, as we have already discussed, the mounting worry over children's future academic success is forcing them into schools or school-like settings at ever earlier ages. Then there is the more obvious and immediate anxiety over measuring up, and as Hart puts it, "the 'fishbowl' effect of being forced to perform in constant fear of ridicule and public failure."[31] Elkind adds to the list the fact that much of the content in the current "teach to the test" form of education is devoid of context or meaning and that the daily routine is unbearably tedious for many. Both factors, he says, are significant stressors.[32]

And so it happens that a growing percentage of schoolchildren are caught in an escalating Catch-22, the term coined by Joseph Heller for the title of his 1961 novel, which has since enjoyed such common use that it can now be found in any desktop *Webster's*. The primary definition is this: "A problematic situation for which the only solution is denied by a circumstance inherent in the problem." The learning kids are now expected to accomplish occurs mainly in the neocortex, and yet the neocortex is the first part of the brain to shut down when a child feels threatened. While most children, writes Hart, can still manage the rote memorization that has become the mainstay of classrooms, the deeper levels of learning—pattern recognition, oral and written language development, and symbolic reasoning—depend on the full participation of the neocortex, which occurs only when a child feels secure.[33]

Students are not the only ones in a bind. Teachers, too, are trapped in a pyramid of pressure that extends from their own school administration all the way up to the White House. No one's job is secure if too many students in a given school have failing scores on the high-stakes year-end exams that are now federally mandated at every grade level. Every teacher I know yearns to inspire his or her students, to engage with them in creative explorations that will enable them to experience the joy and excitement of learning. However, in the present educational climate, the teachers' actions are just as scripted as those of their students. And far too many of the most energetic and idealistic young educators are giving up in despair.

So what does learning look like when children aren't forced into corrals where their thoughts and movements are carefully controlled, where their performance is constantly measured, and where they are graded and sorted like cuts of meat? What if educators, policymakers, and parents stopped viewing education as an extrinsic process that depends on all sorts of anxious orchestration from without?

Let's begin by returning to Deci and Ryan's Self-Determination Theory, which, again, is founded on the premise that children are born with an innate drive to understand and master their worlds. Accordingly, learning is a biological imperative, with every part of our brains finely tuned to enable us to make sense of the environment outside our skin, as well as our inner emotional states.

Such a notion has recently been confirmed by scientists working on the far edge of a number of different fields. For instance, according to Chilean biologist Humberto Maturana and his student, and later colleague, Francisco Varela, life itself is one big learning process. Maturana and Varela started out by trying to explain how it is that we see colors. Somewhat unexpectedly, they discovered that our experience of colored objects is *not* the result of the particular wavelengths of light emanating from those objects and entering the brain through the eyes, the old Newtonian explanation that we were all taught in school. Instead, they concluded, our experience of color "corresponds to a specific pattern of states of activity in the nervous system which its structure determines." That is to say, "We do not see the world. We live our field of vision."[34]

What Maturana and Varela are saying, I think, is that what we "see"—or, for that matter, what we "hear" or "smell" or "touch"—

is not the object itself; rather it is a representation based on how our nervous systems interpret it. Whereas a frog or a fruit fly will see the same object quite differently than we do, the reason we humans agree that the blossoms of a flowering violet are purple and its leaves are green is that, except for the minority of individuals who are born without the receptors for certain wavelengths of light, the structure of our nervous system is extremely similar across our species. So we use a common language to describe said violet and store it in our memories for future use, meaning that "the world everyone sees is not *the* world but *a* world which we bring forth with others."[35]

The deeper Maturana and Varela delved into the biology of perception, the more they became convinced that their distinction between the prevailing belief that our experience is caused by external forces, with information flowing from the outside to the inside, and their discovery that we cocreate our perception in conjunction with the environment, with the information flowing in both directions in a constant feedback loop, applies to all "cognition," or how it is that we know what we know.

The potentially staggering implication of this distinction, which goes straight to the heart of the issue at hand, is that the world as we know it does not exist independently of us. Instead, it is the product of the way in which we continually interact with it. Rather than the world coming to us through our senses, it is you and I who continually "bring forth a world" by means of our experience of it, employing language to describe and share that experience.[36]

Maturana and Varela's revolutionary theory of cognition became the centerpiece of a larger overall explanation of how all organisms function and evolve, which they call "Autopoiesis," from the Greek word for "self-making." "Autopoiesis" refers to the unique ability of living systems to remake themselves by means of their own internal dynamics. Or put differently, living systems are autopoietic because, through their internal interactions with their component parts and their external interactions with the environment, they continually maintain themselves and generate their own organization. Autopoietic systems are also autonomous and have individuality, meaning that they maintain an identity that is independent of their interactions with an observer.[37]

The simplest example of an autopoietic system is the cell. In the cell, DNA produces RNA, which regulates the production of the enzymes that enter the cell nucleus and repair damaged DNA and keep the cell healthy. There are myriad other feedback loops within every cell as well, and even the cell membrane, which keeps the cell intact but is also permeable, participates in the system by using special filters to select what enters the cell as food and leaves as waste.[38] Meanwhile, each cell is unique and able to function autonomously, and its identity does not hinge on being observed. A car, on the other hand, is not autopoietic because it can't produce its own component parts, doesn't generate its own organization, and can't maintain itself, and its identity entirely depends on an observer.

Around the time Maturana and Varela were fleshing out their theory of Autopoiesis in the early 1980s, scientists in other fields were reaching similar conclusions. For instance, Nobel Prize–winning chemist Ilya Prigogine and renowned physicist Fritjof Capra independently coined the term "self-organization" to describe the intrinsic means by which living systems regulate themselves and evolve while in a continuous state of flux. It is self-organization, they write, that explains how cells combine to form tissues, tissues to form organs, organs to form organisms, and organisms to form social systems.[39]

A good example of a self-organizing system is a termite nest. When homeless termites gather in sufficient numbers, individual termites spontaneously undergo certain chemical and behavioral changes. They begin releasing a chemical that attracts other termites, and they also randomly begin dropping bits of earth in a localized area. As more and more termites join in, the earth begins to pile up into pillars that support the nest, which eventually forms around the pillars. This self-organized nest building arises from a feedback loop emerging out of apparently random individual activity. There is no externally conceived plan and no leader. The nest is autopoietic; in effect, it makes itself.[40]

Cognition, according to Maturana and Varela, is autopoietic too; in fact it is the central activity in all autopoietic systems. What we "know" is the result of an interaction between the observed and the autopoietic organization of the observer, which is constantly changing. Moreover, the information that is the raw material of cognition does not exist ready-made in that world. As is the case with the perception of color, which was Maturana and Varela's starting point, cognition is the bringing forth of a world, our knowledge of which is self-generating. It does not depend on structures imposed from the outside.

What does any of this have to do with education? If, as Maturana writes, "learning is not a process of accumulating representations of the environment; it is a continuous process of transformation of behavior through continuous change in the capacity of the nervous system to synthesize it"; and if "man changes and lives in a changing frame of reference in a world continuously created and transformed by him,"[41] then the fixed body of knowledge we hold up as the goal of education might not even exist.

Education, therefore, can no longer be viewed as a process of amassing facts about the world. Again, true learning means being able to adapt to a changing frame of reference in a world continually created and transformed by us. It means that learning is the result of meaningful engagement, not passive storage, which brings us back around to the core reason why we are so exquisitely designed in the first place to be autonomous, self-directing learners; the very essence of life—and in fact all of biological evolution[42]—is a grand exercise in learning.

And thus it should come as no great surprise to us that researchers have recently determined that 95 percent of all learning occurs spontaneously, through play, fantasy, and experimentation—what I call "wild learning." Only the remaining 5 percent of our knowledge—*in our lifetimes*—is acquired through formal instruction, and of that 5 percent, we remember only 3 to 5 percent for any significant length of time.[43]

Does this mean that because wild learning occurs independently there is no place for teaching and mentoring in a child's life? Not at all. While it is true that kids are born with all of the mental structures upon which knowledge is built, it is also true, according to Joseph Chilton Pearce, that "no intelligence or ability will develop unless given the appropriate model."[44] This "model imperative," as Pearce calls it, means that children will develop only those capacities that are modeled for them by the surrounding adult culture. A normal infant born to a deaf-mute mother, for example, cannot develop speech without close and prolonged contact with a speaking person.

But the model imperative stops here. It does not specify how or where the modeling that helps bring forth a child's gifts must take place. I am reminded at this point of a marvelous enlarged photograph of the legendary Louis Armstrong that I once saw in the New Orleans Jazz Museum. In the photograph, Armstrong is giving a trumpet lesson to a young boy who looks about seven or eight on the front stoop of the boy's inner-city apartment building. The utterly intent way in which the boy is gazing up at Armstrong and fingering his own instrument while his teacher is playing for him shows exactly how the modeling process works.

There is no reason why the model imperative cannot take effect in our nation's schools. It's just that in their current pressurized state it is difficult for teachers to be anything more than taskmasters and disciplinarians. If the structure and demands of the classroom are an immoveable impediment to the modeling process, then students should be let out into the world beyond school and matched with adults who are doing whatever they think they might want to do when they grow up.

I will address this crucial issue of modeling and mentoring in greater depth in chapter 8. Let me just say that in my school we encourage students as young as eleven or twelve to explore internship and apprenticeship opportunities. Over the years our kids have worked with chefs, veterinarians, engineers, wooden-boat builders, teachers, wildlife pathologists, attorneys, computer programmers and technicians, Web-site designers, carpenters, artists, dancers, musicians, magicians, archaeologists, comic-book creators, horse trainers, models, videographers, and pilots—even the sky isn't the limit when it comes to finding professionals who are more than willing to share their expertise with an eager-to-learn young person. The only time I was unable to help a student set up an internship was when a boy wanted to shadow a police officer, and for safety reasons the local precinct turned down our request.

It is impossible to measure the amount of valuable learning that takes place thanks to this kind of experience. Suffice it to say that blending a young person's talent and passion with some timely modeling is a potent combination, and students rarely need to be prodded toward pursuing and developing those talents and passions.

Indeed, it has more often been the case that out of my own anxiety and the need to feel like a good teacher, I have regrettably side-tracked a child by trying to assume control of his or her process. For, as Deci and Ryan wrote so eloquently, "Children cannot be pressured into self-determination; they can only be pressured into compliance, reactance, ego-involvement, and helplessness. To achieve self-determination, one must provide informational structures that provide choice and competence feedback in the absence of pressure for specific performance. *And teachers need this as much as the children do*" (italics mine).[45]

I will conclude this chapter with four concrete illustrations of educational environments in which children are encouraged to be self-determining learners. There are many interesting historical examples of schools that recognized the value of wild learning;[46] to show that honoring children's need for autonomy is not a new concept, I'll begin with the story of Yasnaya Polyana, the school that Leo Tolstoy founded and ran on his estate in feudal Russia.

Prior to opening Yasnaya Polyana in 1862, Tolstoy took an exploratory tour of German, Swiss, and English schools to witness firsthand the conditions in them. He was so appalled by the authoritarian posturing in one German school that he wrote in a diary entry, "Terrible. A prayer for the king, beatings, everything by heart, frightened, morally crippled children."[47]

Tolstoy met with the great German educator and creator of the kindergarten Friedrich Froebel while he was in Europe. Although impressed with Froebel's more liberal ideas toward education, Tolstoy went home with the resolve to take them even further. Tolstoy was also influenced by Jean-Jacques Rousseau's philosophy of education; however, he entirely rejected his Social Contract, which was based on the Platonic notion that an orderly society depends on the subjugation of individual freedom to the will of the society. This pointed toward one of Tolstoy's biggest complaints about conventional schools: the rigid conformity by which they operate.

Upon his return to his estate, Tolstoy opened an entire wing of the ancestral manor house to the forty or so school-age peasant children who lived on the estate.[48] Here is a firsthand description of the little school by the American Ernest Crosby, a poet, novelist, and contemporary of Tolstoy:

A little bell, hung over the doorway, rang at eight o'clock every morning, and half an hour later the children appeared. No one was ever reproved for being tardy, and yet there was rarely an absentee at the opening of the exercises. The children had nothing to bring with them, neither book, nor copybook, nor slate; there were no lessons to prepare; neither was there any obligation upon them to remember what they learned the day before.... "They bring only themselves [Crosby quoting Tolstoy], their impressionable natures, and the certainty that school will be as happy for them today as it was yesterday."

No attempt whatsoever was made to enforce order, for [Tolstoy again] "children should learn to keep order themselves." ... The order is perfect; there is no whispering, pinching, or laughing. The hours for lessons are most irregular. Sometimes a lesson which should take one hour is prolonged for three hours, if the pupils are sufficiently interested. Sometimes the children cry out, "Not yet, not yet!" when the teacher is about to close the class. The children are not obliged to come to school nor to remain there, nor are they required to pay attention while there.... In the first place, this disorder, or rather this free order, only appears frightful to us because we are accustomed to an entirely different system, according to which we have been educated ourselves. Secondly, in this case, as in many others, the use of force is founded only upon an inconsiderate and disrespectful interpretation of human nature.[49]

By all accounts, Yasnaya Polyana was a joyful, vibrant place where learning, which was always centered on the children's own interests, inclinations, and rhythms, took place in abundance. Sadly, however, Tolstoy was forced to close the school after only two years due to repeated harassment by the czar's secret police, who were sent to investigate whether Tolstoy was an active participant in the prodemocracy movement being led by the author Ivan Turgenev and other Russian intellectuals.

More recently, the Metropolitan Career and Technical Center, otherwise known as the Met, was founded in 1996 by Dennis Littky and Elliot Washor. This unusual public school is actually a network of six small schools scattered throughout downtown Providence, Rhode Island, with 120 students in each. By state mandate 75 percent of the students come from Providence and the remaining 25 percent come from urban, suburban, and rural areas elsewhere in the state, so the student body is racially and socioeconomically diverse. There are no required courses or credits at the Met, and no set curriculum. Each student creates and updates his or her own individual learning plan by meeting at the beginning of each trimester with a team consisting of an adviser, a parent or guardian, and a workplace mentor. The majority of student learning is project- rather than classroom-based, and students spend two days a week doing internships in businesses or community organizations, developing academic skills through work experience in the real world. Advisers are assigned from the Met's teaching staff, with each teacher overseeing an "advisory" of approximately fourteen students, who form a smaller family within the larger community. Advisories meet almost daily to deal with everything from the particulars of learning plans to personal issues that might stand in the way of learning. Assessment occurs at quarterly exhibitions, where students present to the school community and general public their accomplishments from the preceding period. Family, friends, mentors, and advisers respond to the exhibit with written feedback and recommendations, and advisers then write student narratives for families.

Here is an individual example of how it works: When Chris Emery entered the Met, he was a disaffected ninth grader with a history of school failure and parents who were struggling to get by financially. Emery's first faculty adviser helped him arrange an internship at a commercial bakery, where every Tuesday and Thursday he learned how to mix batter and make cheesecake and tarts. While working as an intern in the Met's kitchen in his sophomore year, he decided to compare the healthy food served at the Met with the nearby Wendy's. This led to a research project on lipids and fat molecules, which concluded with a presentation to fellow students showing that Wendy's food contains unhealthy levels of fat and sodium. Emery was so persuasive that a number of Met students and faculty—including his adviser—stopped eating at Wendy's.

By then, Emery was hooked. Much to his parents' surprise, he began reading science textbooks on his own at home every night, and his adviser, keying off the boy's deepening interest, helped him to set up an internship with a Brown University doctoral candidate in neuroscience. Soon Emery was his new mentor's part-time lab assistant, which gave him access to scientific equipment that most college students don't get to touch until they reach graduate school. She encouraged him to take an introductory neuroscience course at Brown, and despite his shaky academic past, he received a B. Emery, neither of whose parents has attended college, now dreams of earning his PhD.[50]

The Met's track record was so immediately successful—over 98 percent of its initial graduates were accepted to college—that Littky and Washor are now in the process of utilizing a multimillion-dollar grant from the Bill and Melinda Gates Foundation to open forty-four similar schools across the nation, many in struggling cities like Providence.

The Brooklyn Free School, located in New York City, is a privately funded alternative school that maintains its remarkable racial and socioeconomic diversity by offering a sliding tuition scale. The approximately forty students, ages five through eighteen, are free to follow their own interests and direct their own learning with the support of four paid staff and a number of interns and volunteers. There are no grades or standardized tests because, according to its mission statement, the Brooklyn Free School "seeks to minimize, or if possible eliminate completely, undue influence, pressure and stress that accrue from expectations on students to acquire the accepted wisdom of present day society or meet arbitrary standards, so that each child can become an independent learner and thinker." There is no set curriculum; students learn at their own pace by working one-on-one with a teacher, in small groups, or independently, as they see fit. To build on students' interests, the school takes full advantage of the tremendous diversity of individuals, businesses, organizations, and communities that the New York area has to offer. Equally notable, the school operates democratically, meaning that staff members and students of any age can, if they choose, have an equal voice in the day-to-day running of the school thanks to a weekly all-school meeting, at which attendance is optional. Students are thus empowered to help make the rules and set the limits that govern them, and to resolve any interpersonal disputes that might arise during the school day. Founded in 2004 and now in its third year, the Brooklyn Free School has already doubled in size and is looking for a larger space so it can continue to expand.

Finally there is the story of the Colfax family, who gained widespread notoriety in the 1990s when all of their children went on to become successful students at Harvard even though only the oldest had ever set foot in a school (for a forgettable two years).

David and Micki Colfax had been itinerant teachers, David at the college level and Micki in high school, when in the early 1970s they made a radical break and moved with their three young sons to forty-seven acres of remote, logged-over mountainside in Northern California. There they began to establish a self-sufficient, back-to-the-land homestead and to teach their boys at home. The Colfaxes' book about their home-schooling experience suggests how their kids' education unfolded:

> At home, our efforts to restore the land, to plant gardens, and to improve our livestock, stimulated interest in biology, chemistry, and eventually, embryology and genetics. Clearing the badly damaged land provided lessons in ecology, and the construction of the house and outbuildings showed the boys the relevance of seemingly arcane subjects such as geometry. Drew, at seven, understood that the Pythagorean theorem was invaluable in squaring up his sheep shed foundation. Grant, at nine, discovered a Pomo Indian campsite on the ridge and was inspired to delve into Native American archaeology, an interest which later broadened into studies of Mayan and Aztec cultures.
>
> Literature posed no problem at all. We read widely and had acquired a sizeable library of fiction and nonfiction (with more than a smattering of how-to-do-it books!), which the boys began to explore before they were halfway through their reading workbooks. And the county library, some thirty miles away, was virtually plundered every two weeks when we went to town for supplies. And as the boys' interests grew, we built up a rather comprehensive library of reference books, ranging from a set of encyclopedias, which served as a cornerstone, to standard works on genetics, film, sports, and music.[51]

Interestingly, Grant, the oldest, did not begin to read until the age of nine. He had received earlier reading instruction both in school and at home, but the motivation to learn just wasn't there until *he* decided he wanted to find out more about the Native Americans who had once camped on the family's land. With his own interest to propel him, he was reading college-level anthropology monographs within a year and writing essays based on his findings.

When it was time to apply for college, Grant received high scores on his SATs and wrote a long essay describing his home-schooling years on the ranch, his academic accomplishments, and his hopes for the future. He included letters of recommendation from half a dozen mentors who could attest to his work at the community health center, his dairy-goat business, and his general character and intellectual potential. And he traveled to prospective colleges for face-to-face interviews.[52] Both Harvard and Yale accepted him, and he ultimately chose Harvard because of its more generous offer of much-needed financial aid.

Although the vast majority of American children are still forced to digest a daily diet of domesticated learning, an increasing number of genuine educational alternatives are sprouting all over the country. Hundreds of unconventional schools with a wide variety of philosophies and approaches have opened over the last decade, joining hundreds of others. And thousands of parents like the Colfaxes are quietly allowing their children's learning to unfold at home, organically, in the context of family and community.

THREE

NO WORK AND NO PLAY

Play is the child's work.
—Maria Montessori, *Handbook*

ALL WORK AND NO PLAY," as the old saying goes, "make Dick a dull boy." I think it's time for an updated version: no work and no play make Dick and Jane dull boys and girls. Real work and real play are both disappearing from the landscape of American childhood, and evidence of the dimming of children's inner spark is everywhere.

By real work and real play I mean activities in which boys and girls choose to engage in order to feed their instinctive desire for challenge, exploration, excitement, personal autonomy, and connection to others. The work and play may or may not include adults. The key is for the activity to involve a high degree of intrinsic motivation, which again means that the reasons for engaging in it, as well as the meaning and satisfaction, are contained in the activity itself. And it is equally important that the responsibility for determining the structure and conditions of the activity also largely belong to the children.

Forms of work and play that are primarily adult-structured and/or coerced are domesticated forms. There is nothing inherently harmful or wrong with them. Regarding household chores, for instance, which I will discuss in more detail in a moment, I think all parents should insist that their kids do them. It's just that domesticated work and play are of little use to a child's inner wildness.

Because real work has vanished from childhood even more than real play, and because, as a result, the importance of the kinds of work experiences that nourish inner wildness are little understood, let's first examine why they are so vitally important to a child's emerging sense of self. Then in the following chapter I will explore in depth the nature and value of real play.

The Italian educator Maria Montessori, a pediatrician and psychologist by training, preceded Edward Deci and Richard Ryan by well over half a century when she declared that all children are born with an instinctive need to become autonomous individuals. Montessori founded her first school for young children in the slums of Rome in 1907, and within a decade an interest in her highly successful methods developed throughout North America. In her words, "The child's nature is to aim directly and energetically at functional independence.... It is like an arrow released by a bow, which flies straight, swift, and sure."[1] The crux of Montessori's renowned educational method is that children are capable of being autonomous learners from birth onward, and they should be encouraged to be self-directed as soon as possible. All of the learning materials she designed for her students required them to teach themselves through hands-on experience. Her methods were based on her belief that the young are guided by an inner vital force that she called *horme*, an idea that I will explore in greater detail in chapter 5. In a sense, Montessori saw kids as being born with their inner selves already formed. The task of the developmental process, and correspondingly of the adults whose role is to aid it, is then to provide a supportive and stimulating environment in which those selves can actively unfold.

For Montessori, one of the central ingredients of the process is work, by which she did not mean only schoolwork.

The child seeks out independence by means of work; an independence of body and mind. Little he cares about the knowledge of others; he wants to acquire a knowledge of his own, to have his experience of the world, and to perceive it by his own unaided efforts. We must clearly understand that when we give the child freedom and independence, we are giving freedom to a worker already braced for action, who cannot live without working and being active. This he has in common with all other forms of life, and to curb it makes him degenerate.[2]

Were Montessori alive today she would no doubt be shocked by the degree to which the typical child's life has become filled with passive, adult-managed experiences. She would no doubt also look to this highly unnatural state of affairs for the explanations to burgeoning modern-day problems such as childhood obesity and mental and emotional disorders, both of which I will return to in the next chapter.

And so in the Children's Houses, as Montessori's original schools were known, the kids took part in the school's daily upkeep. They cooked, cleaned, gardened, and cared for animals. They painted and drew and made things out of wood and clay. The remainder of their "work"—which, notably, many of us would now consider play —consisted of messing around with Montessori's wide-ranging set of manipulative learning devices, toys, and games that taught them the basic muscular and conceptual skills needed for reading, writing, math, and higher-order thinking. For example, Montessori had some of the fathers of her original students fashion graded sets of wooden pegs and blocks to show the relationships between the primary numbers. Moreover, her students were always free to move about the room and to work with any material for as long as they pleased.

Because Montessori believed that children have an innate drive to overcome obstacles, she instructed the teachers in her charge not to interfere with the kids' spontaneous activity but rather to wait for them to ask for help when they were hopelessly stuck, before stepping in to assist them. Her methods in Rome were so successful with poor and institutionalized children that she soon became a darling of the bourgeoisie throughout Europe and the United States. Today, Montessori schools number over seven thousand worldwide.

A. S. Neill, a Scottish contemporary of Montessori who also founded a school based on principles of freedom and autonomy, offered a similar perspective on work in *Summerhill: A Radical Approach to Child Rearing*, a book that started me on the life path I still follow. Summerhill School, which was founded in Suffolk, England, in 1921 and is now directed by Neill's daughter Zoë Readhead, is residential, so Neill had ample opportunity to study kids in a naturalistic setting where they were allowed to be themselves.

"I have never seen a lazy child," wrote Neill. "What is called laziness is either lack of interest or lack of health. A healthy child cannot stand to be idle; he has to be doing something all day long."[3]

Neill's observation was that a child's attitude toward work depends somewhat on his or her age. Children from ages three to eight or nine, he said, will work like "Trojans" alongside adults on an interesting construction project, for example, without thought of praise or reward. Part of their motivation, he believed, was identifying with the grown-ups and wanting to be like them. After that, most kids have little desire to perform repetitive manual labor but have boundless energy for projects that contain intrinsic meaning for them, examples of which I will give in a moment.[4]

In my experience, children of all ages will work hard at all sorts of tasks, often with great gusto—if certain conditions are met. First, the work must have an inherent, organic purpose. Second, the work must be sufficiently novel. Finally, kids must have some control over their working conditions, and they must be able to see the fruits of their labors directly upon finishing. Under these circumstances, kids will stay with a job until it is done and done well. I know this to be true because I have seen it happen countless times over the years. Even household chores can qualify as real work if parents clearly set the terms and leave it to their kids to get the job done in their own way without a lot of nagging and micromanaging. For instance, in my school the students have regular school chores, which are not optional. They take turns cleaning up the lunchroom once a week, which involves clearing the tables and wiping them down, wheeling the serving dishes and pots and pans to the kitchen (everyone is responsible for bringing in their individual dishes), and sweeping the floor. The kids are organized into crews, and each crew chooses its own leader, who is held accountable for getting the job done properly and on time. The parameters are that the work has to be completed by 1:00 p.m. and that the tables and floors end up reasonably clean. How the kids attack the job, which is not trivial (deciding when to start, for example), is entirely up to the crew. The consequence of not finishing on time is that the crew then has to do the dishes because it has prevented the cook from washing them. This almost never happens.

Watching the process in action is fascinating. Each crew has its own strategy and style. Invariably the crews with the least bossy chiefs cooperate better and perform the task more efficiently. In any event, it is imperative that the teachers stay out of the way and let the kids figure it out for themselves. We have learned over the years that the more we turn the responsibility over to the kids, the less resistance they have to doing it. The work obviously does not thrill them, and they aren't rewarded for it in any way, but they willingly accept the principle of doing their share of school upkeep because they know the teachers are working hard for minimal salaries and the school cannot afford a cleaning person.

Maple-sugaring, which we do in early spring on our school's forested land about twenty-five miles outside the city, is an ideal example of real work that feeds inner wildness. From the outset, the kids are enthralled by the magic of the process. First they drill the trees and see—and of course taste—the first sweet trickle of sap as it emerges from the holes. Later they tramp through the snow to empty the metal, sap-filled pails that hang from the trees into larger plastic buckets. Then they gather the firewood, and lots of it. I have to bite my tongue when I'm tempted to suggest a faster, more efficient way to bring the wood in, because I have learned that if I do intrude, invariably the kids' enthusiasm will disperse like the air out of an untied balloon.

Then they start the fire and keep it going for hours on end, watching the slow transmutation of sap from clear, watery fluid into thick, amber syrup. After all of the sap has been boiled down, they take home a small jar of liquid gold to share with the family. And there is one final step: selling the rest of the syrup to raise cash toward improving the land. The kids love earning money, even when it goes into the school's coffers rather than their own pockets. It adds to their sense of autonomy, and as is the case with performing regular school chores, it strengthens their sense of belonging to and ownership in the school.

An equally memorable project arose when, some years ago, my wife, Betsy, and I took a group of ten-, eleven-, and twelve-year-old boys on a weeklong trip to our founder Mary Leue's farm in the Berkshire Mountains. It was midwinter, and the kids had brought their ice skates so they could play hockey on the frozen beaver pond. The only problem was that the ice lay beneath four feet of snow.

What transpired over the course of our stay astounds me to this day. The first morning, after breakfast, the boys bundled up and slogged their way down to the pond, each with a shovel over one shoulder. Scooping up the soft snow was relatively easy, but then where to put it? They quickly discovered that creating enough space for skating required carrying every shovelful a considerable distance from their starting point. Needless to say, this made progress excruciatingly slow. At the end of day one, the exhausted crew trudged back up the hill with a circle of cleared ice all of five feet in diameter to show for their efforts.

At this rate, it would take the boys all week to finish their coveted rink. Betsy and I were sure they would get discouraged and find something else to do with their time—track animals, build a snowman, or start a snowball war—but the following morning, after breakfast, down the hill they returned for another shift in the snow mine.

This scene repeated itself five times, and it wasn't until our final afternoon that those determined youngsters had cleared enough space for skating. Their "rink" was barely large enough for all of them to fit on without constantly crashing into each other—a hockey game was out of the question—and yet they were triumphant. On the drive back to Albany, Betsy and I heard not one complaint about the efficiency ratio of their project: twenty-five hours of labor to a single hour of play.

It's worth noting that girls are just as eager as boys to engage in physically challenging work. Not long ago, a group of fourth- and fifth-grade girls spent several weeks building a clubhouse in a large tree in a vacant lot behind our school. Construction involved day after day of sawing lumber with a dull handsaw, hauling heavy boards up into the tree, and hammering endless large nails. Sometimes the pieces didn't fit together as the girls had planned, and then they went back to the drawing board. Like the boys' skating rink, this job involved significant perseverance, and yet the girls forged ahead undeterred until the clubhouse was completed to every member's satisfaction.

Our oldest students, the seventh- and eighth-graders, are invited to plan and take a major trip every spring, and groups have traveled to places as far away as California, Spain, and Puerto Rico. These trips belong entirely to the kids. While their teacher helps them arrange and then chaperones the trip, they are primarily responsible for establishing the goals and itinerary and for raising all the necessary funds. This very intensive group process usually entails a great deal of negotiation and debate before everyone is satisfied with the plan.

There are two reasons why we insist that they come up with the money themselves: so that everyone in the class can go, regardless of the financial means of their parents, and so that we can be sure that the students are mature enough, both individually and collectively, to handle the novelty of being away from home for two weeks.

Raising $5,000 to $10,000 is no small task for a bunch of early adolescents; it takes a lot of hard work. The year the class traveled to Puerto Rico to help a poor village that had been ravaged by a hurricane, they brought in more than $9,000 by a wide variety of means, some quite clever and some mundane. A number of the girls liked to sew, and they spent several weeks turning a box of beautiful donated fabric scraps into a magnificently detailed quilt. The raffle they held for the quilt brought in well over $1,000. Other students raked yards and cleaned houses in the neighborhood. The group as a whole staged two major benefit dinners, at one of which they raffled off prizes they had solicited from local businesses. When they returned from Puerto Rico, they published a four-color magazine about their experience. The nearly $2,000 worth of advertising they sold put them well over their fund-raising goal.

Having done all that, the kids proceeded to work their tails off on the island itself, and their task was hardly glamorous. A mudslide had wiped out all the roads in one of the mountain villages, so it became their job first to haul away the tons of heavy wet clay covering the road, and then to build forms and mix concrete for a retaining wall that would ideally prevent the problem from recurring. All of this work—perhaps "toil" would be more accurate—was done under the relentless tropical sun, and yet there was very little complaining. Villagers were so impressed by the kids' moxie that one by one they began to join in. In the end, a retired mason pargeted the wall with a fine coating of cement to give it a smooth finish, and the kids came back in for a grand finale: they painted a giant Puerto Rican flag on the wall and proudly signed all their names. A photo of the group standing in front of the completed project graces the back cover of their magazine. Their satisfied smiles are ample testament to the intrinsic rewards of a job well done.

Last year the students' self-designed trip took them to New Orleans, where they provided relief assistance in the wake of Hurricane Katrina. The kids chose their mission with full knowledge of the fetid conditions they would encounter in the city's ninth ward, yet once again they performed their service willingly, if not always joyfully, given the constant humidity and the devastation that surrounded them.

I could fill this book with examples of kids I have known over the years who chose to pour themselves into hard labor. As Montessori and Neill observed so many decades ago, we seem to have forgotten that meaningful, interesting work is an organic part of young people's instinctive movement toward self-sufficiency and independence. A child's inner wildness hungers for challenge—it yearns for competence, autonomous achievement, and the sense of accomplishment that follows.

The tragic reality is that the only work the majority of American children do today, according to Peter Stearns, is homework. Even household chores have fallen by the wayside in many homes, as more and more parents, concerned about their children's future success, decide that academics should be their kids' only focus.[5] But homework, which is largely a repetition of the material covered in school that day, is hardly the stuff to feed a child's inner wildness. Testifying before a congressional committee in 1933, the national chairman of the Newspaper Boy Welfare Committee put it this way:

> Surely the boy who learns business fundamentals, who meets human nature, who learns the values of business policies on dependability, honesty, courtesy, and promptness, is better equipped to make his way in the world than is the youngster who secures his education wholly within the four walls of a classroom.[6]

So what has happened to work, and how did it vanish from the lives of so many children? Prior to the twentieth century, children worked extensively; indeed, working-class families depended on their kids' labor for survival. The earnings of ten- to fifteen-year-olds amounted to 20 percent of many families' income. Most of that work occurred in the home or on the farm, but by 1890 12 percent of American children between the ages of ten and fifteen were employed in businesses and factories. In 1910 the figure peaked at 18 percent, with fully half of the workforce in many mechanized industries under the age of twenty.[7]

But in a market economy, labor is a commodity traded according to supply and demand. At the dawn of the twentieth century, mechanization was steadily reducing the number of job opportunities in skilled trades, pushing teenage males into unskilled, lower-paying jobs, and automation gradually lowered the need for young male and female factory workers as well. Finally, in 1938, following the massive wave of adult unemployment caused by the Great Depression, children were virtually eliminated from the adult workplace with the passage of the Fair Labor Standards Act. The new federal statute made it illegal for kids under the age of sixteen to work outside the home during school hours, and it limited fourteen- and fifteen-year-olds to no more than eighteen hours during a school week.[8]

At first, displaced young workers did not take these changes lying down. The nation experienced its first mass youth movements when huge numbers of young people marched on Washington, D.C., in 1937 to protest against their collective loss of employment. There the American Youth Congress issued a Declaration of Rights of American Youth, which read, in part, "We want to work, to produce, to build, but millions of us are forced to be idle."[9]

Around the same time, there was a fascinating and interlocking historical segue from the domestication of work to the domestication of play: even before real work had receded from children's daily lives, social reformers launched a concerted nationwide program to organize and supervise their recreation. Reformers were spurred by the perception of a frightened urban middle class that the ways in which children who had formerly spent their days in factories, mines, and sweatshops were using their newfound freedom—hanging out on the streets and in amusement arcades, dance halls, and burlesque theaters, where they drank, gambled, and engaged in other forms of "juvenile delinquency"—was becoming a rampant social problem.[10]

Jane Addams, founder of the famous Hull House, a social settlement on Chicago's West Side, became one of the leaders of those reformers. Here is how the situation appeared to her in 1909, well before all young workers had been legislated out of full employment:

> Let us know the modern city in its weakness and its wickedness, and then seek to rectify it and purify it until it shall be free at least from the grosser temptations which now beset the young people who are living in its tenement houses and working in its factories.... Above all we cannot hope that they will understand the emotional force which seizes them and which, when it does not find the traditional lines of domesticity, serves as a cancer in the very tissues of society and as a disrupter of the securest social bonds.[11]

Addams was particularly concerned about the effects of repetitive labor on urban teenagers:

> As it is possible to establish a connection between the lack of public recreation and the vicious excitements and trivial amusements which became their substitutes, so it may be illuminating to trace the connection between the monotony and dullness of factory work and the petty immoralities which are often the youth's protest against them.[12]

Addams was somewhat unique at the time in noting the psychological tension caused by forcing dull and monotonous work on adolescents. Unfortunately for the future of real play and inner wildness, Addams, rather than call for society to address young-people's need for meaningful work, joined forces with others in lobbying for the end of child labor and replacing it instead with supervised, adult-structured play.

The organized effort to create alternative ways for the youth of the "depraved, socially centrifugal city" to spend their time became known as the Playground Movement. Its mission was to get kids off the streets and onto enclosed play areas supervised by city employees. Once again, it was Boston that paved the way toward designing a universal public institution that would, quite literally this time, fence kids in. Led by philanthropist Joseph Lee, scion of one of

Boston's wealthiest and most prominent families, in the first decade of the twentieth century the city developed a series of large playgrounds that contained specially designed play equipment and sandboxes for younger kids and athletic fields, courts, and sports equipment for older ones. Each facility employed a specially trained staff whose role was to organize and structure the kids' fun and games.

Lee, the "father" of the Playground Movement, was guided by a quasi-scientific philosophy of play that emerged during this time. In particular, he believed that group movement games such as "Ring around the Rosie," which were arranged in circles, taught younger children that "the mark of all morality is subordination." He wrote in 1915: "It is when you lose yourself in the game, give yourself to the cause, and begin to feel that the work is bigger than you are that full life possesses you." Lee also felt that the roots of citizenship and neighborliness lay in the rhythmic songs and movements of circle games. "Rhythm," he wrote, "is the social alchemist."[13]

For older youth, Lee and his protégé Dr. Luther Gulick, the first president of the Playground Association of America, preached the gospel of team sports, which they believed would socialize the same instinctive peer-group loyalty that observers believed was beginning to express itself in gang behavior. According to Gulick,

> The most perfect self-realization is won by the most perfect sinking of one's self in the welfare of the larger unit—the team. . . . This type of loyalty to the group is the same thing as we call good citizenship to the city, and that we call patriotism as applied to the country. The team game is undoubtedly the best training school for these civic virtues.[14]

Gulick advocated structured play not only for healthy physical development but also because he believed that it taught young people to control their emotions, develop greater willpower, and submit more easily to authority. As the Playground Movement gradually spread across the country, it was regarded, according to historian Dom Cavallo, as a panacea for what were perceived to be three of the most acute problems of urban-industrial America: the demise of preindustrial socializing institutions, the process of assimilating young immigrants, and the social anarchy spawned by the youthful "unrestrained" individualism that was so frightening to people like Jane Addams.[15]

While the Playground Movement gathered momentum, there was a parallel growth in other organizations whose raison d'être was to manage young people's extracurricular lives. First to appear was the YMCA/YWCA, which opened its first branch in Boston in 1851 and by 1900 had 1,379 branches nationwide. The National Association of Boys' Clubs was founded in 1906, followed by the Boy Scouts and Campfire Girls in 1910 and the Girl Scouts in 1912. In 1925 the American Legion created the first baseball league for teenage boys, and in 1938 the Little League was founded to provide the same opportunity for younger boys. At the adult level, the years between 1910 and 1917 saw the appearance of myriad civic clubs and community-service groups, such as the Rotary Club, Kiwanas, and the Lions Club, which also placed an emphasis on developing wholesome, adult-supervised activities for kids.[16]

From this point forward the domestication of work and play proceeded hand in hand, still dominated by two key American themes: the Puritan "idle hands are the devil's workshop" ethos and a sticky mix of parental anxiety and guilt. Not surprisingly, the marketplace wasted no time in capitalizing on the growth of kids' free time, and perhaps even more so on the link in the adult mind between youthful boredom and the specter of delinquency. Children's books, toys, games, and other forms of entertainment quickly became highly profitable industries, spurred by a number of other factors as well.[17] IQ testing, for instance, which started in the 1930s, gave a huge boost to the market for "educational" toys that promise to stimulate intelligence.[18] Today, as anxiety over school readiness continues to mount, worried parents—who can increasingly be persuaded that almost any toy is educational—are rushing in record numbers to surround their kids with what play theorist Brian Sutton-Smith calls "images of achievement."[19]

Postwar suburbanization became yet another contributor to the domestication of work and play. Geographic isolation cut down considerably on youth employment opportunities, while suburban affluence eliminated any real need for kids to work anyway. By the 1980s, in many areas, adult subscription services were taking over the few remaining job options for kids, such as mowing lawns and delivering newspapers. Isolation, the perception of cities as danger-

ous places, and the growing idleness of their children has led suburban parents in particular to become more and more involved in
supplying their kids with entertainment. (By the end of the twentieth century, mothers were making 60 percent of the choices regarding their children's leisure activities.)[20]

Driven by anxiety over their children's academic performance,
many of today's parents forged deals with their kids, sometimes
tacit and sometimes explicit: keep up with your schoolwork and
homework, your extracurricular lessons, and the requisite practicing, and we'll reward you with your fill of trips to the mall, tick-
ets to the movies, cell phones, new video games, and so on into the
night. Finally, the safety fears that I touched upon earlier can im-
pinge on work as well as play. Wary parents keep their children
much closer to home than they used to, and may be uncomfortable
letting their kids cruise the neighborhood in search of odd jobs.

Clearly, the near-elimination of young people from the adult
workplace had both positive and negative ramifications. On one hand,
most of the jobs from which they were ousted—we might even say
"protected"—were menial, repetitive, and low-paying. Children as
young as seven or eight often worked long, hard hours in oppres-
sive, if not downright dangerous, conditions. It goes without saying
that they needed protection from ruthless employers who were all
too eager to exploit their youthful energy and naïveté.

On the other hand, there was built-in meaning to the act of
working, because those young people were knowingly and for the
most part willingly contributing to the economic survival of their
families. As a result, they felt needed and important. The experience, even if not inherently fulfilling, provided a true form of en-
trée to the adult world. In granting a preview of what lay ahead, it
supplied a sense of both responsibility and direction and became a
source of confidence and maturity.

Similarly, the Playground Movement was a double-edged sword
in its effects on childhood recreation and play. From one perspective
it marked the beginning of the all-out attack on their undomesticated forms that continues today. From another angle, however,
playgrounds became urban sanctuaries of a sort, safe places for kids
to move and play and congregate, places where they could compete
in sports and develop their athletic prowess. The city of Washington, where I grew up, had just such a system of facilities, born of the

Playground Movement, and between the ages of roughly seven and thirteen I practically lived at the playground up the street from my house. There I learned to play baseball, football, basketball, soccer, tennis, and Ping-Pong—all of which are still a source of joy to me—and there the male playground directors happily served as the father substitutes and mentors I so desperately needed at that tender time in my life.

Thankfully, the majority of our activities there were not adult-structured. The directors tended not to be controlling types, and as long as we kept our behavior within reasonable limits, we were free to do as we pleased. Moreover, the grounds were left open at all hours, which meant that a lot of the time that we were playing and hanging out there were no adults around anyway. So, while the Playground Movement had somewhat of a domesticating effect on the play of my generation, our play was still quite "wild" by today's standards.

With the shift from an industrial to a service economy, young people have, to the extent allowed by law, been gradually allowed back into the marketplace. The number of teens in the workforce ebbs and flows with overall economic conditions; during hard times, the youngest employees are usually the last to be hired and the first to be fired. The good news is that employment opportunities exist for as many as 80 percent of American teenagers, and the experience of working has positive effects on their sense of independence, self-esteem, responsibility, and ability to manage time and money. Moreover, a study by the National Research Council and the Institute of Medicine found that young people who work twenty or fewer hours per week during high school tend to fare better in college and in their subsequent careers, whether or not they complete their degrees.[21]

But the bad news may well outweigh the good. The same study reported that when teens work more than twenty hours per week during the school year, as nearly half of U.S. high-school seniors do, they tend to sacrifice sleep and exercise, spend less time with their families, and cut back on homework. They also tend to have lower grades and higher rates of dropping out of school, behavioral problems, and substance abuse. Plus, they are less likely to enroll in and/or complete college.[22]

The study drew no clear conclusion on why a heavy workload is detrimental to a teen's present and future well-being, but it did offer some clues. More than half of all employed teenagers work in the retail sector, manning cash registers in malls and supermarkets and flipping burgers in fast-food restaurants; 25 percent have jobs in leisure services or low-level health care. The remainder work, as young people always have, in agriculture, industry, and family businesses. Because their jobs are generally entry-level, young workers find themselves changing jobs and work schedules frequently, according to the whims of their employers and the vagaries of the labor market.

Unlike their forebears, however, children seldom contribute their income to their families. Instead, they tend to spend their paychecks on "discretionary items" and individual wants and needs: clothing, entertainment, cars, and so on.[23] And what the authors of the National Research Council report failed to mention is that real earnings for young workers, adjusted for inflation, have dropped by 25 percent since 1985 and continue to fall.[24]

So the problem, in my view, is that many young people are trapped in yet another Catch-22. The employment options available to them are for the most part dulling and mindless. They do thoroughly domesticated work, devoid of any creativity or purpose apart from making money. But because the pay is so low, they often have no choice but to work long hours to meet their financial goals —and this is after a full day of often tedious, repetitive school routines. At the end of the week, these young workers rush to spend their hard-earned cash on an endless array of goods and entertainment sources to alleviate their boredom and frustration. Before they know it, they have been lured so deeply into our addictive consumer economy—to the tune of nearly $200 billion a year[25]—that they can't seem to find their way out. Around and around in this vicious, exhausting, and often self-defeating circle they go.

One of the last remaining bastions of hands-on labor for children, and therefore a crucial source of self-discipline, competence, responsibility, and other important life lessons, is household chores. Unfortunately, as I mentioned earlier, many parents no longer require their kids to help out around the house. Some mothers and fathers feel that their children already have enough on their plates with homework and other extracurricular activities. Others have a strong need to be liked by their kids and so tend to back down when the kids resist doing chores. "It's easier to do it myself," becomes an all-too-common fallback position for these parents.

Still other parents, according to psychologists and parent educators Jean Illsley Clarke, Connie Dawson, and David Bredehoft, get trapped in a pattern of overindulging their children. In their insightful book *How Much Is Enough?: Everything You Need to Know to Steer Clear of Overindulgence and Raise Likeable, Responsible, and Respectful Children*, which is based on interviews with nearly 1,200 adults who themselves were overindulged as children, the authors define overindulgence as "giving them too much of what looks good, too soon, and for too long." It means devoting a disproportionate share of family resources to a child in a way that appears to be addressing the needs of the child when in fact it addresses the needs of the parents.[26] Because we live in a culture of such excess, write Clarke, Dawson, and Bredehoft, and we are constantly bombarded with messages that more is better, it's almost inevitable that parents today will try to give their kids too much food, clothing, money, attention, and entertainment.[27] While overindulgence occurs in all types of families and different parents overindulge their kids in different ways, they argue, overnurturing is the common denominator.[28]

Overnurturing parents make a serious mistake when they do all of the housework instead of insisting that each of their children carry a share of the workload. A majority of the participants in the study said in hindsight that they would have preferred to do chores as children in order to earn a feeling of pride in helping the family succeed.[29]

Clarke et al. then point to a fascinating study conducted by Marty Rossman, associate professor of family education at the University of Minnesota, which followed a group of eighty-four children, starting in preschool, and concluded that the best predictor of a child's success—not using drugs, having high-quality relationships with others, finishing school, and getting a good start in a career—is helping with household chores beginning at age three or four. The study went on to find that early participation in household chores was more important to adult success than any other factor—including IQ. The bottom line is that the sooner kids learn they aren't a burden, and in fact can make important contributions to household life, the better.[30]

Again, while washing the dishes, taking out the trash, and mowing lawns aren't the "wildest" forms of work, performing such mundane tasks strengthens children's inner wildness because it helps them to forge a template of purposeful involvement in life at home that they can gradually transfer to the larger world as they grow more competent and mature.

The bottom line is that it behooves parents to stop and consider how important real work is to the ecology of childhood, and the disconcerting extent to which it has disappeared since the turn of the twentieth century. Parents—and teachers—who understand the vital part that meaningful work plays in a child's development will look beyond chores and routine academic exercises to more creative and satisfying work opportunities. Moms and dads who have hands-on skills—sewing, woodworking, cooking, building, photography, gardening, and so on—need to model those skills for their kids and find ways to involve them in projects that are pleasurable and mutually rewarding.

Likewise, teachers need to encourage students to get involved in projects that put their ideas and creativity to practical use. Schools need to break out of their isolation from the community and forge a multitude of connections that get students out into the workplace and professionals into the schools.

It has never been more urgent that all of us who want to play a significant role in children's lives constantly be on the lookout for ways to support their right to their own spontaneous, authentic, and self-generated experience—which, as we shall see in the following pages, is what sustains our inner wildness and is the very essence of what makes us human.

FOUR

REAL PLAY

Play is the highest expression of human
development in childhood for it alone is the
free expression of what is in a child's soul.
—Friedrich Froebel, *The Education of Man*

REAL PLAY, THE KIND that arises out of children's spontaneous
urge to experience excitement, wonder, and meaning, is the best
friend of inner wildness and without a doubt its greatest ally. The
freely chosen and pleasurable imagining, exploring, manipulating,
experimenting, relating, learning, laughing, and risk-taking that
constitute real play enable kids to integrate their minds and bodies
into a unified, coherent, and *undomesticated* whole.

It is through real play that children make some of their greatest
discoveries: whom to trust, how to differentiate true from false and
reality from fantasy, when they are ready for the next challenging
experience, where their boundaries end and the next person's begin, and why things are the way they are. Deci and Ryan call these
growth steps the "psychological work" of childhood.[1]

Real play contributes to every aspect of a child's mental, physical, emotional, and social development. To begin with, it is one of the
driving forces behind the instinctive unfolding of intelligence that
starts the moment we are born. Everything babies do in the first
few months, aside from eating, eliminating, and expressing emotions, is essentially play, according to the esteemed Swiss psychologist Jean Piaget, whose model of the stages of cognitive growth in
children that he mapped out between the early 1920s and 1960 is
still widely accepted today. Moreover—and this is one of Piaget's
lasting contributions to the psychology of learning—it is a baby's
early sensory-motor and imitative play, well before the development of language, that paves the way for intelligent thought.[2]

Piaget was fascinated by the role the mind plays in a child's progression from a babbling, flailing, and unpredictable tangle of needs and impulses to a rational, orderly being capable of a deep understanding of both its inner and outer world. He fundamentally disagreed with the behaviorists, who ruled psychology at the time and who saw learning as an essentially passive and mechanical process controlled by environmental stimuli and reinforcements.

Like Maturana and Varela, whose theory of cognition I outlined in chapter 2, Piaget's goal was to get down to the biological roots of learning; and similarly, Piaget concluded that learning is a dynamic, creative act. Knowledge isn't something children acquire and store. They build it by making novel mental structures out of materials supplied by the outside world. For example, the infant who first realizes that objects fall when you drop them is creating a mental structure and not waiting to be taught about the law of gravity at a later date.[3]

The linchpin of the knowledge-construction process, Piaget believed, is real play, which he defined as "actions that are an end in themselves and do not form part of any series of actions imposed by someone else or from outside."[4] At each stage play supports the kind of learning that is supposed to occur at that time. During the initial "sensory-motor" phase (birth to age two), for instance, play is characterized by the urge to taste and touch every new object and to endlessly mimic patterns of movement and sound—which is how we all learned to walk and talk.

In the "pre-operational" stage (ages two to seven), the child learns to use complex language and to represent objects with symbols; and so, correspondingly, Piaget named the type of imaginary play that fuels that learning "symbolic play." "The symbol is the very structure of a child's thought," he wrote in Play, Dreams and Imitation in Childhood. It concretizes and animates everything in young children's reality, enabling them to express and understand their experience at a time when their verbal/logical thought is not sufficiently developed.[5]

As children enter the "concrete operational" phase (ages seven to eleven), they are able to think logically about concrete objects and events. At this point, Piaget writes, kids become less interested in symbolic play and start to be more interested in games characterized by rules and structure, which he calls "social play." Because they can now use reason to make sense of the world, they no longer need their make-believe orientation. Finally, during the formal operational stage (eleven and up), children can think logically about abstract ideas, and so their play consists mainly of group competitive games and sports.[6]

Real play not only funds children's intellectual development but is an important source of emotional learning as well. This is because emotions are almost by definition nonrational; and make-believe, or imaginary play, which is one of real play's purest forms, likewise operates outside the bounds of rationality. In the world of make-believe, children enjoy the freedom to act out their fantasies without having to adapt to the conventions and requirements of external reality.[7] They can work or, more accurately, play their way through the emotional spectrum by imagining themselves in all sorts of evocative roles and situations. All they need is unstructured time and access to a few simple props.

This is why we always have a readily available trunk of dress-up clothes in our preschool area. By donning a man's hat, a boy can suddenly transform himself into a stern, punitive father. A girl can become a strict, domineering mother simply by slipping a pair of women's shoes onto her feet and a purse over her wrist. Alternately, they can reverse the polarity and pretend to be loving parents, doting over the imaginary offspring that their friends have agreed to playact. Without any accessories at all, a group of young boys can turn themselves into a litter of puppies wrestling and climbing over each other. Just like real puppies, they test their strength and explore the safe boundaries of their aggression without hurting each other. If anyone hits, pushes, or squeezes too hard, the others will quickly let him know, and ninety-nine times out of a hundred the aggressor will immediately tone it down a notch.

If you wander downstairs into our elementary classrooms, chances are you'll find any number of children engaged in imaginative play of one kind or another. These days there is a group of seven- to thirteen-year-old boys who devotedly play the interactive role-playing game Dungeons and Dragons, or "D & D" as they like to call it. Without any adult input whatsoever, the players create a changing array of heroic fantasy characters—fierce warriors, evil rogues, powerful wizards—which they guide through an ongoing series of trials and adventures, working together to battle dark enemies and defeat terrible monsters.

D & D is essentially an improvisational fairy tale that the boys cocreate as they go along. It is driven by their imaginations—there is no technological component of any kind. They begin by drawing elaborate illustrations of their characters and writing down descriptions of the characters' powers. Then one player is chosen as the Dungeon Master, whose responsibility it is to narrate the action and referee the game. Together, the Dungeon Master and the players bring the game to life by rolling multisided dice to help determine the outcomes of the life-and-death scenarios they dream up. The game involves a great deal of cooperation and social interaction. It is intensely absorbing, and the boys will often play uninterrupted for hours at a time. Ironically the game is rarely, if ever, marred by real-life conflicts between the combatants, even though it contains a lot of fantasy blood and gore.

The girls in the school tend to prefer a different style of pretend play. Last year, for instance, a group of six- and seven-year-olds were in the middle of an intense love affair with horses. Aster, the leader of the group, was fortunate enough to engage her passion in the real world during weekly riding lessons, but the rest of the time, she and her fellow urban-dwelling classmates would invent an alternate reality replete with horses. Sometimes they would bring their miniature toy horses to school—Aster has a nearly life-size stuffed toy pony given to her by her grandmother—and dream up one horse drama after another.

The girls would sit together for hours, drawing their favorite horses, and then make up elaborate stories about them. Aster was already a fluent writer, so she often served as the group's scribe, and it was she who invented a way of "galloping" on her hands and knees across the carpet in our largest room, which, when her friends joined in, sounded uncannily like a herd of real horses thundering down the home stretch. Every so often they decided to stage "horse races," to which the whole school came to cheer them on. All of these antics took place without any adult participation whatsoever.

Piaget extolled the absence of adult-imposed rules in make-believe play. "The conflict between obedience and individual liberty," he said, "is the affliction of childhood." In real life the only options are submission, rebellion, or compromise, whereas in make-believe play there is an endless supply of magical alternatives.[8] Piaget also termed pretend play "practice" play because it allows kids to reenact experiences that have moved or delighted them, and thereby to reinvoke, rethink, and integrate those feelings.[9] A child can "liquidate" anxieties caused by traumatic situations by reliving those experiences in make-believe.[10] As an example, Piaget tells the story of a girl who is feeling painfully jealous after the birth of a sibling. The girl addresses the unhappy emotion by playing with two dolls of unequal size and making the smaller one go away on a trip while the larger one stays home with Mommy.[11]

In *The House of Make-Believe*, the husband-and-wife psychologist team Dorothy and Jerome Singer recount the experience of their neighbors' three-year-old son after the parents had to have the family dog euthanized because it was suffering from a fatal tumor. Unsure how best to handle their son's feelings, the parents had told Michael they were taking the dog to the "dog doctor" to see if he could help the dog get better but that the dog might still die. After his parents returned without the dog, Michael built a house out of large cardboard blocks. Soon the house became a doghouse, and Michael led his mother on all fours inside. At first he was gentle with the "dog," and gave her a bone and scratched her behind her ears. But then he became angry and began scolding the dog, finally "locking" her in the doghouse and going off to play.

Michael returned a short while later, made up with the dog, and then pretended to drive her to the vet's office. When they arrived, Michael ended the fantasy and changed his mother back into her original form. Through his make-believe play, the Singers say, Michael was able to express the confusing mix of love and anger he felt toward both the dog and his mother over the loss of the dog, until he reached a place of acceptance and completion.[12]

This is the basis of contemporary play therapy, which enables children to heal deep emotional wounds through the modality of imaginary play. A good example, again from the Singers, is the case of a six-year-old boy whose parents divorced after many months of fighting, often in front of Mark. To make matters worse, Mark's dad's job required a lot of travel and he began canceling many of

Mark's weekly visits to his house. Mark's behavior in school soon became intolerable. He started hitting and biting other kids and even threw a chair at the teacher when she tried to intervene.

In his play-therapy sessions, Mark used superhero action figures to reenact his conflicts. He placed himself in complete control of everyone around him, bullying, commanding, and winning every battle. Then one day, after he had watched scenes of a destructive hurricane on the six o'clock news, Mark pretended that the hurricane was descending upon the large dollhouse in the play therapy room. He knocked over furniture and toy people and threw objects out the dollhouse windows. Then he took a toy doctor kit, pretended it was a toolbox, and repaired all the damage. After several similar sessions, Mark stopped playing at the destruction of the house. Instead he began using the miniature people in scenarios that involved caretaking, nurturance, and having fun together. His behavior in school improved dramatically.[13]

It is also through real play that children accomplish a great deal of social learning. Play is almost the exclusive medium within which young kids connect with their peers, which brings into the discussion the third of the three innate psychological needs that anchors Deci and Ryan's Self-Determination Theory: interpersonal relatedness. According to this model, human beings can't thrive without meeting all three needs; an environment that promotes the first two needs, autonomy and competence, but not relatedness will result in some measure of "impoverishment of well-being."[14]

It's no coincidence that the dictionary term for a companion with whom a child plays is "playmate." You might say that kids mate through their play, because play is the social glue that binds them together. It provides the common ground—the "playing field," if you will—on which kids can meet as equals and begin to discover each other's likes and dislikes, wishes, and dreams.

Play, I might add, is an extraordinarily efficient means of exchange. In my school, it never ceases to amaze me how fast kids who meet for the first time can initiate a friendship once they discover a form of play that is mutually satisfying. This is because, according to Israeli psychologist and family therapist Shlomo Ariel, play— especially make-believe play—is a special communication medium.[15] Make-believe play is so "remarkably flexible and sophisticated" that it serves a number of purposes. It can function as a "diplomatic language" when kids use it to work out their interpersonal differences and conflicts in imaginary ways. Safely inside their shared fantasies, they can vie for power and control without resorting to physical aggression. They can negotiate how close to allow themselves to get to one another and how much trust to invest in each member of the group; who is inside the group and who is out; and who gets to be in charge and how much of the time.

Ariel calls these "issues of proximity and control," and he writes that they underlie the interactive dance that is the basis for relationships among all animals, not just humans. Here the players are free to try out all kinds of social configurations because they aren't bound by the normal "chains of reality and social conventions," the pressure and stress of which often contribute to less than harmonious outcomes.[16] Anyone who has spent time observing children at play knows how quickly war can break out when they try to work out their proximity and control issues in a sport or some other competitive game of skill.

Kids also utilize make-believe play as a "legal language" to negotiate territory and possession issues, two more universal sources of conflict. A key step in structuring their fantasy play is the process of making their own rules and establishing consequences for violations, which they seldom do with adult logic.[17]

The Singers, who have spent nearly fifty years studying play, also cite it as an important source of emotional and social learning. Only rarely have they observed children exhibit strong negative emotions while they are pretend-playing. What they do see is kids acting out their fear and aggression on a fantasy level, using toys and make-believe characters in such a way that no one is actually harmed. In one longitudinal study, the Singers recorded the social-interaction patterns of children from eight nursery schools during indoor and outdoor free-play periods over the course of a year. They found, not surprisingly, that the children who engaged in the most make-believe play exhibited the most joy and liveliness; and the more imaginative the child appeared, the less he or she seemed anxious, sad, or fatigued. Numerous other studies have produced the same results.[18]

Conversely, according to Ariel's extensive research, children who are not skilled in make-believe play are often rejected by their peers, which can have serious negative effects on their self-esteem.[19]

However, according to two studies conducted by research psychologists Stephen Davis and John Fantuzzo, peer-led play-treatment sessions helped rejected children learn how to engage in make-believe play, which in turn led to significant improvements in their social competence and their overall behavior.[20]

Real play makes perhaps its greatest contribution to inner wildness by providing the impetus for the creative process. It is a marvelous feedback loop: inner wildness thrives on the dynamic energy of creativity and, in turn, creativity needs inner wildness's hunger for novelty, originality, and free and full expression.

At the end of a long, illustrious career spent studying a number of classical periods, the Dutch cultural historian Johann Huizinga argued that all culture arises out of play, because play permeates human activity. Language for the most part is learned through play, and then we use it playfully when we create metaphors, humor, and so on. Myth, Huizinga writes, is based on an imaginary concept of the world, and the spirit of mythology "is playing on the borderline between jest and earnest."

Huizinga called his last and most unusual work *Homo Ludens*. Latin for "Man the Player," the title is a takeoff on the biological classification for human beings, *homo sapiens*, or "man the knower." His reasoning: "We play and know that we play, so we must be more than merely rational beings, for play is irrational." The bulk of the book is spent tracing what Huizinga calls the "play-element" through each province of culture. In the arts the critical involvement of play is obvious. Poetry is playing with words and metaphors; music—which one *plays*—is playing with sound and rhythm; dance is playing with movement and rhythm; and the plastic arts with color, shape, and texture. Philosophy is playing with ideas and in fact has its origins in the art of making up and solving riddles. Science is playing with observations, measurements, and patterns.[21]

Later we will look at Huizinga's dire projections for a culture that fails to value and sustain its sense of playfulness and creativity.

Since Huizinga's time, several social scientists have conducted extensive studies of the creative process in order to understand its essential characteristics. For instance, the eclectic thinker and writer

Edith Cobb spent many years studying the lives of famous artists, writers, and scientists in order to pinpoint what fueled their creative genius. She eventually concluded that the name for the place where real play and creativity intersect is wonder.

In her book *The Ecology of Imagination in Childhood*, Cobb wrote:

> The sense of wonder is spontaneous, a prerogative of child-hood. When it is maintained as an attitude, or point of view, in later life, wonder permits a response of the nervous system to the universe that incites the mind to organize novelty of pattern and form out of incoming information. The ability of the adult to look upon the world with wonder is thus a technique and an essential instrument in the work of the poet, the artist, or the creative thinker.[22]

Wonder, for Cobb, is what play was for Piaget. It causes babies to delight in the discovery of their hands and in the reappearance in their line of vision of a familiar person or object. Long before recognizable play is possible, all of an infant's actions are marked by a sense of wonder "and an expectancy of more wonders to come."[23]

Although Cobb lacked the formal training of other explorers of the child psyche, she is often one of the first to be cited in well-known books and articles that deal with imagination and creativity in children. She was strongly influenced by the concept of ecology that was emerging in the 1960s, when she was gathering the research for her seminal book. As a child ecologist, she was especially concerned with how the exchanges between kids' inner and outer worlds determine the kind of person the kids will become, and particularly whether or not they will grow up to lead creative, original lives. The bottom line for Cobb was this:

> In the creative perceptions of poets and children, we are close to the biology of thought itself—close, in fact, to the ecology of imagination, in which the energies of the body and mind as a unit, an ecosystem, and the energies of nature combine in a mutual endeavor to adapt to nature, to culture, and to the societies devised by man to embody culture.[24]

Cobb viewed the imagination as "the gift of childhood to human personality." A child's future mental, social, and physical health depends upon a well-developed imagination, she firmly believed, and the purpose of childhood is to serve as a special time set aside for its incubation.[25] She saw great danger in forcing children to overdevelop the mind at the expense of a child's creative drive.[26] One can only imagine what she would have to say today about the state of affairs in our nation's homes and schools, a subject I will return to shortly.

The social psychologist Teresa Amabile, who has been researching the creative process for more than three decades, also began by studying hundreds of well-known creative individuals to find out what they had in common. Her widely accepted analysis of creativity reveals all of the chief characteristics of inner wildness. For instance, Amabile found that the personality trait all shared was independence, which she defined as an absence of conformity in thinking and an absence of dependence on the approval of others.[27] Creative people look first to themselves for an assessment of the quality of their creations, and only secondarily to the opinions of others—as when Woody Allen skipped the Academy Awards ceremony after winning an Oscar for *Annie Hall* because to him it was more important to play his clarinet with his jazz group at their regular weekly gig in Manhattan.[28]

The subjects of Amabile's landmark study also stressed the importance of playfulness and freedom from external constraints in bolstering creativity. Here she offers the story of Einstein's schooling as an example. As a child, Einstein attended rigid, militaristic lower schools, where he was a less than illustrious student. Then, at the age of fifteen, he ended up enrolling in a Swiss boarding school after he failed his university entrance exams. Fortunately, this school stressed the students' need to search for knowledge on their own terms. There was little emphasis on memorization; instead the focus was on individual lab work, student-initiated investigations, and relaxed, democratic exchanges between students and teachers. Einstein later wrote about the school:

It made an unforgettable impression on me, thanks to its liberal spirit and the simple earnestness of the teachers who based themselves on no external authority. . . . There were altogether only two examinations; aside from these, one could just about do as one pleased. This was especially the case if one had a friend, as I did, who attended the lectures regularly and who worked over their content conscientiously. This gave one freedom in the choice of pursuits until a few months before the examination, a freedom which I enjoyed to a great extent and have gladly taken into the bargain the bad conscience connected with it as by far the lesser evil.[29]

It was at his new high school that Einstein devised the first experiment that would eventually lead him to the theory of relativity.[30]

At the conclusion of her research, Amabile assembled this definition of creativity: "The process that results in a novel work that was arrived at in an original, trial and error manner, and that is accepted as useful or satisfying by a group at some point in time." In other words, following a recipe to bake a cake is not an example of creativity, but it is when the baker improvises and experiments with the ingredients and turns out a tasty delight.[31]

Then Amabile constructed the following five-stage model of the creative process. It begins with the individual choosing to create something or to solve a problem for his or her own reasons. The greater the extent to which the motivation is intrinsic, the greater the degree to which the individual will be able to approach the task playfully and with a willingness to take risks, and thereby attend to aspects of the environment whose relevance might not be immediately obvious. Extrinsic motivation—rewards, deadlines, assessments, approval—undermines creativity at every turn because it causes the individual to focus narrowly on achieving the extrinsic goal. Meanwhile, creativity often depends on stepping away from the goal and being free to pay attention to seemingly incidental aspects of the task or problem and the environment. The more single-mindedly we pursue a goal the less likely we are to explore alternative pathways and thereby come up with something original and unique.[32]

In the second stage the individual builds up or accesses both new and already-learned technical skills, special talents, and information that are relevant to the project or problem.

It is the third stage that determines the level of novelty of the creation or solution. The individual's repertoire of what Amabile terms "creativity-relevant processes"—deep concentration; uninhibited risk taking; and the ability to take new perspectives on problems, generate unusual ideas, and use the imagination in novel ways —will determine the flexibility with which he or she proceeds. Intelligence alone, she stresses, does not spark creativity.

In the fourth stage the individual pauses to analyze the usefulness and satisfaction—by definition, novelty is not enough to make something creative—of the work in progress. Finally, in the fifth stage one decides whether or not to continue the process based on the results of the self-evaluation in step four. If one determines that the goal has been reached or that one doesn't have the wherewithal to reach the goal, one will terminate the process. If there has been some progress toward the goal, the individual will elect to return to step one and move through the five stages again.[33]

After Amabile felt that she had successfully mapped out a basic outline of the creative process, she turned her attention toward children. Creativity, in her opinion, isn't an inherited characteristic that some of us have in greater abundance than others. Rather it is a potential within every child, and its development—or lack thereof— depends a great deal on environmental conditions.[34]

In a pamphlet commissioned by the National Education Association, Beth Hennessey and coauthor Amabile include a chapter entitled "How to Kill Creativity." They list five ways:

1. Have kids work for an expected reward. Rewards make children much less likely to take risks or to approach a task with a playful or experimental attitude.
2. Set up competitive situations for some desirable reward or other form of recognition.
3. Have children focus on an expected evaluation. When kids are performing for a successful assessment of their performance, their motivation automatically becomes extrinsic and creativity dies.
4. Use plenty of surveillance. The mere presence of a watchful audience can be all it takes to undermine the intrinsic motivation that sustains creativity. Quoting Hennessey and Amabile, "If you want to lessen your students' chances of coming up with creative solutions, make your presence felt

at all times. Watch their every move, and shift their focus away from the task at hand and toward your implied evaluation of their progress."

5. Set up restricted choice situations by forcing kids to choose from a predetermined set of options.[35]

Hennessey and Amabile went on to write that unstructured and make-believe play stimulates creativity because it gives kids the opportunity to discover new properties of objects, and this nourishes the imagination. To support their claim, the researchers cited a study they conducted with a group of preschool children. First, they unobtrusively observed the kids while they were involved in unstructured activities and classified those who tended to engage spontaneously in make-believe play as "players" and those who didn't as "non-players."

Then the test subjects were placed in one of the three following situations: free play with a set of objects, imitating an experimenter's actions with the objects, or engaging in straightforward problem solving with the objects. The free play group outperformed the other two groups every time, but it was only the "players" among that group who scored high on the creativity scale.[36]

Hennessey and Amabile end with a bit of advice to teachers. Give students ample time for free play and allow them to engage in make-believe. Eliminate the restrictions, rewards, evaluations, and competition from the classroom as much as possible; instead help kids to focus on the enjoyable aspects of what they do. They even suggest that teachers actually talk with their students about what they find interesting or fun about school.[37]

It would appear that their words have fallen largely on deaf ears.

Inner wildness cannot survive without real play, and yet the enemies of real play seem to be everywhere. So much of what passes for play today—sports, passive entertainment, and all types of electronic toys and games—is not really play at all. These are forms of what Johann Huizinga called "false play" because they do little to enhance a child's imagination or creativity.[38]

Real play is fading from every context of a contemporary child's life. At home, as I will explore in depth in chapter 7, it is being overrun by TV and videos, video and computer games, and the Internet. The problem is a compound one. Electronic media are intensely alluring and potentially quite addictive; and yet, as we have already discussed, many parents, fearing for their kids' safety, hesitate to encourage them to play outside or allow them to roam very far from home. To make matters worse, children are becoming increasingly cut off from nature—the subject of chapter 6—and passive, technological substitutes like the Discovery Channel and the Internet are rushing in to fill the void.

Real play is also being squeezed out by the rampant busyness and heavily structured and overscheduled nature of many kids' lives. Real play requires open time and space, and it simply cannot flourish on a survival diet of play dates and trips to the movies or commercialized play emporiums. And while there is certainly nothing wrong with parents playing with their children, it can slip all too easily into becoming another form of management by adults. Again, real play springs forth from inner sources of energy and inspiration.

Then there is real play's public enemy number one: school. At this point most conventional schools have entirely erased play from the list of daily options on the chalkboard. I know of many schools where students are no longer permitted to go outside for any reason. Once they're inside, the doors are locked behind them, and that is that.

Some schools still pay lip service to a supposed kind of "educational" play—the use of games, toys, and puzzles that teach academic concepts—but according to Sheila Flaxman, a public elementary school master teacher for the past thirty-five years, such activities don't promote the same enriching qualities as play that is nonliteral and self-motivated. "Children direct and invent this kind of play," she wrote in an article entitled "Play: An Endangered Species," "no one presents them with a task or a set of standards to follow.... [It] provides the flexibility for children to experiment, grow, and discover, without the pressure of failure or adult evaluation.... Today's young children are controlled by the expectations, schedules, whims, and rules of adults. Play is the only time they can take control of their world."[39]

But let's not be lulled into thinking that the failure of our schools to value real play is a recent phenomenon. Consider the words of Piaget a half-century ago: "In spite of the prophetic vision of the great educators, play has always been considered, in traditional education, as a kind of mental waste matter, or at least as a pseudo-activity, without functional significance, and even harmful to children, keeping them from their homework." And yet, he continued, "Teaching at its best requires creating situations where structures can be discovered; it does not mean transmitting structures. . . . Children have real understanding only of that which they invent themselves."[40]

The last vestiges of creativity are being steadily eliminated from the conventional school day as well. More schools every year, either for budgetary reasons or because of the demands of the No Child Left Behind Act, are cutting art and music out of the curriculum. But even in those schools that haven't, as we have seen, the prevailing carrot-and-stick approach to education is antithetical to the creative process.

Modern mechanical and technological toys are yet another foe of real play because they have become so realistic and multimodal that they leave very little to the imagination. For this reason we keep the toy supply in our preschool as basic and—except for our collection of wooden blocks and three different sizes of Legos—as small as possible. We keep large quantities of these building materials on hand for two reasons: so that the kids won't fight over them and so that they can build elaborate structures when they are so inclined.

At any given time you will also find in the toy corner a basket of stuffed dolls and animals; the aforementioned trunk of dress-up clothes; a large toy stove, sink, and refrigerator for playing "house"; a container of toy trucks and cars, preferably metal; an old discarded telephone; a Fisher-Price castle and airport; a tumbling mat; two small slides; two spin-around toys; two old-fashioned tricycles; a wooden rocking horse; and a couple of plastic kick balls and cartons of tennis balls. Additionally, there are a handful of items that we keep in the closet and bring out only when kids ask for them: an old suitcase full of plastic food and dishes, a small Indian tepee, a parachute, a long balance beam, and a big box of multicolored wooden beads and shoelaces to string them on.

While I am by no means against toys, there's nothing I enjoy more than watching kids invent their own toys out of whatever materials might be on hand. For instance, this year two big five-year-old boys, rather than play with the wooden blocks, prefer to build with the dozen or so square plastic milk boxes that contain the blocks. They like to construct skyscrapers with them, or staircases that go too high for us to allow them to climb. They will do this several times a week, even though it involves the onerous chore of putting all the blocks back in the boxes when they are done. In another example, a couple of years ago several imaginative four- and five year-olds decided to tie an old piece of fabric across the climbing structure upstairs to form a hammock to hide and swing in. The idea caught on fast, and before we knew it there were six to eight hammocks at different levels inside the structure, which suddenly looked like a tree infested with tent caterpillars.

When we go to the park, we usually bring no toys at all, apart from an occasional ball or Frisbee. There the kids create the toys that their fantasy play calls for out of whatever they find lying around. The stick is perhaps the supreme all-purpose raw material. It can alternately be a knife, sword, gun, spear, airplane, rocket ship, shovel, or the fuel for an imaginary campfire. A discarded soda bottle filled with dirt becomes a bomb, and leaves and berries from the bushes bordering the park become the ingredients for "fairy tea" or a witches' brew, depending on the players' mood.

My conservative position on toys finds ample confirmation in Brian Sutton-Smith's book *Toys as Culture*, in which he addresses the question of whether modern toys promote or suppress creative play. Sutton-Smith provided one possible answer from mythologist Roland Barthes:

> Faced with this world of faithful and complicated [toys] ... the child can only identify himself as owner, as user, never as creator; he does not invent the world, he uses it; they are prepared for him, actions without adventure, without wonder, without joy ... they are supplied to him ready-made; he has only to help himself, he is never allowed to discover anything from start to finish.... [However] The merest set of blocks, provided it is not too refined, implies a very different learning of the world; ... [with them the child] creates forms which walk, which roll; he creates life, not property; objects

now act by themselves, they are no longer an inert and complicated material in the palm of his hand. But such toys are
rather rare.

Barthes went on to disparage toys made of modern plastic, which
he says "destroy all the pleasure, the sweetness, the humanity of
touch."[41]

Sutton-Smith quotes another critic of contemporary toys from
a UNESCO paper on children's play:

> More serious still is the fact that an industrially made toy,
> stereotyped and technically perfect, forfeits much of its value
> as a plaything. It is a closed object, setting up a barrier against
> creativity and imagination. In almost all instances an ele-
> mentary plaything is preferable, be it stick or pebble, which
> the small player can turn into a musical instrument, a tool, a
> weapon, a car, or a boat, as his mood dictates.[42]

A study by research psychologist Mary Ann Pulaski of a group
of kids in kindergarten through second grade confirmed these sentiments. Pulaski found that the play of children who were given
minimally structured toys and materials—paper, paints, Play-Doh,
wooden blocks, cardboard boxes, pipe cleaners, rag dolls, dress-up
costumes—was much more varied and richer in fantasy than the
play of children who were given highly structured stuff, such as a
miniature gas station, Barbie dolls, and action figures accompanied
by specific outfits to dress them in.[43]

Other studies the Singers cite show that younger children need
more structured toys representing commonplace objects—dolls, toy
appliances, miniature cars and trucks, and so on—to stimulate their
pretend play, and then, as they become more adept at it, they
are more and more able to use less realistic objects in imaginative
ways.[44]

Sutton-Smith ultimately takes a much more middle-of-the-
road position than mine on the issue of toys and their impact on
the quality of children's play. His answer to the above question is
that it is open to debate whether toys are a training ground for dis-
tractibility and therefore an "opiate" for the social control of chil-

dren or a way of transmitting novelty and unique information to them.[45]

He cautions us not to blame toys themselves for whatever effect they may have because they merely echo the larger cultural patterns found in the family, technology, schools, and the marketplace. Toys are at the center of children's play today, and so children automatically inherit the pressures that the society brings to bear on families. And, he writes, it is not so much toys in themselves that define their effect but the way in which children use toys to express how those pressures affect them. Different toys at different times can encourage solitary, competitive, or cooperative play; a toy can offer autonomy by allowing the child to control it, education by discovering how it works, novelty by exploring all of the toy's possibilities, and consumer pleasure by showing off the toy as a status symbol.[46]

All of which brings us to another double-edged sword. On the one hand, writes Sutton-Smith, "Indeed it is the nature of play that children will engage with toys in such ways to increase their own autonomous excitements by manipulating their world of fantasy in ways that, in the same act, both mimic and defy reality."[47]

Here he is talking about the genre of toys that stretches from baby rattles, dolls, toy telephones, and coloring books for younger kids to board games, bicycles, and craft kits for older ones. But on the other hand, when he gets to the emerging new genre of toy, the video game, he has this to say:

> But the video game as a toy, although it illustrates a liberation of human beings by technology, also illustrates the tremendous power that technology comes to exercise over human beings.... This toy, as a machine, not only isolates the child, it possesses him.... What brings us more control may end up controlling us.[48]

I will explore electronic media at greater length in chapter 7.

Games that are organized and managed by the young players themselves, such as baseball, football, basketball, soccer, tennis, and so on, were once a vital source of inner wildness. Sadly, today these games are known as sports, which means they are modeled after the adult version of the game and entirely run by adults. Organized children's sports have grown astronomically over the last generation and now involve over twenty million kids in this country. My objection to children's sports has nothing to do with the idea of kids' playing competitive games. It is the adult structure, the overlay of adult rules and costumes, the weeding out, the rewards, the pressure of adult expectations, and the stigma of losing and failure that concern me; these elements violate the spirit of real children's play.

Again, real play is freely chosen. It is nonliteral, based entirely on self-motivation and self-direction, and non-goal-oriented. Above all, it is about fun. I once was a Little League baseball coach and got to witness firsthand how many obstacles there are between the kids and their having a good time: the overbearing parents, the grumpy umpires, the coaches' egos, and, always, the bottom line of the final score. I would do what I could to downplay those antiplay elements, but my efforts usually seemed to fall short, which was why I eventually quit.

Wendy Grolnick, on whose work I drew extensively in the opening chapter, cites a study of a group of children aged thirteen and under who were participating in competitive ski racing. At question was the amount of pressure exerted by parents as well as the effect of that pressure on the kids. The results showed that 62.8 percent of the children rated their parents as a source of either moderate or heavy pressure to compete and not to withdraw. Twenty-seven percent said their parents forced them outright to participate. Asked how they felt about their parents' involvement, only half responded that it was okay with them. Twenty-seven percent of the kids had a neutral opinion, and 24 percent reported being unhappy.

Grolnick doesn't conclude that competitive sports are bad for children. In fact, sports can have a positive effect if the participation of the child is truly voluntary and if the conditions are in line with the nature of real play. Her advice to parents is to be involved; to encourage but not pressure; to help children focus on the pleasure of competing and not on winning and losing; to let children set their own performance goals; and above all to monitor the coach's attitudes.[49]

It was such a different situation when I was a child. For instance, even though I participated in many organized sports, the overwhelming majority of my athletic play took place without any adults around. My friends and I would arrange our own games, tailoring the rules and structure to the number of players, the equipment we could manage to scrounge up among us, and of course our personal idiosyncrasies.

I remember one period in particular when boys spanning a couple of grades in my elementary school got together for a kid-run Saturday-morning football league. There were usually more than twenty of us, and so we were able to play regulation-size games. In our case, however, the rules and structure were always negotiable, and arguing over them was an important part of the experience and a key source of its wildness.

I'll never forget the secret strategy sessions we held between games. With no grown-up coaches to provide us with scripted game plans, we made up our own plays. During the week at school, each team would sneak off to a deserted corner of the playground during recess to draw up new ideas in the dirt. The planning and the anticipation of next Saturday's game were as exciting, if not more so, than the games themselves.

Sometimes we would hybridize our own unique games. One day, when there were only a handful of us and a single tennis racquet and ball, we invented a brand-new game we named racquetball, so called because it was half tennis and half baseball. This was many years before the appearance of the adult indoor sport by the same name. The marvelous thing about the game was that it was simple to play and required very little in the way of equipment. Using a tennis ball eliminated the need for mitts, and because the infield was a basketball court at the playground, the bases were provided by the intersecting white lines painted on the concrete. It also meant that if the baseball diamond was too muddy for real baseball, we could always play racquetball.

Our invention was very flexible, too. If there were plenty of players, we would expand the field to include the hedge at the end of the court and the grassy area above the bushes. We would also play by more traditional baseball rules. If there were only a few of us, on the other hand, we would make the "outfield" out of bounds and alter the rules so that a fielder could get a base runner out by hitting him with the ball when he was between bases. We would also reduce the number of outs per inning. The game suited our needs so perfectly that it became a neighborhood tradition that endured throughout my childhood.

I should note that we also played a seemingly endless variety of games that were non-sports-oriented. Some were traditional games like Rover Red Rover, dodgeball, hide-and-seek, tag, and Spud; and others, again, were our own concoctions. For instance, in the fall we would rake all the leaves on our street into a pile, four or five feet high and ten or fifteen feet long, alongside the curb. Then we would all get on our bicycles, and the contest would become who could blast all the way through the pile without stopping.

The secret to success was to start the game a block or more away and build up a real head of steam. This made the moment of impact exhilarating, to say the least. Leaves would explode outward in every direction, and the world suddenly grew dark. Then, if you could maintain your balance and keep the pedals churning fast enough before the spokes became choked with leaves, you might just make it out the other end.

One summer, forty years or more in advance of Paintball technology, the kids on my block made slingshots with coat hangers and rubber bands and divided into teams for a neighborhood-wide war game. We discovered that the unripe grapes from a neighbor's large arbor were the perfect ammunition because they didn't cause serious injury when you hit your enemy, and yet they did leave enough of a telltale mark that the enemy couldn't get away with saying your shot had missed. The only downside to the war was that the very nice neighbor returned home from vacation to discover that there would be no grape harvest that fall. We felt so bad that we never played that particular game again.

Another integral element of real play is risk taking. Taking risks is how we challenge our limits and stretch our capacities. It's one of the primary means by which we learn to transcend our fear of the unknown. For children especially, it's a vital and necessary source of nourishment for their inner wildness.

Risk taking can assume myriad forms, not just physical ones. For many of us there is a certain risk involved in reciting a poem in front of a group, declaring our friendship to someone we've recently met, or investing money in the stock market. But so much youthful learning has a bodily component that kids urgently need opportunities to test themselves on the physical level in order to survey just where their edges lie.

Here I'm reminded of one of the students in the aforementioned class that traveled to Puerto Rico. Jesse, who came to us at the age of twelve with a long history of academic and behavioral troubles, was a paradoxical character. Well versed in the hip-hop lingo of the inner-city streets, on occasion he wore a pager to school, even though it wasn't activated. He wanted the world to see him as a tough, sophisticated teenager, but the pudginess left over from early childhood signaled that he was still timid and immature inside.

Like so many kids who grow up amid too much poverty, addiction, and loss, Jesse had received too much of the wrong kinds of attention. There were too many trips to the corner store for candy and sugar drinks and to the mall for designer clothing and hundred-dollar basketball shoes—even though he rarely played the game. At the same time, he never got enough of the right kinds of attention in the form of hugs, bedtime stories, and reasonable and consistent limits on his behavior.

And so, when it came time for Jesse to climb into the school van with his classmates and ride to the airport, he was really scared, though he would never admit it. The immediate tip-off was his enormous travel bag, which contained enough clothing to last him several months. Another sure sign was the constant stream of cocky, annoying wisecracks spewing from his mouth.

As soon as the jet soared into the air and pointed its nose southward toward San Juan, Jesse grew uncharacteristically silent. He remained this way for quite a while.

Simply boarding that plane represented a staggering risk for a child who had never been very far from home and whose life had never known a firm footing. It does the same thing for many of the kids we take on these long trips, which indeed is one of the reasons we do it.

Let me fast-forward the story to the moment when Jesse took a particular risk that I think changed him forever. At the conclusion of every workday, the group drove up into the rain forest in the northeastern corner of the island to cool off with a swim in a large, deep pool at the base of a waterfall. As is often the case in such spots, there is a series of rocky ledges above the water that kids can jump from if they have the nerve. The first day we arrived there, a bunch of local teenagers were jumping—and some were diving—from the highest ledge, about twenty feet up.

Naturally, some of our kids couldn't wait to follow suit. Two of the older, more athletic boys were the first to try. Because the area was so remote, I told them they could go only as far as the middle ledge, which was about fifteen feet above the water—and no diving. They groaned a bit at my caution but clambered lightly up the rocks and began having the time of their lives. Before long, several of the braver girls joined in on the adventure, as did Sandy, the female chaperone. Not at all fond of heights, I was quite content to sit by the edge of the pool and play lifeguard.

Much to my relief, Jesse showed no interest in jumping either. He was clumsy and impulsive enough that I was concerned he might slip and seriously hurt himself. But by the third visit to the swimming hole, he had decided he wanted to be like the other kids. He looked to me for the okay, and without changing my expression I made a quick mental calculation of the danger. I hadn't been especially worried about the other kids. But this was *Jesse*, which of course was precisely why I had to let him attempt it. It was Jesse, more than any of them, who needed to take this kind of physical risk. I did insist that he start with a "practice" jump from the ten-foot-high lower ledge, and he groaned just like the other boys. While I held my breath, he slowly and deliberately navigated the climb. Then, when he reached the ledge, he stood and gazed pensively down at the sparkling pool below. He looked a lot like he did after the plane took off. Thankfully, none of the others egged Jesse on—they too sensed the delicacy of the moment—and he didn't launch himself outward until he had fully centered himself.

The jump was flawless, and Jesse's head bobbed back above the surface of the water to whoops and cheers from the others and a relieved thumbs-up from me. His smile was as wide as Chicago. It had been a veritable leap of faith for us both.

Some years after Jesse graduated, he returned to visit the school. His solidly built body had lost every ounce of its former doughiness, and his expression was warm and confident. That smart-alecky smirk seemed to have vanished without a trace. He told us he had gone on to have a successful high-school career, and that he and a friend were about to start a business venture about which he was very excited.

And yes, he remembered the leap.

Thus in my school we recognize and honor children's need to take risks. Thankfully, the ones they take are seldom as dramatic as Jesse's; in fact, usually they are quite ordinary. For instance, we have the large, aforementioned climbing structure upstairs on the pre-school floor of the building, and another one in the backyard. For safety's sake there is a padded carpet and thick mattress beneath the indoor structure and a springy layer of wood chips under the out-door one. To prevent little ones from prematurely reaching what could be a dangerous height for them, we removed the lower rungs from both structures.

After that, all bets are off; which brings us to the sensitive sub-ject of injury. The way I see it, risks aren't real risks without the pos-sibility of someone getting hurt. Occasionally kids do slip and fall from our climbing structures. In the case of the younger students, I can happily report that there has never been a serious injury in the school's history, just a bruised fanny here and a bumped head there. Once, many years ago, however, two older boys were playing chase on the outdoor structure, and when thirteen-year-old Joey tried to jump from one section to another, he fell short and snapped his up-per arm in two. This injury turned out to be an important growth experience for the boy. Finding out that he could deal with the pain and discomfort became a needed source of inner strength. The cast —which all of the kids signed, of course—became a badge of cour-age. His overall maturity leapfrogged forward after that.

Another time, ten-year-old Crimson decided to take a forbid-den shortcut to the park. Her misadventure entailed scaling an old chain-link fence with a sharp-edged top, which is why we have always told kids not to climb it. But Crimson was determined to do it anyway, and as fate would have it, she lost her footing as she was crossing over from one side to the other and severely cut her forearm.

To this day Crimson will proudly recount that the jagged tear took thirty-eight stitches to close. She will also proudly show her scar, which by now has grown faint. The injury was both painful and frightening, and the emergency room attendants, as well as Crim-son's dad, were amazed by her ability to remain calm under fire. They told her so more than once, and she's still proud of that too.

It goes without saying that injury is a double-edged sword. No one wants to see a child have to endure the accompanying pain and fear. But I can honestly say that every childhood accident I have witnessed—and there have been surprisingly few, given that we allow kids to take many more risks than do most schools—has contained important lessons for the child involved.

The conglomerate issue of safety, risk management, and liability is fast becoming the last nail in the coffin of real play. As I have already discussed, safety has become a modern-day obsession. Continual efforts are being made to remove risk entirely from the lives of children, which has led to the domestication of both real work and real play. And I rarely hear anyone asking, at what cost?

Liability fears and the high cost of insurance rank as perhaps two of the leading causes of the domestication of work and play over the last thirty years or so. How often, over the course of that time, has a child heard the phrase, "I'm sorry; we can't let you do that anymore. You know—for insurance reasons." Our fiercely litigious society has led insurance companies to charge higher and higher rates and issue stricter and stricter guidelines to any setting where children are playing on a regular basis.

The problem reached an acute stage during the so-called liability-insurance crisis of the mid-1980s, when the U.S. Chamber of Commerce reported that 40 percent of its members saw increases of 100 to 500 percent in their insurance costs, and 20 percent had their policies canceled altogether. The insurance industry blamed the problem on "cyclical forces" within the insurance market. However, prices only continued to rise after that time, and the effect was similar to the Halloween candy scare: a permanent hysteria took root and caused dark clouds to form around the issue of children and risk.

Thankfully, when our school's insurer announced that it was going to triple our rates in 1985, our founder, Mary Leue, made the bold decision to cancel the school's liability policy and instead began putting the premium we were paying into an escrow fund that would enable us to become self-insuring. It was a visionary move on her part because I am sure by now, were we still carrying a commercial policy, things like our indoor climbing structure would be a relic of the past.

Mary's plan has worked brilliantly thus far. We tell parents that in the event their child gets hurt at school, we will cover any treatment-related expenses for which they don't have insurance. The fact of the matter, Mary realized, is that most parents do have some form of coverage. Then we ask them to sign a liability waiver, whereby they promise not to sue us. To date, there has been only one glitch, when, many years ago, a boy fell head first off a stepladder and knocked out his front teeth. His young single mother was so frightened and angry that she took us to court anyway—liability waivers aren't legally binding in New York State—but the judge threw the case out because the school was clearly in a position to assume responsibility for the necessary dental work.

However, the organizations that are willing to assume responsibility for their own risks are few and far between theses days, and, notes Peter Stearns, by 2001 even traditional games like dodgeball came under scrutiny for the threat they allegedly pose to physical and moral safety.[50]

A culture that has forsaken its ability to play has negative consequences not only for its children but for society as a whole. Unfortunately, as we have seen in this chapter, there is evidence everywhere you look that we have already reached that point. Every aspect of play in mainstream life has become thoroughly domesticated, and far too few of us are noticing the price we are starting to pay.

I am hardly the first person to make this observation. Nearly seventy years ago and then in the twilight of his life, Johann Huizinga decided to attempt one final book, in which he wanted to alert the world to the reality that Western civilization "is no longer played."[51]

The timing of the book—1938—was as profound as its contents. With the Nazis closing in on his native Holland, Huizinga decided to plunge himself into a study of the history of play because of the deep connection he sensed between real play and a free society. "Play *is* freedom," he wrote at one point, and the passion and self-absorption of real play are its "primordial essence."[52]

And then: "Real civilization cannot exist in the absence of a certain play element., for civilization presupposes limitation and mastery of the self, the ability not to confuse its own tendencies with the ultimate and highest goal, but to understand that it is enclosed within certain bounds freely accepted."[53]

Huizinga's research led him to declare that the Renaissance, when the idea of childhood as we know it today was born, was the "golden age of play," arguing it was that era's omnipresent spirit of playfulness that provided the impetus for its extraordinary cultural awakening. In the nineteenth century, however, the psychological and sociological effects of industrialization and the explosion of technology began to take a heavy toll on play in all its forms. Huizinga cites as an example the fact that this marked the period when organized adult sports originated. What had formerly been playful contests for the most part began to become serious business—first for grown-ups and later for children—and no longer fit the definition of real play. It's no accident we stopped calling them games.

At the same time, scientists became more and more motivated by the applicability and profitability of their work and less by the hunger for pure discovery. And nations at war no longer followed any codes of conduct or laws of humanity, and all of the ancient associations with ritual—the "play element"—were rapidly disappearing, a development to which Huizinga was personally forced to bear painful witness.

Tragically, Huizinga died while being held captive by the Nazis in 1945, and *Homo Ludens* was published posthumously.

After spending thirty years studying the nature and value of children's play around the world, Brian Sutton-Smith reached a conclusion very similar to mine, which is that real play is disappearing at a frightening pace. He noted in the early 1980s that the total amount had already diminished drastically since he began his research in the early 1950s, a development that is leading, in his words, to the "zooification" of children.[54] In *A History of Children's Play*, Sutton-Smith had an interesting take on the roots of childhood domestication:

> Antithetically, but equally pessimistically, the idealization of childhood in children's literature, art, and play, as well as the cognitive view that children's thinking is preoperational or primitive can be regarded as justifications for treating children as especially innocent and requiring control. Like the noble savages of the 18th century and the idealized women of the 19th, children in this conservative view are seen as ir-

rational, emotional, and rhythmic, justifying colonization, exploitation, or indoctrination at as early an age as possible in the basics of our civilization.[55]

Thus he saw the domestication of play as part of a larger pattern, one that parallels the shift in society's prevailing view of the child from savvy and competent to naive and dependent, which I described in chapter 1. Sutton-Smith's conclusion that one of the most significant determinants in the history of childhood from the turn of the twentieth century to the present is the increasing subordination of children through their play and an educational system based primarily on indoctrination.[56]

He was deeply concerned, as I am, about the dulling effects of the domestication of play on children's wherewithal to adapt in successful and satisfying ways to today's unpredictable, rapidly changing world. Real play, the essence of which is its flexibility, spontaneity, and open-endedness, is childhood's training ground for sustaining and fine-tuning the abilities and characteristics kids need to shake off the shackles of control and blossom into their true selves.

FIVE

THE WILDNESS WITHIN

> Intellectuals or eggheads like to think that we can live in
> a world of ideas that we invent, as we create the domestic
> plants and animals. But in some part of our skulls there is
> wilderness. We call it the unconscious because we cannot
> cultivate it the way we would a field of grain or a field of
> thought. In it forces as enduring as climate and bedrock
> maintain our uniqueness in spite of the works of progress.
> It is the source of our private diversity. Together, our
> collective unconscious seems almost to exist apart from
> ourselves, like a great wild legion where we can get in
> touch with the sources of life. It is a retreat where we
> can wait out the movers and the builders, who scramble
> continually to revamp our surroundings in search of a
> solution to a problem that is a result of their own activity.
> —Paul Shepard, *Place in American Culture*

I T IS HARDLY A NEW IDEA that human beings are enlivened by
some unseen essence. Down through the ages, that essence has
been a subject of great speculation by philosophers, theologians,
mystics, and psychologists alike. Some have called it the soul, others the spirit—both of which, according to *Webster's*, mean "that
which animates human life." Still others have called it the imagination. Socrates and subsequent Greek philosophers recognized it
as the daimon. The Romans had a similar notion, the *genius*. Sig-
mund Freud named his version the *id*, Maria Montessori hers
horme, and Henri Bergson his the *élan vital*. More recently, Chellis
Glendinning, who specializes in what she calls eco-psychology,
wrote about the "primal matrix," by which she means our natural state of being beneath the overlay of society and culture. Jean
Liedloff, an accidental anthropologist who spent two and a half

years living deep in the South American jungle with a Stone Age indigenous group, refers to this state as the "continuum."

All of these conceptualizations have a great deal of common ground, but many carry with them too much religious, scientific, or New Age spiritual baggage to suit my purposes here. Besides, I want a term that evokes the sparkling effervescence and originality of children—hence my use of "inner wildness" to describe that ineffable spark and to draw attention to the intimate connection between its outer and inner forms. For, as Henry David Thoreau once wrote, "It is in vain to dream of a wildness distant from ourselves. There is none such. It is the bog in our brains and bowels, the primitive vigor of nature in us, that inspires that dream."[1] I realize there are risks in associating "wildness" with children. One is the potential confusion regarding the link between inner wildness and outward behavior. Let me make it clear from the outset that all children, whether their natural temperament is quiet and delicate or noisy and frenetic, are born with a certain wildness inside. While some children express it by behaving in ways that some might deem "wild," others do so through art, imagination, fantasy play, a deep sense of wonder, and unique perceptions of the world around them.

Because of my philosophy of education and of life, which grants children a high degree of physical and emotional freedom and empowers them to direct their own learning and resolve their own conflicts, I have always had to dance on a razor's edge of advocating inner wildness without inspiring images of *Lord of the Flies*: destructive, uncivilized children run amok, answerable to no one. It is my belief, however—again based on decades of experience—that William Golding's iconic morality tale is a myth steeped in fear and ignorance. Few are aware that Golding was a schoolmaster in an elite Church of England grammar school when he wrote *Lord of the Flies* and other novels with similarly dark, Hobbesian themes. I will argue that the savagery into which those marooned schoolboys descended is a projection of the author's Calvinist heritage and the accompanying fear of wildness that I described in chapter 2. That said, perhaps if some of Golding's students really had been shipwrecked on some deserted island, they would indeed have sunk to such depths. It's not too hard to picture a group of upper-class English boys, raised by surrogates in a rigid atmosphere of emotional denial and fierce competition, being reduced to the lowest common mammalian denominator in the absence of adult control.

I can flatly state that this would not be the case for students in my school, a true community where people work cooperatively and share responsibility for the well-being of the whole, and where the awareness of feelings and their honest expression are highly valued. Why? Because children whose inner wildness is respected and nurtured are inherently civil. They accept limits that are natural and reasonable. And their God-given instincts guide them toward making constructive, life-enhancing choices. Here I unabashedly join the ranks of the so-called Romantics, who believed that children are inherently pure and good. I stand shoulder to shoulder with Freud's radical student Wilhelm Reich, who declared that children at their core are loving, responsible, and sociable beings. It is only when they are neglected, traumatized, excessively managed, or over-indulged that they develop a defensive "middle layer" of distrust, aggression, and out-of-control impulses.[2] Again, my belief is not merely theoretical; it is built upon intimate interactions with hundreds upon hundreds of different kinds of children, including two of my own, in an environment where they are not pressured into conforming to a set of standardized expectations, where they are loved and touched and spoken to honestly, where they can associate freely with people of all ages—in short, where they can be themselves.

To exemplify just what I mean by inner wildness, allow me to illustrate how it has manifested itself in some of the individual kids with whom I have worked over the years. Speaking in generalizations is the downfall of much of the literature about children, because every child is a unique combination of traits and characteristics.

Gabrielle was a student of mine from the age of two until she moved on to high school at fourteen. Long-legged and lithe, with bright blue eyes and a head full of wispy blond curls, Gaby, as she prefers to be called, was a gentle, placid child who possessed her full share of inner wildness. Occasionally that inner wildness could be seen in outwardly naughty behavior, like the time she and a fellow four-year-old decided to coif their own hair and try on the lipstick they had purloined from Gaby's unsuspecting mother. But for the most part Gaby was a carefree, dreamy little girl who liked to dress up, play house, sing, dance, and listen to long stories. Most of all, she loved to paint and draw. Even at a very young age her artistic output was prodigious, and her gift was evident in her earliest crayon sketches and tempera portraits. By the time she was five, she was creating unicorns with a striking level of detail.

When Gaby reached first grade, her passion for art and fantasy was all-consuming. Reading, writing, and arithmetic usually remained well below the action level on her daily agenda; she much preferred fashioning her own make-believe realm filled with dragons and princesses, and she would spend hour after hour drawing the characters that later became the heroes and heroines in makeshift plays that she and her friends liked to put on.

First grade zipped by, then second, and then third, and still Gaby showed little inclination to tackle the three R's. Her postponement of learning in these areas was partly a matter of personal choice, but perhaps it was due even more to the fact that the right side of her brain—the seat of imagery and imagination—was highly developed, while the left side, which handles the linear sequencing and data storage needed for literacy and numeracy, was not. Because she was given the freedom to learn at her own pace and pursue her own inclinations, Gaby focused squarely on her art.

However, it wasn't as though she lacked interest in literature. She loved being read to, which we did every day in school and her parents did at home. By the time she was eight, she had listened to Tolkien's entire *Lord of the Rings* series and many other classics. Gaby also loved to compose poetry, as long as someone else handled the writing process, which she found tedious and cumbersome. She was such an accomplished poet that one of her dictated poems won first prize in a contest sponsored by the Albany Public Library, in which a substantial number of area students participated.

Fortunately, Gaby's parents, who operated a law partnership out of their home, were strong supporters of our school's approach to education, and in fact they had moved into the neighborhood in order to be closer to the school. We were able to reassure them that when Gaby was ready to learn to read, learn she would. Their concern understandably grew as their daughter got older, but their trust in their daughter's innate intelligence enabled them to keep their fingers off the panic button.

It was in the fourth grade that Gaby finally decided it was time. Working diligently in school every day, plus two afternoons a week with a private tutor, she was reading fluently within months. Most impressive was the fact that as soon as Gaby had sufficiently broken the code, she began reading sophisticated material, not kids' stuff. And while reading never replaced art as her first love, it did become a close second; she could often be found with a good novel in her hands.

As Gaby's reading experience increased, her writing skills fell into place as well, but Gaby and math remained distant cousins. As is often the case with extremely right-brained kids, she struggled mightily with mathematical concepts. There was nothing about the subject that she enjoyed. It was not until eighth grade, her final year with us, that Gaby decided to tackle the ins and outs of arithmetic. Her motivation had nothing to do with this newfound interest, but rather with the hard, cold reality that she wanted to attend Albany High School the following year, and she would have to pass four years of math in order to graduate. Thanks to sheer hard work and commitment on Gaby's part, she mastered the entire K–8 math curriculum in a single school year.

As proof that she was completing middle childhood with her inner wildness fully intact, Gaby prepared a skit for our big end-of-the-year talent show that to this day remains one of the funniest children's-theater productions I have ever seen. She called it *TV Sucks Your Brains Out*, an obvious loving poke at her parents, who had put away the family television years earlier because they didn't like the effect it was having on their kids. The skit went something like this: two children lived in a home where the TV was kept in the closet, strictly off-limits. One Sunday afternoon, the kids' father tricked them into going outside so he could sneak out the TV to watch a little football. The kids quickly caught on, and somehow managed to trick their dad in return so they could get in a little TV watching of their own. Unbeknownst to the audience, who could only see them sitting in front of the TV that Gaby had cleverly constructed out of cardboard, the two siblings had clear plastic bags filled with cooked spaghetti hidden under their hats. Each bag was attached to a strand of clear monofilament fishing line that ran along the floor and into a hidden pair of hands behind the TV screen. All of a sudden, after the kids had been sitting spaced out in front of the set for a while, their accomplice yanked the kids' "brains" out from under their caps and slowly dragged them across the stage and into the hungry mouth of the TV. It was an ingenious sight gag. People were laughing so hard that some literally fell out of their seats, and it took several minutes to restore enough order to bring on the next act.

Not surprisingly, Gaby's transition into high school was a bit rocky. The conventional curriculum is almost entirely a left-brained affair, and the option of learning according to her own pace and her own interests was a thing of the past. Moreover, now she faced the daily pressures of grading and testing, challenges entirely new to her. The way Gaby handled the situation wonderfully demonstrates the value and the importance of inner wildness: Gaby developed personal relationships with her teachers, and when she needed extra help she didn't hesitate to seek it. She saw through the meaninglessness of much of what she was required to do, but she quickly learned to play the game. Determined to succeed, she was on the honor roll by the middle of her first year, a status she would maintain for the rest of her high-school career.

Naturally, Gaby took every art class on offer, and it was probably that which sustained her more than anything else. More precisely, it was her relationship with her favorite art teacher that enabled Gaby to look forward to going to school every day. Miss Schmader became an important mentor for Gaby; like any good teacher, she recognized Gaby's gift and went out of her way to feed it by helping Gaby win scholarships to prestigious summer camps for young artists. Miss Schmader would later be an honored guest at Gaby's high-school graduation party.

Gaby went on to a well-known private college where she could pursue her love of art in earnest. It was there that her passion for drama fully asserted itself. She entered a special playwriting program that eventually required her to script, direct, and produce a full-length dramatic production. I was fortunate to attend one of her performances, and I saw with my own eyes the stunningly professional quality of Gaby's work.

The story of the unfolding of an interesting life continues. When Gaby returned home after graduation, she was immediately struck by the upsurge in gang activity in the neighborhood during the years she had been away at college. She observed what is often the case in the inner city—the utter lack of anything constructive for children to do—so she and a couple of friends decided to start an outdoor arts-and-crafts and gardening program on the street where most of the hanging out and drug dealing occur. The program was an immediate success. At summer's end, Gaby and her cohorts set their sights on moving it indoors so they could continue to run it year-round. They concluded that an abandoned Catholic church, situated on one of the neighborhood's gateway corners, would be the perfect site. After a series of meetings with the bishop of the archdiocese, they persuaded him to sell them the building for $5,000.

As I write, this band of intrepid activists has expanded into a full-scale not-for-profit organization that is currently developing the plans and raising the funds needed to renovate the hundred-year-old church and convert it into an arts-based community center.

And so begins a quirky, bold, and imaginative young woman's first foray into the adult world.

Then there is Paul, in many ways the temperamental opposite of Gaby. Whereas Gaby was like a softly played violin, Paul was a blaring trumpet. The youngest of four children, he was born howling, as his mother, Missy, teasingly likes to remind him. As an infant he was fretful and colicky, his fierce brown eyes shining out from a face the color of light chocolate.

Paul's emotional weather was easy to forecast. When life was going his way, there was nary a cloud in the sky. His infectious smile had the power of the sun. But if ever misfortune should strike in the form of injury, unfair treatment by a peer, or being refused his way by a grown-up, the chances of a thunderstorm were nearly 100 percent.

As soon as Paul could walk, he was a blur of motion and activity. He was, as the old saying goes, a handful, testing Missy—a single parent from the beginning—on what seemed like an hourly basis. His willfulness and tenacity often led him to trample over normal limits and consequences. In extreme instances, Missy would resort to shutting him out on the front porch until he promised to bring his behavior back within reasonable bounds. Then his howls could be heard from a block away.

Because Missy was a teacher in the school at the time, Paul began attending at a very early age. His spirited energy filled the forty-foot-square, high-ceilinged preschool space. By the time he was three, the school had attracted five other little boys who were just as high-octane as he was. They roamed the room like a pack of wolf cubs, alternately scaling the indoor climbing structure, wrestling on the king-size mattress that lay beneath it, or building towers in the block corner and then toppling them over with gleeful abandon. Chase, whether indoors or out, was probably their favorite game of all.

Their play was endlessly inventive. They would arrange the little kids' lunch-table chairs in two parallel lines in the middle of the floor, and suddenly they were on a bus cruising around town. They would get down on all fours with no props at all and morph through a series of four-legged creatures. One moment they were approachable, tail-wagging dogs; the next they were dangerous, snarling lions. Sometimes the boys would join organized activities, and at other times they preferred to assert their independence and do their own thing. They longed for novelty and fluidity. They abhorred routine.

All six boys moved through the next ten years of school together. Their long and eventful association eventually culminated in a film they created as eighth-graders, a zany, slapstick affair filled with daredevil stunts that no child should ever try at home. I have little doubt that these six are bonded for life.

Paul expressed his inner wildness through his unquenchable physicality and his thirst for adventure and risk taking. In all of the years I had the challenge and the pleasure of working with him, I don't ever recall seeing him bored. When one lives fully in one's body and is comfortable inside one's skin, one is never at a loss for something interesting to do. Boredom appears when a child is forcibly denied the freedom of movement that was once the birthright of all children. By the time Paul was seven or eight, his gifts as an athlete were obvious: his sinewy build, natural coordination, and abundant physical confidence enabled him to excel in any sport he chose to attempt. Baseball became his favorite, and, as a perennial Little League all-star, he set the record for the highest number of home runs hit out of the park in a single season.

Like Gaby, Paul was also a so-called late reader, but for different reasons. In Paul's case, it was his predilection for speed and motion that made reading difficult as a younger child. His eyes tended to scan the symbols faster than his brain could process the information; or they would impulsively jump to the end of the word first, or even over several words at a time, throwing him into a frustrating state of contextual confusion. When Paul was twelve, he slowed down enough to make a serious attempt at learning to read. Still, his early efforts were amusing to watch. An irresistible restlessness would quickly set in, and before long you would see him standing up over the book and shifting his weight nervously from one foot to the other. A few minutes later you might find him sprawled on top of the table; not long after that, you might find him underneath it. But somehow he maintained his concentration, and his ability to pace himself and focus grew week by week. By the end of the seventh grade, he was reading at grade level with ease and pleasure.

Paul's biggest developmental challenges were managing his impulsivity and controlling his fiery emotions. In both cases he was fortunate to have a tolerant, open-hearted mother who managed to set firm, consistent limits at home without squelching Paul's frequent need to discharge some of the intensity that inevitably built up inside him. Missy patiently helped her son learn to put words to his feelings, and she didn't punish him for his outbursts. Instead she established a baseline of honesty and respect from which he rarely, if ever, wavered.

The same was true at school, where we worked with Paul on recognizing his anger before it rushed to his muscles and developing effective alternatives to striking out at his perceived adversaries. How much of Paul's bubbling rage was simply inborn temperament and how much was the result of being repeatedly abandoned by an absent father struggling to overcome cocaine addiction no one will ever know; but thanks in part to adult and peer support, Paul's ability to tolerate disappointment and modulate his anger gradually increased. His anger by no means disappeared, but he learned not to automatically blame the environment for his upsets and, when anger toward others was appropriate, to measure it to fit the circumstances.

By the time Paul was ten, he was becoming a powerful student leader. He had done enough of his own emotional homework to begin helping other children understand the sources of their strong feelings. He still overreacted sometimes, but he was relentlessly truthful about his motives and almost always willing to admit that he was wrong. His built-in "bullshit detector" was finely tuned, and he didn't hesitate to call out his friends—or even his teachers —when he spotted hypocrisy or inconsistency in their stories. His courage and his frankness earned him universal respect.

Like Gaby, Paul chose to go on to public high school. Although his energy level had toned down enormously, the sedentary rhythm and nature of the ninth-grade curriculum proved a formidable obstacle at first. But Paul was determined to show that he could excel in academics just as he did in athletics, and by the end of his freshman year, his name was on the honor roll. I should add that he made the decision, entirely on his own counsel, to pass up baseball in the spring in order to focus on his studies.

Having proven himself academically, Paul renewed his love affair with sports in the fall of his sophomore year—with a vengeance. Even though he had no prior experience with organized football, he was chosen as a starting receiver on the junior varsity team. In the winter, he tried wrestling—also for the first time—and made the varsity team. He had a very successful season, defeated only by older boys who had been wrestling for many years.

Paul tried out for the baseball team that spring, and not surprisingly he made the varsity team as the starting center fielder. In his first game, which was covered by all the local TV news outlets because the high school had just revamped its field, Paul hit one out of the park his first time at bat. The entire Capital District got to see it on the six-o'clock news.

How Paul will enter the adult world remains to be seen, but I think it is safe to assume that his well-nourished inner wildness will enable him to invent a life that is at once original and rewarding.

Lest the reader think there is a correlation between inner wildness and learning to read beyond the average age, let me include the story of Elinor, who entered our school at the age of eleven, having been a competent reader since the timely age of six. Elinor was born in Malaysia to Irish parents, who at the time were itinerant teachers of English as a second language. When she was two, the young family moved to the island of Brunei, where they lived until they came to settle permanently in Albany.

Elinor's most striking feature was an enduring sweetness. If she were a Native American child, her totem animal would probably have been the deer. When she smiled, her soft blue eyes smiled, too, and when she was amused, a timid giggle was more likely to emerge than a throaty laugh. Elinor possessed a penetrating intellect and a persistent curiosity to match, but her almost painful shyness tended to keep her mental gifts under wraps. Part of Elinor's diffidence no doubt came from her mother and father, both of whom are soft-spoken; but an equal measure came, I suspect, from growing up in an Asian culture, where feminine submissiveness was the rule.

When Elinor first arrived, the effects of her regimented school-ing in Brunei were all too apparent. She had grown so accustomed to having someone else structure her experience for her that even though her academic skills were well honed, she had few clues as to what her real interests were. For a while she kept herself busy with texts and workbooks, the staples of her education to date. When she tired of her self-imposed routine, she began to hint that she was bored. Her inability to think for herself prevented her from seeing the possibilities and options that were so readily visible to the other kids. Whenever a teacher asked her what she wanted to do, she sim-ply said, "I don't know."

Elinor's reserve and social inexperience held her back from join-ing the free-form play at the core of our school's "curriculum," and it took her most of her first year with us to discover how to enter the flow. It was in the art room that she began to feel her way out of her isolation. Among other things, she started taking weekly pottery lessons from my wife, Betsy, who had taught full-time in the school for many years and now volunteered whenever her mid-wifery schedule permitted.

Elinor's greatest gift turned out to be her hands. Soon she was working independently on the potter's wheel on the days when Betsy couldn't be there. It wasn't long before Elinor had learned everything Betsy had to teach her and was turning out cups and bowls that were good enough to sell. By her second year in our school, Elinor was feeling entirely at home. She was well liked by all of her peers, who valued her insightfulness and subtle presence, and she gradually developed a quiet confidence that made her for-mer uncertainty almost entirely a thing of the past.

At one point Elinor pursued an interest in anthropology by in-terning at the New York State Museum with an anthropologist who was cataloguing Native American remains that had been dug up at highway construction sites. Elinor's job was to carefully clean the remains, and she was excited to learn how much information can be gleaned about people by studying the condition of their bones.

Another passion emerged while Elinor was with us: travel. When she was in the eighth grade, she and her two closest friends orchestrated a two-week class trip through the southern states in the school van. Elinor's class had already journeyed by train to the West Coast the previous year for an international alternative-education conference, but this year's trip was their pièce de résistance. The three girls meticulously planned a five-thousand-mile itinerary that took them as far south as Saint Augustine, Florida, and as far west as Saint Louis. While some of her classmates were thrilled simply because they were away from home, Elinor was fascinated by the history, culture, and architecture of each stop along the way, as she lingered in the museums and galleries that many of her peers casually breezed through. In Saint Augustine, America's oldest city, she stopped to read every historical plaque and marker, and in the French Quarter of New Orleans she took dozens of detailed photos of the extraordinary buildings. The following summer she and one of the two girls with whom she had planned the road trip flew to San Francisco, where they stayed with relatives. The veteran travelers spent a week exploring the nooks and crannies of the city, almost entirely on their own.

Elinor elected to go on to Albany High. Academically, high school was a walk in the park, but the school's massive size, impersonality, and raw edges didn't suit her at all, and at the end of the year she had the inner wisdom to know that Albany High was not for her. On her own she found out about a private boarding school in neighboring Massachusetts, applied there with the blessings of her parents—who couldn't even begin to afford the tuition—and was accepted with a full scholarship. Elinor thrived in her new school, which strove to maintain the same sense of community that she had enjoyed in our school. There she intensified her focus on ceramics, and by her junior year she was producing professional-quality pieces.

One thing Elinor missed by being away at school was cooking with her mother, something the two had loved to do together since Elinor was very young. She began hanging around the school kitchen, where she struck up a friendship with the school baker, and before long she was helping prepare the bread and cakes. A new passion involving her hands had caught fire.

Elinor graduated from high school with honors and immediately set out to pursue her love of baking. She approached the owner of a prestigious pastry shop in a small city just north of Albany and asked whether he would take her on as an apprentice. "Absolutely not," he responded. "A seventeen-year-old couldn't possibly handle the pressure." Not to be denied, Elinor wedged her foot in the door by taking a job in the shop's soup and sandwich kitchen. Her daily strategy was to finish her work as early as possible and then hang around in the bakery after hours, just as she had done in high school. Naturally, the head baker took a liking to this determined, winsome girl with an Irish accent. Before long, he was teaching her the secrets of fine-pastry making and giving her small tasks to do.

Elinor had applied to college and been accepted, but she was not sure she wanted to move immediately on the following September. By the end of the summer, however, she had tired of making sandwiches for a living and decided to give college a try. She attended a small, innovative institution where she was able to pursue almost exclusively her interests in ceramics and archaeology.

The first year went well for her, but when she contemplated returning for a second year, she realized that something was missing: it was dough she wanted her hands in, not clay. So back to the pastry shop she went. Impressed by her work the previous summer, the owner relented this time and agreed to her request for a yearlong apprenticeship. Elinor's natural skills and her drive to learn were so strong that within two months this nineteen-year-old was the head baker on the night shift, the most critical shift of all.

At year's end Elinor decided to continue her baking education in Germany. She applied to a government exchange program that was originally intended for students pursuing political careers, and in so doing became the first applicant to seek an internship in a nongovernmental trade. At this writing she is happily baking away in a small Bavarian city. She has been accepted to several well-known universities in New York, a city carefully chosen so that she can work and learn in some of its many fine bakeries while she completes her undergraduate degree.

It is the kind of inner wildness Elinor has in such abundance that enables young people to blaze their own trails into adulthood. Though the outside world may perceive her to be shy and lacking in confidence—indeed that is one facet of her appearance—on the inside she has a sure sense of direction because she learned to trust the inner voice that tells her what she is supposed to do next and why she is supposed to do it.

The search for a less culturally burdened conception of that which animates us led me all the way back to the ancient Greeks and Romans, the first Westerners to try to understand in earnest the essence of our humanity and of a life well lived. I found myself rereading Plato's *Republic,* a dusty paperback copy that had sat on my bookshelf since my freshman year of college. I am no devotee of Plato—there are many things about which we simply do not agree—but at the very end of his treatise on enlightened society, I found exactly what I was looking for. There, through a retelling of the Myth of Er, Socrates' best-known student expressed his mentor's idea that everyone has a daimon, an inner compass and source of wisdom that guides—and sometimes goads—us through life. The story goes something like this: Er, a soldier slain in battle, suddenly comes back to life while he is lying on his funeral pyre and begins to report what happens to the soul after the body dies. He can do this because he was allowed to witness the journey the soul takes after it departs.

According to Er, the souls are first brought together in a large group before the three Fates—Lachesis, keeper of the past; Clotho, keeper of the present; and Atropos, keeper of the future. Taking charge of the proceedings, Lachesis sets out before the assembled souls an array of lots, or samples of potential lives, for them to choose from. "Souls of a passing day," she incants, "here beginneth another cycle of mortal life that leads to death. No daimon shall be allotted to you, but you shall all choose your own daimon. Let him who draws the first lot choose a life, and thereto he shall cleave of necessity." After all the lots are chosen, Lachesis sends off each soul with the daimon it has selected, which will then be the guardian of its life and the "fulfiller of the choice." The souls then undertake a day's travel that renders them so thirsty they are compelled to drink from the River of Forgetfulness, after which they remember nothing of their underworld journey. At midnight they are reborn into their new lives.[3]

No one knows for certain, but it is possible that the idea of the daimon originated with Socrates, who reported that his daimon appeared to him on several occasions as a distinct inner voice and gave him important counsel at critical life junctures. In the *Apologia* he refers to his daimon as an "internal oracle," writing, "This sign, which is a kind of voice, first began to come to me when I was a child."[4]

The Romans had their own version of the daimon, the *genius*. Their term has fared much better down through the ages: in English, it stills means exactly the same thing it once meant in Latin, "an attendant spirit." The daimon, on the other hand, made a 180-degree turn somewhere along the way, shifting from a beneficent (albeit double-edged) presence to its contemporary English definition: *demon*. The daimon's linguistic descent into hell warrants a closer look, because its redefinition goes straight to the heart of why I felt compelled to write this book. Let's start with a more precise examination of the two terms. The Roman *genius* is a far simpler construct, suggesting only that we each have within us a sort of protector akin to the Christian guardian angel. The daimon, on the other hand—daimon meaning in Greek "unpredictable, out of control"—carries with it the much more complex notion of an independent—one might say, "wild"—inner force that urges on the soul and is the "fulfiller of the choice."

It is interesting to note that the Greek word for happiness is *eudaimonia*—a well-pleased daimon. However, the notion that the key to a good life is to live in harmony with one's passions and follow an inner rather than an outer guide didn't sit too well with early Christian theologians. As far as they were concerned, we are all guided by an external God with a single master plan. They were quick to turn the polarities of good and evil and light and dark into the opposing archetypes of angels and devils. Western science would later join religion in opposing the belief that that which animates us has a will and a wisdom all its own. The same idea of a master plan—minus Jehovah on his heavenly throne—took root in the Newtonian revolution of the sixteenth and seventeenth centuries. The moment Sir Isaac demonstrated that the movement of physical objects, both on earth and in the heavens, could be mathematically determined, a school of thought was born which held that every-thing—ourselves included—is reducible to a set of objective, verifi-able laws. The universe is wound up like a giant watch, it was now assumed, and it is just a matter of time before science learns all of its secrets and seats itself at the controls.

The history and philosophy of science fall beyond the scope of this book, but the role that scientific paradigms play in shaping the way in which we view reality remains in the background through-out, because in the last four centuries Newton's universe-as-machine model has come to govern all of the domains of childhood. The ancients' idea of the daimon remained essentially on life sup-port until it was revived in the mid-twentieth century by the exis-tential psychologist Rollo May. As a therapist, May encountered the same problem with his clients on a practical level that Friedrich Nietzsche had attempted to address philosophically in the latter part of the nineteenth century. Nietzsche's observation was that the dominance of Newton's entirely rational and mechanical model was stifling human originality and creativity. Add to the mix the "slave morality" of Christianity, he warned, with its innate distrust of sensuality and instinct and its preoccupation with the hereafter, and you wind up with "Theoretical Man," a one-dimensional fig-ure devoid of desire and imagination. After another century of relentless scientific and technological progress, the linguist Mar-shall McLuhan would rename him "Mass Man," and the sociologist David Riesman would call him "Plastic Man."[5]

Similarly, what concerned May the psychotherapist was a per-vasive pattern of inner emptiness in his clients. Something had ren-dered them passive and immobile, unable to take charge of their lives. His response was to construct a model of the psyche that ze-roed in on human motivation, the centerpiece of which became the daimon, or, in his own modern translation, the "daimonic." He defined the daimonic as "the urge in every being to affirm itself, as-sert itself, perpetuate and increase itself. . . . Its source lies in those realms where the self is rooted in natural forces that go beyond the self and are felt as the grasp of fate upon us."

"The daimonic will never take a rational 'no' for an answer," May went on to write. "In this respect it is the enemy of technology. It will accept no clock time or nine-to-five schedules or assembly lines to which we surrender ourselves as robots." According to May, the daimonic is humanity's helper toward self-realization. Among other functions, it warns us when we are about to lose our autonomy. The trouble is that we evade the daimonic by getting lost in the herd, allowing modern-day conformity and anonymity to keep us from listening to the inner voice about which Socrates spoke.[6]

A generation later another radical psychotherapist, James Hillman, took up the cause of the daimon and wove it into what he called the Acorn Theory. The idea of the Acorn Theory, which is more of a myth and a metaphor, is that just as the oak tree is contained within the acorn, every child is born with a unique innate paradigm—a calling, if you will—that cannot be reduced to biological or psychological explanations. Hillman writes eloquently about the daimon:

> The *daimon* motivates. It protects. It invents and persists with stubborn fidelity. It resists compromising reasonableness and often forces deviance and oddity upon its keeper, especially when it is neglected or opposed.... It is out of step with time, finding all sorts of faults, gaps, and knots in the flow of life—and it prefers them. It has affinities with myth, since it is itself a mythical being and thinks in mythical patterns.... It has much to do with feelings of uniqueness, of grandeur and with the restlessness of the heart, its impatience, its dissatisfaction, its yearning. It needs its share of beauty. It wants to be seen, witnessed, accorded recognition, particularly by the person who is its caretaker.[7]

For Hillman, just as for his near-contemporary Rollo May and for Plato and Socrates before them, life is not a series of predictable causes and effects. There is no recipe for raising children that makes it a simple matter of measuring out and mixing together the right ingredients. Each baby is born with a distinct identity and a set of special gifts to match, and its development becomes an unpredictable process of unfolding that is driven as much from within as from without. Yes, children need nurturing, protection, and guidance, but it is imperative, as Hillman is careful to point out, that parents, teachers, and mentors not confuse themselves with a child's daimon.[8] Rather they need to allow children, as historian of childhood Stephen Mintz wrote (see the introduction), to undertake the "odysseys of self-discovery" that will enable them to live the lives they are intended to live.

Soul, daimon, inner wildness, or whatever we choose to call it—inside every child is a unique and oh-so-precious spark that has its own impetus and its own internal guidance system, as can be clearly seen in the marvelous examples of Gaby, Paul, and Elinor. But that spark is only a spark. It is vulnerable, from the moment a child is born, to being extinguished by conditions that are becoming increasingly inhospitable to its existence.

All of this begs the question: what would have become of my three former students had they been forced to toe the line in conventional schools? What if their parents had joined forces with those schools and fallen into patterns of anxious management and nervous control?

My guess is that Gaby's reading delay would have been diagnosed as attention deficit disorder, and her alarmed parents would have administered Ritalin or something even more potent in the hope of sharpening her focus and improving her academic performance. When told that their daughter was suffering from a genetic brain imbalance, they probably would have tightened the reins on Gaby considerably rather than allow her to dance to her own drummer. The bottom line is that everyone would have agreed that Gaby had a problem with a capital "P." The drugs would have biochemically squelched her dreaminess and her penchant for fantasy and make-believe. Her self-esteem would have suffered, perhaps severely; and, given her gentle personality, she might very well have begun to shy away from expressing her creativity. Her art, poetry, plays, and hilarious spoofs might have been replaced by years of remedial classes in school and special exercises at home.

It is not at all unlikely that as she approached adolescence, Gaby's carefree air and girlish silliness, already under direct attack, would gradually have been replaced by depression, and Gaby might have joined the growing legion of teenagers who depend on antidepressants in order to cope with their lives. Recent studies show that adolescent use of antidepressants nearly doubled in only five years between 1997 and 2002.[9] Twice as many adolescent girls as boys are diagnosed with depression, and antidepressant prescriptions are increasing faster for girls than they are for boys, with teen girls more likely to get antidepressants than any other population group. In 2002 antidepressant use was highest among girls aged fifteen to eighteen years, at a whopping 6.4 percent nationwide.[10]

There is little doubt in my mind that Paul would have been labeled ADHD, or something even more ominous like ODD (oppositional defiance disorder), and given a cocktail of biopsychiatric drugs: one to help him sit still and concentrate, another to dampen his impulses, and yet another to control his anger. A psychologist probably would have instructed Missy to place Paul on a strict behavior-modification program at home, invalidating her instinctive ways of dealing with such a temperamental, energetic boy. Both mother and son would thereby have lost sight of the highly positive side of Paul's personality, and the tenderness of their connection, which is still so evident today, might have suffered enormously. Even with the support of drugs and remedial classes, I suspect, Paul would still have struggled with reading in the early grades in a conventional school. As a result, he would have internalized the idea that he was "dumb," a stigma that would have followed him into high school and almost certainly compromised his chances for the academic excellence he is now enjoying. Whether Paul's athletic prowess also would have suffered is anyone's guess, but I have my own theory on this score: one of the secrets of highly successful athletes is that their inner wildness is still intact. Through years of training and discipline, they are able to bring all of their inner sources of strength and confidence up to bat with them, as it were.

It pains me even to think about what might have happened to Elinor's inner wildness had she been forced to go through twelve years of factory education instead of the six that she did endure. She would not have been labeled and medicated like Gaby and Paul, but something even worse might have occurred: because she learned with relative ease and never made waves, she would have become invisible, trapped in the role of the "good girl." Given how shy she was by nature, so polite and eager to please, she might never have discovered her adventurous side, the side that refuses to conform to convention.

And what a loss to humanity that would have been.

SIX

THE IMPORTANCE OF SOLITUDE

You think that I am impoverishing myself by withdrawing
from men, but in my solitude I have woven for myself a
silken web or chrysalis, and, nymph-like shall ere long burst
forth a more perfect creature, fitted for a higher society.
—Henry David Thoreau, *Journal*

A S I BEGIN WRITING THIS CHAPTER, I am sitting at an outdoor
table beside the home of my friend Rosalie, whom I mentioned
in the introduction and who resides here with her husband, Paul.
The house, where my friends are still sleeping, is perched on a steep,
isolated, piñon- and ponderosa-covered slope over seven thousand
feet up in the Zuni Mountains of northwestern New Mexico. It is
moments after sunrise. Just now, a hummingbird buzzed so close by
my ear on its way to the feeder, which hangs from a low branch of
an old cedar, that I started halfway out of my chair. I can hear the
faint trilling of hermit thrushes somewhere in the distance. The
rumblings of an early-morning thunderstorm to the southwest are
warning that soon I may have to move back inside.

On my first evening here, Rosalie and Paul took me down to
Dowa Yalanne, or Corn Mountain, the nearby Zuni Indians' most
sacred site. I marveled at the way you can see how the earth built up
the different layers of mud and stone over the course of eons and
now how wind and water are slowly wearing them back down. As
we walked silently alongside the mesa, we could hear the yipping
and whining of a pack of coyotes. Suddenly, without any prelude,
the slanting rays of the setting sun lit up the reddish-brown sand-
stone as though it were on fire. All three of us stopped and stared in
utter awe. There were no words to describe what we were witnessing, so we barely spoke, and the stunning, otherworldly effect lasted

only two or three minutes. When it was over we turned back toward the car, each of us lost in his or her private thoughts.

On my second day there, I walked alone for a couple of hours on a deserted dirt road that led I don't know where. The sky was on the march with thick, moisture-laden clouds, a sign of the arrival of much-needed summer rains. Thankfully, they held on to their water, because the road would have quickly turned to gravy and I was wearing sandals.

The farther I went, the more I noticed my senses sharpening. The warm afternoon breeze filled my nostrils with the sweet smell of sage. I could hear the staccato screaming of an unseen jay in the forest that rose up from the road. Up ahead, a large and gangly raven ruled over a meadow from the top of a tall, dead pine. Whenever the road climbed, I felt my heart and lungs working overtime to compensate for the thinner air at this altitude, to which I was not yet accustomed.

And so this morning, my third in the mountains, I notice most of all that I am growing quieter. This is not insignificant, because as a rule I am a loud, gregarious person. My wife sometimes has to remind me not to shout when I am excitedly sharing a new idea with her. I once spent a week at an ashram in southern India, and the elders of the place were constantly wagging their fingers to remind me to keep my voice down. In school, my favorite kids are always the rowdy, high-spirited ones.

Thus I have come here not only to spend time with special people whom I have known and loved for many years, but also to get away from the incessant ringing of doorbells and telephones, the constant noise of cars and buses, the never-ending e-mail requests, and all of the myriad distractions that are part and parcel of living and working in the bustling downtown of a capital city. On the flight west, I found myself questioning my decision to take such a long journey when I have a book deadline looming directly ahead; but not anymore. Already, there is greater clarity in my thinking. Old ideas that have been knotted up inside my mind over the last several months of writing are coming untangled. New ideas are appearing out of nowhere, as it were. I can feel my message coming into sharper focus.

Here I should stop to quote from the book I thought I had

brought along just to read for pleasure, suggested by another good friend. It's by the western author Terry Tempest Williams, who lives in the Four Corners part of Utah—the corner directly opposite the one I am visiting. The book, *Red*, expresses Williams's deep concern for the fragile beauty of this vast red-rock region and the ever present threat posed by the greed of men who want to exploit it for its natural resources and commercial potential: "As the world becomes more crowded and corroded by consumption and capitalism, the landscape of minimalism will take on greater significance, reminding us through its blood red grandeur just how essential wild country is to our psychology, how precious the desert is to the soul of America."[1] Williams's words are apropos because she is calling for the defense of outer wildness with the same urgency as I am on behalf of inner wildness. She goes on to say:

> I believe that spiritual resistance—the ability to stand firm at the center of our convictions when everything around us asks us to concede—and that our capacity to face the harsh measures of life comes from the deep quiet of listening to the land, the river, the rocks. There is a resonance of humility that has evolved with the earth. It is best retrieved in solitude in the stillness of days in the desert.[2]

I also quote Williams because she speaks so magnificently to the natural parallel between inner and outer wildness. She sees how interdependent the two are, and that one of the key components of the nexus between them is solitude.

There is no doubt that the solitude I am enjoying here is better connecting me to my own inner wildness, to my deepest reasons for undertaking this long and complicated project that sometimes keeps me awake at night wondering what is the most important thing to say next. Indeed I made the right choice in coming, because I am certain I will get more work done here, and the quality of that work will be far higher.

For many reasons, some of which I have already discussed, solitude is fast disappearing from children's lives. In *Dumbing Us Down: The Hidden Curriculum of Compulsory Schooling*, veteran teacher John Gatto analyzed a typical child's week. He concluded that after you've added up all the hours kids spend in school, commuting to and from school, doing homework, attending after-school activities such as music lessons or organized sports, eating meals, watching TV, playing video games, and surfing the Internet, young people have only about nine waking hours per week left in which to explore, imagine, and reflect. The equation varies somewhat according to social class, but the end result is about the same, writes Gatto: that's all the time there is for them to get to choose what to think and do.[3] It's simply not enough.

Gatto made this estimate in 1990, and I suspect that figure has been cut in half since then, with technology intruding so aggressively into children's inner lives. More and more kids now own cell phones and take them wherever they go. There may be no one next to them while they're walking down the street, but they're rarely alone because they're usually on the phone. Between calls, there is always text messaging to fill the time. As for the ubiquitous portable music players, you rarely see a young person outdoors without one, except, perhaps, in neighborhoods like mine where teenagers are far too generous about sharing their music with any and all who are within earshot. In the workout room at the YMCA, where I am a regular, I almost never see anyone under thirty without headphones on.

Some of you may beg to differ with me and argue that listening to music facilitates solitude, that it stimulates internal communication. But I strenuously disagree, because to me solitude means being alone with one's thoughts. It involves experience that is unmediated by anything except nature and her forces. I am so grateful that there are no televisions, radios, or music players at Rosalie and Paul's. Here the only music comes from the scores of birds they feed, the wind in the trees, the thunder, the rain on the metal roof, and occasionally Paul's guitar. I draw support on this issue from a recent magazine interview with one of my favorite authors, Barry Lopez, who travels to remote corners of the globe to write about the relationship between people and their landscapes. For many years Lopez has lived overlooking the McKenzie River in western Oregon, and he writes that he resists the temptation to turn on the radio or a CD player when he's driving because he knows it will inevitably pull him away from the present moment. He wants to make sure he is available to witness every new detail as he goes along, and he knows that listening to another source of input, no matter how pleasant, will at least partly divert his attention.[4] This discipline is no doubt part of what makes Lopez such an acute observer, a quality that continually infuses his writing and earns him universally high praise. Meanwhile, Pulitzer Prize–winning author Annie Dillard, another favorite of mine, in *An American Childhood* paints a picture entirely different from Gatto's in which she tells her story of growing up in Pittsburgh in the 1950s. Dillard, too, went to school, and took regular piano and dance lessons on certain afternoons. She had homework, and for a time she went to Sunday school, even though her parents weren't religious. But none of these things prevented her from leading a thoroughly undomesticated childhood, with countless hours to attend to what she calls "the inward life." Hours to cruise the dusty stacks of the branch library and hours to read the endless variety of books she brought home. Hours to capture and identify the insects with which she shared the tree-lined streets and grassy yards of her well-heeled uptown neighborhood. Hours to label the hundreds of rocks and minerals in the collection the newspaper boy passed on to her from a customer who had given it to him before the old man died. Hours to operate a "private detective agency" with the boy next door. Hours to play baseball and football in games the kids themselves organized. Hours to teach herself to draw.

Why? Of course, part of the answer is that technology had only just begun its assault on solitude when Dillard was growing up. However, another piece of the answer, one with perhaps an even greater impact, can be found in the following scene from her memoir. One morning, after weeks of searching in her microscope for an amoeba in the hay infusion she had concocted, Annie the budding young scientist finally spotted a prime specimen. She ran up the basement stairs to tell her parents and ask them to come and see it, too. I'll let Dillard finish the story in her own words:

> Mother regarded me warmly. She gave me to understand that she was glad I had found what I had been searching for, but that she and Father were happy to sit with their coffee, and would not be coming down.
>
> She did not say, but I understood at once, that they had

their pursuits (coffee?) and I had mine. She did not say, but I began to understand then, that you do what you do out of your private passion for the thing itself.

I had essentially been handed my own life. In subsequent years my parents would praise my drawings and poems, and supply me with books, art supplies, and sports equipment, and listen to my troubles and enthusiasms, and supervise my hours, and discuss and inform, but they would not get involved in my detective work, nor hear about my reading, nor inquire about my homework or term papers or exams, nor visit the salamanders I caught, nor listen to me play the piano, nor attend my field hockey games, nor fuss over my insect collections with me, or my poetry collection or stamp collection or rock collection. My days and my nights were my own to plan and fill.[5]

Dillard's experience points to the glaring generational shift in parental attitudes toward involvement in their children's lives. Today, some might consider her mother's blithe disinterest rather selfish or an outright assault on Annie's self-esteem, rather than a show of respect for her daimon; but if that is the case, perhaps today's parents are erring in the opposite direction. In any event, it is clear that Dillard's parents took care not to confuse themselves with her daimon. They respected her ability to guide herself to the experiences that would bring her innate gifts to fruition. And interestingly, she ultimately chose to become a writer, utilizing a talent that neither of her parents particularly shared.

Dillard went on to describe how her mother gave her free rein of the neighborhood once Annie was old enough to remember her phone number, and how she lay in bed drawing mental maps so that she wouldn't get lost during the next day's explorations. Her favorite haunts were the alleyways and other out-of-the-way places where she would find all sorts of hidden treasures. She even managed to persuade her mom to let her go to the park that her father had told her to stay away from because there were bums living under the bridge. It is interesting to note that Dillard makes scarcely a single reference to school in this entire book. All of the formative experiences that she deemed worthy of mention happened when she was out and about in her world, very often alone. Thus was she able to undertake the "odysseys of self-discovery" that enabled her to dig deeply into herself and come into full possession of the treasures hidden there.

Now let me tell you about Madison, to give you a more contemporary picture of what solitude in childhood can look like. Madison entered my school at the age of two and is now in the eighth grade. I got to know this exceptional boy especially well because for several years he lived with his parents in an apartment across the street from me, meaning that I often had the opportunity to observe him playing outdoors when school was not in session.

When Madison was a scrawny, towheaded, crew-cut five-year-old who could have passed for four, he developed the solitary habit of bouncing a worn-out tennis ball against the side of his building, which he did by standing in the driveway of the garage next door, where two attorneys from a neighborhood law office parked their cars on weekdays. Of course, Madison would say he was pitching, not just throwing the ball. He imagined himself as a major-league hurler, and before long he developed his own unique windup and delivery. His mother and father were both ardent baseball fans, so during baseball season there was almost always a game beaming into the twenty-four-inch screen in their living room. This gave Madison plenty of opportunity to study his heroes' techniques.

The little lot next door was his testing ground, and to a certain extent his stage. If you listened carefully while you were walking by, you could pick up his soprano play-by-play: "Alomar swings and misses—Cone strikes out the side!" Or "Line drive to center field. Bernie Williams runs in and makes the catch!"

Madison's dad was such a Yankees aficionado that he watched their games with the TV muted, preferring the audio track to be the radio commentary of the Yankees' own announcers. This was the source of Madison's stylized call when someone managed to get hold of one of his pitches and drive it deep. When this happened, his shrill voice rang up and down the block: "It is high; it is far—it is GONE!!"

Sometimes Madison kept score, and sometimes he played just for fun. Always, however, he was alone out there in his private world of baseball. It wasn't because there were no kids in the neighborhood with whom he could play ball; there were, and sometimes he did. Rather, what appeared to most people as just another deteriorating downtown parking lot, with its asphalt cracking, paint peeling, and mortar missing from the cinder-block walls of the garage, was Madison's personal field of dreams. And he was content to keep it that way.

Early one evening, having waited all day for the owners of the cars to go home, Madison disappeared downstairs to get in a game before supper. He returned a minute or two later, his head weighted down with dejection. I happened to be in his apartment at the time, and I saw the depth of his frustration.

"There's still a stupid car parked in the lot," was all his poor father could get out of him when he asked what could suddenly be so wrong.

Another time Madison's game was interrupted by rain. When his mother called down to tell him it was pouring and he had to come in, he was beside himself. "Oh, Mom, do I *have* to? The game's not over yet!" he implored. The next thing I heard through my living-room window was Madison stomping angrily up the two long flights of stairs to his apartment.

I knew Madison well enough to know he wasn't spoiled. His parents were careful to teach him that little boys don't always get their way. Then why such a reaction to a disappointment so seemingly trivial? Why such a deep-seated desire to throw a ball against a wall?

On yet another evening, while I was coasting down the hill looking for a place to park, Madison appeared suddenly out of the lot and began running alongside the car, shouting, "Hey Chris! Wait up! I gotta tell you!" I stopped and hastily cranked open my driver's-side window.

"Yankees lead the Mets two to one," he said, breathing hard. "The Mets were ahead one-nothing, but Strawberry just hit a two-run homer!" His sparkling eyes vibrated in synch with his larynx. He was wearing a brand-new New York Mets hat that had no doubt inspired this interleague rivalry.

When Madison tired of pitching and decided to practice his fielding, he simply walked to the edge of the lot, tossed the ball as far as he could up our steep, meandering side street, and waited for it to come bounding back down. Since he wasn't allowed to pursue the ball into the busy avenue below, the stakes were high if he missed it. As a result, his fielding percentage was nearly perfect.

Madison's dream is to be a professional baseball player when he grows up. Toward that end he started playing Little League "tee ball" the summer he turned five, but he hated hitting off the tee. I think he felt insulted by the way they've dumbed down the game for young kids.

Whether or not Madison ever realizes his dream is beside the point. The object of his imaginings happened to be baseball, but it could have been just about anything else. The point is the purity and simplicity of his solitary play, despite the incessant action-filled TV shows and video games that now fill kids' waking hours. Here was a child who needed only a used tennis ball and a brick wall to create an entire summer of endless drama and excitement. Here was a boy who had been set free to follow his own wild imagination—alone and unsupervised, with occasional check-ins with his parents—wherever it might take him.

Fortunately, in these fear-ridden days, Madison's mom and dad didn't feel moved to overprotect him. Instead they seemed to possess an innate respect for his need for the solitude in which to construct his own reality. Thanks to the ample space they allowed him, he's already well on his way to building his own inner structures and inventing a free-flowing, confident sense of self. I have no doubt that when he comes of age, he won't be dependent on others to do this for him.

The importance of Madison's solitary realm to his developing young psyche must not be understated. It was his way of satisfying the human need to imagine and to dream, gifts that a great many of us seem to lose as we grow older. A great many children today seem to be cast adrift without the freedom to develop these gifts; their one-of-a kind, self-generated images have been crowded out by an endless barrage of external, mass-produced ones, much as townhouse tracts devour farmland and forests. Fewer and fewer young people are developing the capacity to decorate their inner rooms lavishly, with fine tapestries on the walls and thick, intricate carpets on polished stone floors. Instead their minds are becoming threadbare cubicles, the only furnishings a Formica desktop, stool, and computer.

So how can children learn to fashion their own rich, unique selves today? There are no foolproof recipes, but one essential ingredient is time alone, away from the clatter of modernity. This private time can be spent just about anywhere: a bedroom, a tree, a backyard, a park, or a pristine place like the mountains where I am writing these words. It doesn't matter all that much what children do while they're alone, either. They can pursue a solitary hobby as Annie Dillard did, or play alone as Madison did, or draw alone as Gaby used to do for hours on end, or walk alone, or write in a diary, or read, or sit privately listening to music—or do nothing at all. The only activities I would rule out are watching television and playing video and computer games, because, as we will see in the next chapter, these electronic media have the power to hypnotize children and take possession of their psyches. What matters is not so much the nature or location of the activity but the existential experience of aloneness, of uncluttered time and space within which children can think their own thoughts, feel their own feelings, and hear the inner voice that Socrates described.

Henry David Thoreau, one of the world's best-known champions of solitude, wrote, "I love to be alone. I never found a companion so companionable as solitude. We are for the most part more lonely when we go abroad among men than when we stay in our chambers. A man thinking or working is always alone, let him be where he will."[6] The year was 1837, and the recent Harvard graduate was back home in Concord, Massachusetts, working in his father's pencil factory. It would be another eight years before he moved out to the pond that he made so famous, to live in a small cabin he built himself, "to live deep and suck out all the marrow of life."[7] Thoreau's reflections, including those in *Walden; or, Life in the Woods*, on the vital necessity of being in touch with both outer and inner wildness struck an immediate chord with the American public, and the book has since been published in well over a hundred editions and translated into virtually every modern language.[8]

Like Tolstoy, Thoreau once founded a school in his hometown. Upon graduation from college he had tried teaching in the public grammar school in Concord, but after only two weeks there a member of the local school committee criticized his "lax discipline" and ordered him to begin caning the students. Thoreau immediately resigned in protest, and in the fall of 1838 he and his brother John opened their own school in a building that had once housed the private academy they attended as children. Thoreau never wrote at great length about education, but clues to his philosophy can be found in a letter to a friend, in which he wrote that his educational approach "supposes a degree of freedom which rarely exists. It hath not entered into the heart of man to conceive the full import of that word—Freedom—not a paltry Republican freedom, with a *posse comitatus* [the power of the sheriff to compel people to assist law enforcement] at his heels to administer it in doses as to a sick child —but a freedom proportionate to the dignity of his nature."[9] Later, in his journal, Thoreau wrote about the conventional educational process: "What does education often do? It makes a straight-cut ditch out of a free, meandering brook."[10]

Representing a significant departure from convention, Thoreau's school reached maximum enrollment by its second year. True to his beliefs, Thoreau began each day with an informal talk—to which one former student said the kids always listened in rapt silence—on such subjects as nature, beauty, the indigenous people who first occupied the land, the rotation of the seasons, and the miraculous design of the universe. The windows of the building were kept open for ventilation, and the brothers emphasized learning by doing instead of by drill and recitation, the prevailing method at that time. Field trips to town businesses and industries were common, and the brothers suspended classes on Fridays to take all twenty-five boys and girls—Louisa May Alcott and her sisters among them—out to tramp through woods and fields, sail or row on the river, or swim in one of the nearby ponds.[11]

Sadly, the little school closed after only three years, when John contracted tuberculosis, the same disease that would later strike down Henry David at the age of forty-four.

Solitude and nature are like brother and sister: such has been my daily lesson here in these austere mountains. And what better way to help children learn about solitude, and keep open the pipeline to their inner wildness, than to immerse them in the natural world the way I have been immersed these last several days?

Unfortunately, according to naturalists Gary Paul Nabhan and Stephen Trimble, authors of *The Geography of Childhood: Why*

Children Need Wild Places, childhood is rapidly becoming *dena-*tured. Part of the problem is simply demographic: only 2 percent of Americans live in the country, and even in the relatively rural West, 75 percent live in cities. One out of four Americans who lived on the land in 1979 moved to a town or city ten years later. A generation ago, most of us still had rural relatives, but nowadays most of us don't.[12]

In 1992 the authors conducted a national survey of fifth- and sixth-graders to find out where and how they learned about nature. Fully 53 percent said they got their impressions through electronic media, 31 percent said they learned about nature in school, and only 9 percent said they experienced nature at home or directly in nature herself.[13] Taking their research further, Nabhan and Trimble decided to survey children who still live where they have primary contact with wild places, so they interviewed fifty-two Anglo, Hispanic, O'odham, and Yaqui/Mayo children, ages eight to fourteen, in the desert area of southern Arizona. The results were shocking. Despite their rural homeland, a vast majority of the kids reported gaining most of their knowledge of the natural world vicariously. An overwhelming 77 percent of the Mexican kids, 61 percent of the Anglos, 60 percent of the Yaqui, and more than a third of the desert-dwelling O'odham youngsters felt they had seen more animals on television and in movies than in the wild.

It gets worse. When asked if they had ever spent half an hour alone in a wild place, none of the Yaqui children and only 42 percent of the O'odham, 47 percent of the Anglos, and 39 percent of the Mexican kids responded in the affirmative. Only half of all the children surveyed said they had found and kept a treasured natural object such as a special stone, feather, or animal bone.[14]

Nabhan and Trimble didn't bother to investigate kids on the opposite end of the geographic spectrum because the results would have been all too obvious. Those who are trapped in inner-city environs—soon a quarter of the U.S. population—are the first to suffer what the authors call "the extinction of experience" because they have virtually no access to wild places, and therefore no choice but to subsist on second- and thirdhand contact with the natural world. My own experience with inner-city youth tells me that in terms of maintaining an instinctive connection with their inner wildness, they have but one advantage over their uptown and sub-urban counterparts, which is that their caregivers either intention-ally or through a certain neglectfulness allow them to roam about freely and seek adventure in their unnatural surroundings.

In any event, the sad fact is that just as nature and solitude walk hand in hand, so do the denaturing and domestication of childhood. This is a crying shame, especially when we consider all the forms of duress children are under today, because forging connections with plants, animals, and wild places is such an important part of one's sense of personal meaning and self-worth. As Nabhan and Trimble put it, "The natural world does not judge. It exists. One route to self-esteem, particularly for shy or undervalued children, lies in the out of doors. . . . The sun, the wind, the frogs, and the trees can reassure and strengthen and energize."[15]

While hardly encouraging, Nabhan and Trimble's analysis stops short of despair. Recognizing the harsh reality that children's access to truly wild places will only continue to become more restricted, they are careful to look at outer wildness from a child's perspective. For kids, wilderness isn't about gazing at scenic backdrops. It's about adventure, exploring the unknown, and observing interesting bugs, plants, and animals. Above all, the underlying essence of the wil-derness experience is "playing with abandon."[16] Having worked with children primarily in the inner city throughout my career, I agree that while it will always be important to find ways to get kids out to truly wild places—and at my school we do so whenever we can—possibilities for "roaming beyond the pavement" do exist within the confines of our cities. For instance, here in our neigh-borhood in Albany we are blessed to have a wonderful little city park only a block away from the school; the kids call it the Swing Park because it has a swing set and other traditional playground equipment. For years, the park had an old, corroding merry-go-round that the kids delighted in spinning round and round on, sometimes at quite high speeds if the pushers had enough muscle and endurance. It was by far the most exciting piece to play on, with the chance of being downright dangerous. Sometimes the cocky kids who refused to hold on to the handrail would go flying off onto the surrounding dirt track, at which point the scene began to re-semble a rodeo: if the fallen child failed to spin out of the way in time, he or she risked being trampled by the pushers. I rued the day when the Parks Department discovered how rusted out and wobbly the merry-go-round was becoming, because they would surely replace it with a tamer playground piece, something stationary and plastic, with lots of rounded edges. Such has been the case in parks and playgrounds across the city over the last two decades, as recreation officials are forced to accede to mounting safety and liability concerns.

Finally the dreaded moment arrived. We knew it immediately when we showed up one morning with a group of kids and saw that all the equipment had been repainted in bright primary colors. Hesitantly, I glanced toward the spot occupied by the old merry-go-round, and much to my joyous disbelief, there sat a brand-new, royal blue one, good for yet another generation of breathless children crying out, "Push me again! Push me again! PLEASE!"

But the best thing about the Swing Park is that it is covered with grass, except for one sandy area where kids can dig for worms and grubs and buried treasures, and the fence that surrounds it is lined with trees, bushes, and various kinds of wild vegetation. In particular, there is a flowering crab cherry by the park entrance that makes an ideal climbing tree for young children because the lowermost branches are invitingly horizontal and only about four or four and a half feet above the ground. Our only rule for the tree is that no one is allowed to help anyone else up. This prohibition screens out the precocious kids who wouldn't know what to do when they got up into the first crotch, and it also provides a good, safe training ground for steeling nerves and preparing the necessary muscle groups.

Once kids have conquered their fear and mastered the fine art of tree climbing, the upper branches of the tree become a lovely source of solitude. And the kids seem to know this, because those who can climb to the top invariably do so alone, and there they sit staring off quietly into space. It usually takes a very compelling reason—like, say, lunch—to get them to come down. And there are other wild adventures to be had in our little park; in fact, what an observer would quickly notice is that our kids don't spend all that much time on the play equipment. Left to their own devices, they prefer to climb the tree, build little forts in the bushes, harvest the intensely sour wild

Concord grapes that appear along the fence in the fall, sword-fight with sticks, play chase, and otherwise invent their own forms of excitement.

In case you're wondering about safety, only once in over thirty years has one of our students fallen from that crab cherry, and ironically it was at the end of this past school year. A five-year-old girl who had been climbing the tree for nearly two years slipped out of the tree and fractured her collarbone, which at the time of this writing has mended nicely and is an injury she is quite proud of.

As I mentioned in chapter 4, our school is self-insuring. Part of the process involves informing the parents of incoming students that we believe in allowing kids to take reasonable physical risks, and that minor injuries do occasionally occur. This initial openness seems to prevent parental concern from escalating when kids do hurt themselves in school. In the school's entire history, only one parent declined to enroll her son when she learned of our liberal safety policy, and even that boy enrolled several years later after his mother had a change of heart.

By practicing the art of the possible, then, and by allowing children to be inventive and take physical risks, we can offer them plenty of sources of nature and solitude away from the wilds of these Zuni Mountains. Parents can directly help their kids gain access to nature and solitude by taking them hiking, camping, and walking for hours by the river. They can locate summer camps for their kids that include wilderness experiences. The rustic YMCA camp where my wife and I sent our daughters start the younger campers out with a single overnight stay in lean-tos on the deserted side of the lake, opposite from the lodges and cabins, and by around age twelve the kids go on five-day hikes and canoe trips.

Parents can help indirectly by not filling up their children's lives with managed activities, by not keeping the TV on incessantly, and by not constantly entertaining them, either as a reward or as a way to forestall boredom. Actually, boredom can become a teacher, for often within that empty space of nonactivity and nondistraction we begin to look and listen inward, and we get to know ourselves in a deeper way. When children have enough empty space in their daily lives, they learn to use it constructively, in ways that support their relationship with their inner wildness.

I'm reminded of a wonderful essay by the award-winning science, nature, and travel writer David Quammen about his close relationship with the hundred-year-old black walnut tree that grew in one corner of the half-acre lot occupied by his childhood home in suburban Cincinnati. It was a towering specimen, with two low-lying horizontal branches about eight feet off the ground, from one of which his father hung a child's swing. According to Quammen, the tree took the place of the dog and the grandfather he never had. Gradually he learned to extend the height of his climbs, memorizing with his body the requisite knobs and crotches, until finally one day he reached the "crow's nest" at the top. I'll let Quammen tell the rest:

> At one point, having outgrown the little kids' swing, I hung a trapeze from a higher limb. But I never built a tree house or defaced the trunk with a ladder-line of plank steps. Driving nails into this living xylem would have seemed barbarous, both to me and to my father, himself a great lover of trees. The tree in its unsullied state embodied all the stairway and structure that seemed necessary. Besides, a board shack furnished with old carpet and comic books and a flashlight, forty feet off the ground, was not what I wanted. What I wanted was a tree. When the urge struck me to daydream, or to pout, or to gaze out across the landscape, I went to the crow's nest.[17]

Forty years later, Quammen still thinks about that old walnut, and about how "it amused me, it nurtured me, it challenged me, it taught me in ways I can guess at but not measure. It showed me the possibility of a deep fondness for an individual living creature beyond the usual channels of sentiment—that is, beyond the easy reciprocal relations of boy-to-dog, girl-to-horse, boy-to-snake."[18]

Quammen's story wonderfully illustrates the simplicity of the needs of inner wildness. In an ordinary Midwestern suburb, a young boy was able to find the solitude that enabled him to begin to explore his own inner nature. Today's children face a much greater challenge because the number and intensity of the distractions have multiplied in ways that can't be calculated. Kids absolutely need our help with this dilemma. More accurately, they need our protection —but not from danger. What they need, again, is protection from the distractions and the busyness, so they can preserve and multiply their opportunities for inner listening.

And so, as I prepare to leave the blessed silence of these unspeakably beautiful mountains, I know I will return home with an important reminder about children's critical need for solitude and for our help in defending their ability to enjoy it.

SEVEN

CHILDHOOD LOST

Children are the living messages
we send to a time we will not see.
—Neil Postman, *The Disappearance of Childhood*

NOW IT IS TIME TO WRANGLE with perhaps the sharpest of all double-edged swords: technology. As we will see in the following pages, the increasing dominance in children's lives of a constantly growing array of electronic media poses both explicit and implicit threats to their inner wildness. TV, cinematic and music videos, computer and video games, the Internet, and the myriad forms of cyberspace communication are all major sources of childhood domestication.

Electronic media are so enticing and provide so much instant and effortless gratification that they are severely eroding kids' desire and ability to engage in real play. These technologies render the consumer passive, a state that is the antithesis of real play, removing the physicality, the imagination, and the interactivity upon which inner wildness feeds. There is one exception: video and computer games. Unfortunately, as I will discuss at length below, the active and interactive components of video and computer games make them perhaps even more hypnotic and harmful than television.

Electronic media also have a tendency to discourage children from being in genuine physical and emotional contact with one another. For instance, while teenagers' preferred means of staying in touch with friends—e-mail, instant messaging, and text messaging—may increase the quantity of communication, this comes at great expense to its quality. My concern here is that the ease and speed of cyberspace communication foster a sense of connectedness that is often illusory. If we consider a recent national survey, which revealed that the average American adult reports having only two friends with whom he or she can talk about important matters,[1] and if we remind ourselves again that interpersonal relatedness is one of the three most important and basic human needs, then we must question whether the Internet is really a friend to inner wildness.

The impact of cyberspace as a medium of information and communication is not well understood, but it is certainly a mixed bag from the standpoint of inner wildness. On the one hand, the Internet gives young people private and independent access to information and to each other in an era when much of their experience is mediated by adults. On the other hand, that privacy and independence may be illusory. While some adolescents intentionally seek out pornography on the Web, 25 percent of youngsters who use the Internet say they are subjected to such material involuntarily, according to a national survey conducted by the University of New Hampshire Crimes against Children Research Center. The survey also found that 20 percent of kids who use the Internet regularly have been solicited sexually while online, and in 15 percent of these incidents, the solicitor attempted to contact the youth in person, over the phone, or by mail. Meeting youngsters online is easy for predatory adults because kids often reveal too much information about themselves in chat rooms or create member profiles for themselves when they register with their service providers.[2] While the Internet, unlike the media, is not controlled by any one group of people, it is just as rife with commercial and sexual exploitation and is a heavily corrupted source of potentially harmful imagery and information.

I will also examine the pervasive extent to which the entertainment and advertising industries influence children's thoughts, feelings, and values, and the sometimes irreversible personal choices children make based on that influence. Finally, I will attempt to show in a section devoted to the neurological effects of TV and video games that these two overwhelmingly popular media may well have profoundly negative effects on the thinking ability of children who are heavy viewers and players, meaning that here we face a juggernaut that affects both the content and the structure of our children's minds.

Much has been and is still being written about technology's schizophrenic nature, the fact that it comes bearing great gifts at what turns out to be great costs. The Canadian scholar and social critic Marshall McLuhan was one of the first to sound a warning about technology's high price tag, which he saw as the way in which technology has the power to modify and even control us without our awareness. It was McLuhan who in the 1960s uttered the iconic and oft-repeated statement "The medium is the message," by which he meant that it is the process, not the content, of technology that affects and alters culture. For example, he wrote, it doesn't matter whether a machine is turning out corn flakes or Cadillacs. The medium of mechanization and mass production carries the message of restructuring human work and association, and very often the content of the medium blinds us to its actual effects. We are so pleased by the ease and comfort of traveling in a Cadillac that we fail to recognize the fragmenting and dehumanizing effects of the manufacturing process on the people who produced it, and beyond that the environmental havoc wreaked by a car-based society.

As another example, McLuhan discusses the invention of movable type, which, in making it possible to mass-produce books, made literacy a nearly universal phenomenon. The positive effect of this development is easy to see: the joy and great usefulness of reading became available to everyone. The not-so-visible cost is the effect of the medium of printed text on human consciousness. Printing fostered the modern idea of individuality, but at the same time it destroyed the medieval sense of community and social integration. In a literate society, McLuhan argued, uniformity and sameness become dominant characteristics, and the linear nature of printed language supports the development of left-brained rational thinking at the expense of other forms of intelligence.[3]

McLuhan was forming his ideas in the 1950s and '60s, just before television and its subsequent electronic cousins assumed their cultural dominance. It was left to a student of McLuhan's to apply McLuhan's insights to the onslaught of electronic media that began in the late 1970s and its impact on childhood in particular. Picking up where his mentor left off, Neil Postman took an ecological approach to the issue of young people and electronic media in order to understand the full range as well as the roots of the media's effects. He founded the Media Ecology Department at New York University, which he chaired until his death in 2003, and, after a decade of research, came to the profound and disturbing conclusion that childhood itself is in danger of extinction.[4]

Postman's reasoning proceeds thus: childhood is a social construct, not a biological given. Childhood as a distinct life phase generally didn't exist in Western cultures prior to the Renaissance because, as Postman sees it, everyone shared the same information environment, and, since information was transmitted orally, young people had the same access to information that adults had. Because families lived in very small spaces, everyone also shared the same intimate social environment, so young people were exposed to all aspects of adult experience from the very beginning. But this state of affairs changed radically with the fifteenth-century invention of the printing press. The rapid spread of books created a knowledge gap between adults and children, because now access to adult information required the ability to read. "Literate Man left behind the children," Postman wrote, and from that point on, children were forced to acquire their reading skills in a drawn-out, step-by-step manner in schools created expressly for that purpose.

So it came to pass that childhood gradually evolved into a prolonged period of intellectual development for which the dominant form of information was written and controlled by the adults, who made it available to children through a sequential schooling process. Only a fully literate individual, in other words, had access to the secrets of the adult world, which meant that children, for the most part, did not. That was what made them children. And as childhood and adulthood became increasingly differentiated, children could no longer share the language, learning, appetites, and social life of adults, as they had previously been able to do when knowledge was passed down orally.

Not until the invention of the telegraph, which made communication instantaneous, did adults begin to lose control over the flow of information. Television sped up the change exponentially, because it not only transmits information instantly but does so through visual images, thereby reducing the power and importance of the written word. And of course the Internet, which did not exist when Postman was working out his theory, now provides children with almost infinite access to adult knowledge entirely on their own terms.

As a result, writes Postman, the distinction between childhood and adulthood today is like a movie playing in reverse. TV has collapsed the information hierarchy because it requires no skills and does not segregate its audience. All programming is reduced to the same accessible level, and what was formerly adult material is available to children at the push of a button, which means they now have more knowledge about the adult world than they have had at any time since the Middle Ages. The merging of childhood and adulthood is inevitable when a group that is socially (as opposed to biologically) constructed is largely defined by the exclusivity of the information it possesses. If everyone knew what lawyers know, in other words, there would be no lawyers.[5]

The changes I have been observing in the children I have worked with over the last thirty-five years confirm Postman's theory. Far too many kids are thinking and acting on adultlike thoughts before they are ready. The violence and pornography spewed out by electronic media are robbing them of that irreplaceable period in their lives that our culture has set aside for exploration and innocent discovery, for child's play, and for testing and retesting their personal place in the scheme of things before they have to begin making irreversible choices. To quote Postman, "It means—to use a metaphor of my own—that in having access to the previously hidden fruit of adult information, they are expelled from the garden of childhood."[6]

Let's first examine some of the effects of the electronic media that may appear obvious to many readers. I want to do this in some detail because, while I think most of us already know that watching too much TV is unhealthy for children, as is violent and heavily sexualized programming, we may not realize the extent to which these media have taken over many young people's lives. Nor am I sure that we fully appreciate the disturbing implications of daily exposure that grows heavier every year, and in some cases is extending to outright addiction. I think it is important that we all have a thorough understanding of the issues so we can stand firm in our roles as protectors of childhood.

Young people today spend an enormous number of waking hours interacting with one electronic medium or another. According to media researcher Emory Woodard, while 98 percent of American homes have at least one television, the average number of televisions in homes with children (ages two through seventeen) is now at nearly three per household. Virtually half of all American kids (47 percent) have a TV in their bedroom, and that figure increases sharply with the age of the child. An overwhelming majority (78 percent) have basic cable, and 31 percent have premium cable. More than two-thirds (68 percent) have video-game equipment, and that figure is rising steadily. More than 90 percent of homes with children have at least one personal computer, and 75 percent of those computers have online access, another number that is climbing fast. The bottom line: the average American child spends over four and a half hours a day *sitting in front of some kind of screen*. And perhaps the most shocking finding of all: that figure was up by nearly 10 percent from just the previous year, 1999.[7]

Another survey of media use by communications researcher Donald Roberts, which measured the overall media exposure of young people ages eight to seventeen (including the hours added when they use more than one medium at a time, for example, checking e-mail while listening to music), found that the average child is exposed to nearly eight hours of media daily. The rate varied somewhat by race, with African American youth reporting ten hours, Hispanic youth nine hours, and whites seven hours every day. The rate of exposure was inversely related to income level, whereas there was a positive correlation between income and computer use.[8]

Communications researcher Frank Bocca took a glance into the future. He noted that youth born into the television generation spend the equivalent of seven years of their lives watching television. But what about members of the so-called Internet generation—those born after 1993? The computer, Bocca wrote, has reached the status of "meta-medium" because of the way in which it potentially combines a TV, book, magazine, newspaper, typewriter, radio, and game console in a single interface. Based on current estimates of the amount of time young people spend with these various media, Bocca guessed that an average member of the Internet generation might spend as many as *twenty years* at a computer during his or her lifetime. At this point, so early in the computer era, with cyberspace expanding so rapidly—the size of the Internet has approximately doubled every year since 1990—the long-term effects of this new trend are anyone's guess.[9] Thus it behooves us to heed McLuhan's cautionary analysis and begin giving far more careful consideration to the impact on children of the computer in particular, to explore its potential downsides before we become entirely blinded by the exciting aura of this powerful new form of technology. Unfortunately, at the present time very little research is being done in this area.

It's not that children don't still interact with traditional media forms; it's just that they no longer spend much time with them. Outside of school the average child reads books for only fifty minutes a day, and newspapers and magazines for twenty-one minutes.[10] So we can see that electronic media severely cut into the amount of time children interact with older media forms that require independent thinking and that stimulate the imagination. And the chronic passivity and inactivity that electronic media engender have another, even more alarming effect: childhood obesity. According to a recent government report, the number of significantly overweight kids has reached epidemic levels, with the number doubling in the last two to three decades. Currently one child in five is fat, and that figure is still rising. The increase is taking place in both children and adolescents, and in all age, race, and gender groups.

Obese children are now turning up with diseases like type 2 diabetes, which used to occur only in adults. They also tend to be overweight as adults, which of course puts them at greater risk for heart disease, high blood pressure, and stroke. But perhaps the most devastating effect of all to an overweight child is the most immediate one: social stigmatization. Children who are teased a great deal because of their physical appearance are very likely to suffer from low self-esteem and depression.

Let's turn to what should be the equally obvious effects of the violent and sexual content of the media that kids spend over 480 minutes a day absorbing. It took researchers a while to wake up to the importance of understanding the media's influence on children's social, emotional, and psychosexual development, but the results are pouring in, and none of the news is positive. One of the most comprehensive reports on the subject to date was assembled by pediatrician Victor Strasburger and social scientist Edward Donnerstein. It was based on a comprehensive review of all the relevant studies over the past twenty years, and in their introduction the authors cut straight to the chase: a serious problem exists that should elicit the serious concern of parents, educators, physicians, mental health advocates, and politicians. Every year, young people view an estimated ten thousand acts of violence through electronic media. In addition, an analysis of music videos of all genres showed that 22.4 percent of MTV's offerings portray overt violence, and in 80 percent of those, highly attractive role models are the aggressors. On the extremely sensitive and complex issue of sex and sexuality, so integral to an adolescent's and young adult's sense of well-being, the media have virtually nothing constructive to say. Teenagers annually view nearly fifteen thousand sexual references, innuendoes, and jokes, of which only 170 deal with birth control, abstinence, sexually transmitted diseases, or pregnancy. Prime-time television's so-called family hour, from 8 to 9 p.m., presents more than eight sexual incidents per hour—four times as many as in 1976 —with nearly one-third of family-hour shows containing sexual references.[11]

In another major research review, child psychiatrist Susan Villani cites a Kaiser Foundation study of sexual behavior on television. Researchers analyzed 1,300 shows across ten channels and reported that while 50 percent of all shows—and 66 percent of prime-time shows—contained sexual content, only 9 percent included any references to the possible risks or responsibilities of sexual activity or any mention of contraception, protection, or safe sex.[12] And those unfortunate facts pale next to the reality that the Internet grants unprecedented access to hard-core pornography with a few strokes on the keyboard.

Strasburger and Donnerstein pose the question: does media exposure actually cause violence, drug and alcohol abuse, and unfulfilling and unsafe sexual activity among young people? Or, as the entertainment and advertising industries maintain, do the media merely mirror an increasingly violent, drug-oriented, and sexualized society? The authors state that research on the relationship between media violence and real-life aggression is "voluminous" and very clearly reveals a direct causal relationship between the two. The available data, they say, include detailed cross-sectional studies, naturalistic studies, longitudinal studies, and two highly regarded government reports. The consensus among the researchers, in their view, is that the violence seen on television, in videos, and in movies leads to aggressive behavior in children and teenagers.[13] Moreover, according to Villani, numerous studies show media violence to have the greatest effect on preschoolers. Even though their aggressive behavior was "less problematic" because of their young age and small size, researchers warned about the long-term influence on subsequent behavior.[14]

Not all children become aggressive, of course, but the correlations between violence and aggression are undeniable. In fact, as Strasburger and Donnerstein emphasize at the end of their report, media violence is as strongly correlated with aggressive behavior as any other behavioral variable *that has ever been measured.*[15] They are quick to point out that media violence is hardly the sole cause of violent behavior; poverty, racism, inadequate parenting, and the dissolution of the family may all have a larger impact. However, the use of violence to achieve goals or settle conflicts is learned behavior. Such learning, they say, occurs in social groups such as the family, peer groups, and gangs; and here, perhaps, is the keynote in their review of the scientific literature: "Television and other media may function as a *'super peer'* in this respect." On a broader cultural level, media violence can not only encourage antisocial behavior but also increase a young person's perception that the world is a mean and dangerous place. In light of the fact that many parents already perceive the world to be unsafe and keep their kids on tight leashes as a result, this media-generated effect on the next generation of mothers and fathers has huge implications for the future of inner wildness.

Unfortunately, write Strasburger and Donnerstein, in contrast to the more than one thousand studies linking media violence to real-life violence, very little research has been done on the connection between children's steady diet of sexualized media content and their sexual attitudes and behavior. Here the authors can only suggest that if children and teenagers can learn aggressive behavior from the imagery they view and the music they hear, it is reasonable to assume that they are learning unhealthy sexual attitudes and behavior as well.

A study that appeared subsequent to Strasburger and Donnerstein's report unequivocally confirms their suspicions. A team led by research psychologist Rebecca Collins conducted a national longitudinal survey of the TV-viewing habits and sexual experience of nearly 1,800 adolescents ages twelve to seventeen. Not surprisingly, the results showed that the more sexual activity teens watched on television, the more likely they were to be initiated into sexual intercourse, with those ranked in the ninetieth percentile of TV sex-viewing twice as likely to become sexually active as those in the tenth percentile, for all ages studied.

Collins and her team surmised that one of the reasons for the strong link between viewing and engaging in sex is that high exposure to sex on TV affects adolescents' developing beliefs about social norms. The content of the shows they watch may convey the illusion that sex is more central to daily life than it actually is; and because the sexual relationships portrayed on the screen are glamorized, casual, and generally overwhelmingly devoid of the emotional risks and physical complications that go hand in hand with real sex, teenagers are far more likely to try it out for themselves. Often they are not yet fully informed or emotionally prepared, as is evidenced by the high rate of sexually transmitted diseases among sexually active adolescents (one in four) and a teen pregnancy rate that is one of the highest among industrialized nations.

The study, the first of its kind, included a follow-up survey a year later to track changes in subjects' behavior vis-à-vis their viewing habits. Researchers found that the most significant changes occurred in younger teens, who are statistically far more vulnerable to STDs and early, unwanted pregnancies. For instance, twelve-year-old respondents who had high exposure to media sex behaved in ways that resembled fifteen-year-olds with low exposure.[16]

On top of the effects of TV programming, there is the army of advertisers that have young people in their crosshairs. The average child views forty thousand commercials each year, of which nearly two thousand are for beer and wine. For every "Just say no" or "Know when to say when" public-service announcement, teenagers view twenty-five to fifty beer and wine ads. Alcohol and tobacco advertisers are an increasing presence on the Internet as well, with more than thirty-five alcoholic beverages represented, a Budweiser online radio network, interactive games, free giveaways, brand spokescharacters, and specially designed chat rooms. The tobacco and alcohol industries annually spend $6 billion and $2 billion respectively trying to entice young people to "just say yes." Does that enormous investment pay off? The answer, according to Strasburger and Donnerstein, is an unequivocal "yes": "The preponderance of the evidence indicates that children and adolescents who are exposed to greater amounts of tobacco or alcohol advertising are more likely either to use or intend to use such products."[17]

Advertising is so effective in reaching younger audiences in particular that the journal *Pediatrics* issued a cautionary special report on the subject in 1995. As evidence of the frightening power of the advertising medium, the authors pointed out that despite the ban on cigarette ads on TV, two million teenagers start smoking every year. The report cites the example of the infamous Joe Camel billboard and magazine campaign, for which the Camel cigarette company admen created a new logo featuring a friendly, slouchy old camel with a cigarette jutting out of his mouth. One study showed that one-third of all three-year-olds and nearly all kids over the age of six could recognize the logo; in fact, Old Joe was as familiar to them as Mickey Mouse. Another study found that the ad campaign was more effective among children and adolescents than among adults. Not coincidentally, Camel's share of the underage cigarette market equaled $476 million in annual sales—one-third of all cigarette sales to minors.[18]

In *Consuming Kids: The Hostile Takeover of Childhood,* Susan Linn, a professor of psychiatry at Harvard Medical School, takes an even closer look at the effects of advertising on what she calls, tongue-in-cheek, "the consumer group formerly known as children."[19] Linn investigated every dimension of the marketplace exploitation of our young people, not just those in the realm of alcohol and tobacco. She estimates that the combined budget for advertisements aimed at kids is more than $15 billion a year—two and a half times the 1992 figure. The fact that children influence $600 billion in annual spending has not been lost on corporate America. Regarding alcohol and tobacco in particular, Linn is quick to point out how important it is to those industries to get to kids early. For instance, she writes, research shows that people who start drinking before the age of fifteen are four times more likely to develop an alcohol dependency than those who don't start until they're twenty-one. Moreover, lifetime alcohol abuse is the highest among individuals who take their first drink between the ages of eleven and fourteen, and the industry depends on alcoholics for a large share of its profits. Together, underage and adult problem drinkers account for nearly half of all alcohol sales. Tobacco companies, likewise, are well aware of the research showing that the younger the kids are when they start smoking, the more likely it is they will become regular smokers and the less likely they will successfully quit. If a young person can reach the age of twenty without taking a puff, Linn notes, he or she has almost no likelihood of ever starting to smoke, as 90 percent of all smokers pick up the habit before they turn eighteen—the legal age for buying cigarettes.[20]

Linn then turns her focus to the relationship between advertising and sexuality. She notes that sex has always been a favorite tool of advertisers, but now it is also being used to sell the very media offerings that attract the young viewers whom sponsors want to reach. Ads for TV programs, movies, and music highlight sexuality just as they highlight violence, and the messages aren't only about sexual behavior. Equally important, they are about what it means to be male and female, what attracts us to each other, and how males and females treat one another.[21] Again, the media influence on young people's sexual attitudes and activity is a woefully understudied issue, but Linn has gathered the following data to support her claim. One-third of ten- and eleven-year-olds surveyed in one study reported that the pressure on them to have sex is a big problem. Another study shows that girls in the early stages of puberty are especially vulnerable to media messages regarding sex, and the younger a girl is when she has intercourse for the first time, the more likely she is to feel that it was unwanted. Furthermore, in a national survey of sexually active young people, 81 percent of twelve- to fourteen-year-old boys and girls said they wished they had waited until they were older.

For Linn, the crux of the problem of the media's effect on young people's tender sense of themselves as sexual beings is this: many parents are reluctant to talk openly with their kids about sex, and only half of all public schools in the country offer sex-education classes that teach birth control other than abstinence and address broader sexual issues. This information gap leaves young people, who are having their first sexual experiences at a younger age than ever before, with little choice but to get most of their information or advice about sex—64 percent, according to one study—from the media, not from parents, teachers, or even friends.[22]

• • •

It goes without saying that violence, drug and alcohol abuse, promiscuity, unsafe sex, and unwanted teenage pregnancy are major public-health issues, but that is not my main reason for exploring them in such depth. My primary concern remains with inner wildness, and thus the two-part question that preoccupies me is: do advertising and the media represent yet another form of control over children's minds, bodies, and spirits, and when it's time to decide whether and when to experiment with alcohol, drugs, or sex, are young people making their own choices? Without a doubt, the answers are yes to the first question and no to the second. If cigarette companies can generate logos that rival Mickey Mouse in their power over a child's imagination, toy manufacturers can produce entire prime-time Saturday-morning children's programs—and "program" is the operative word here—that continually and subliminally market their products for thirty minutes at a stretch, and TV and advertising combined can profoundly alter young people's sexual attitudes and behavior, how can we see it any other way?

I have saved for last the issue of video and computer games because they are the latest electronic media to come on the scene and are spreading like wildfire. What began as a handful of simple games confined to bulky home machines has evolved into a dazzling array of increasingly realistic simulations that can be played on special consoles, personal computers, handheld systems, PDAs, and even cell phones.[23] Sales in the video-game market increased from $100 million in 1985 to $7 billion in 1994 and are probably rising even faster today.[24]

Researchers are just beginning to determine the effects of this new medium on children. According to research psychologist Nicholas Carnagey, with over 85 percent of games containing some violence and approximately half featuring seriously violent acts, the growing consensus among video-game researchers is that exposure to violent games causes more aggressive attitudes, emotions, and actions, and a corresponding decrease in helping behaviors. When leading video-game researcher Craig Anderson conducted a study involving over five thousand participants, he was so alarmed by the magnitude of their increased measures of aggression after they had played a series of violent games that he made the following comparison: the magnitude of the effect of violent games is greater than the effect of condom use on HIV risk and the effect of secondhand cigarette smoke on nonsmokers. Because so many young people are being exposed to so many hours of media violence, he warned, even a small effect can have enormous social consequences.[25]

In another study, researchers Eric Uhlmann and Jane Swanson uncovered the unsettling depth of the problem. Because most video-game enthusiasts, according to Uhlmann and Swanson, insist that the games they play have no adverse effects on them, the two investigators administered an unconscious association test after their subjects had finished a round of violent games. As predicted, when the subjects were asked directly whether they felt more aggressive after the games, they said they did not. The results of the unconscious association test, however, told a very different story, which led Uhlmann and Swanson to conclude that repeated exposure to video-game violence influences the players "automatically and unintentionally." Moreover, violent video games, because of their interactive nature—which requires players to assume an active role for which they are increasingly rewarded as they master the game —and because they are having fun while they are busy "killing" and "destroying," may contribute even more than watching violent TV and movies—essentially a passive experience—to the learning of aggressive attitudes and behaviors.[26]

Perhaps the most disturbing effect of all, however, is the tendency of violent video games to desensitize children to real-life violence. To study this possibility, researchers took a group of older adolescent test subjects and randomly gave half of them a violent video game to play and the other half a nonviolent game. After twenty minutes both sets of players were shown a ten-minute clip of real-life violence in four different contexts: courtroom outbursts, police confrontations, shootings, and prison fights. In one scene, two inmates repeatedly stab another prisoner. To measure the players' unconscious emotional responses, researchers hooked them up to electrodes that monitored heart rate and galvanic skin response, both of which are reliable indicators of emotional arousal, while the participants were playing the games and while they were viewing the violent film clips.

Interestingly, there was very little variation in the subjects' heart rates and skin response regardless of the type of game they were playing. It was a totally different story, however, once they began watching the clips of real-life violence. Researchers found a dramatic difference in both arousal indicators between the violent-game players and the nonviolent-game players. In both cases, the rates of the nonviolent players went up, suggesting that they were emotionally affected by what they were seeing on the movie screen. Then came the most disquieting result of all: the heart rates of the violent-game players remained the same as when they were playing the game, and their galvanic skin response *went down*, meaning they were entirely unmoved by the real-life violence.

Once again, these effects were caused by only twenty minutes of playing video games. The researchers take care to note that the U.S. military is now finding violent video games a highly effective training device in desensitizing recruits to the idea of killing others. Their report ends with a chilling statement:

> Children receive high doses of media violence. It initially is packaged in ways that are not too threatening, with cute, cartoon-like characters, a total absence of blood and gore, and other features that make the experience a pleasant one, arousing positive emotional reactions that are incongruent with normal negative reactions to violence. Older children consume increasingly threatening and realistic violence, but the increases are gradual and always in a way that is fun. In short, the modern entertainment media landscape could accurately be described as a violence desensitization tool.[27]

Finally, there is the question of whether or not video games are addictive. Do children really choose when and how much to play? Or is the medium so exciting and alluring that it begins to control them? My review of the literature turned up no relevant studies, only comments from experts in news articles suggesting that video- and computer-game playing may very well be habit-forming. For instance, David W. Kaplan, chair of the American Academy of Pediatrics Committee on Adolescence, is worried that computer activity is taking over the lives of some young people, causing them to ignore important functions like eating, sleeping, and face-to-face socializing.[28]

My own anecdotal observations have confirmed Kaplan's concern. Because students in my school enjoy a lot of freedom to structure their own day, we didn't establish any limits on playing portable video games in school when they first hit the market. This state of affairs inadvertently gave me the opportunity to witness the behavior of certain kids who turned out to have a serious addiction to video games. The telltale signs were always the same: they would begin refusing to do other activities that had previously been very important to them, such as eating lunch, playing sports and other real-life games, going out to the park, and so on. These children were not in the majority by any means, but they were very often the ones we felt were the most vulnerable to the games' negative effects. At first we decided to let the game playing take its natural course, hoping that if we let those kids play to their hearts' content, they would eventually get bored and go back to eating and playing outdoors. When the expected change failed to materialize and we realized how serious the problem was, we called together all of the elementary- and middle-school students and teachers and discussed the issue.

As it turned out, enough students had been noticing how addicted some of their friends appeared to be that, in the end, it was one of the older kids who proposed that video games be allowed only during the last hour of the school day. Even the "addicts" voted for the motion, although one had to be monitored for cheating for some time after.

Now let's examine the not-so-obvious: the hidden neurological effects of electronic media, especially TV and video and computer games. I present the following material, which is quite technical at times, because it is so little known and because the implications for inner wildness are so ominous. Harkening back to McLuhan's prescient warning, here we're no longer talking about the impact of the content of the medium on children's thoughts and feelings but about the effects of the medium on the brain.

Once again we enter an area where not nearly enough research has been done, so some of the conclusions about the neurological damage caused by TV and other media must come from tangentially relevant research. This was the challenge social scientist Merrelyn Emery faced when the Australian government hired her in the 1970s to study the potential psychosocial impact of wiring her country for cable television, and in particular of the educational programming that would then be possible. Emery's first crack at the available literature turned up only early versions of the kinds of studies referred to earlier, studies that address the mental and behavioral impact of programming content on young viewers. When she dug deeper, however, she began finding bits and pieces of clues that gradually formed a pattern so strongly suggestive that she would ultimately conclude, very much to her own and the government's surprise, that TV suppresses the thinking and imagining centers in the brain so severely that it renders the medium absolutely useless as an educational tool. All of the available research showed, without a single exception, that the kinds of brain-wave activity associated with cognitive thought drops significantly almost immediately after an individual begins watching television—and the effects can persist for several days even if no more TV is viewed.

In one such study, an adult subject was first asked to read a magazine and then to switch to watching television. Researchers monitored brain-wave patterns in the left hemisphere of the subject's neocortex—again, where the majority of our thinking and learning takes place—throughout both activities, and the results were quite conclusive. The beta, or fast-wave, activity (thirteen or more cycles per second [cps]) indicative of the information processing that occurs when people are talking, reading, or engaging in other everyday pursuits fell from 56 percent to 24 percent. The concentration of slower wavelengths, theta (four to seven cps), and delta (one to three cps) associated with hypnagogic states such as daydreaming and sleep rose from 10 percent to 46 percent, almost a fivefold increase. This change occurred only *thirty seconds* after the subject began watching TV.

In another study, the brain-wave bands of two dozen thirteen-year-olds were measured while they watched four different programs. Each teenager was found to have roughly twice as much slow-wave activity as fast-wave activity, regardless of program content. Elsewhere, researchers compared the EEGs of eight dyslexic boys from the Learning Disabilities Clinic at Children's Hospital in Boston with a control group of boys reading at or above grade level. The results showed a significantly higher percentage of slow-wave activity in the dyslexic boys, indicating, according to Duffy, an "idling" of the left hemisphere of the brain—precisely the effect television is known to cause.[29]

A number of other studies have been designed to test whether television causes memory impairment, a major ingredient of dyslexia. In one such study, a large group of adults in San Francisco were telephoned immediately after they finished watching the evening news. More than half of those surveyed could not remember a single news item that they had just seen reported.[30] In another, researchers asked three groups of subjects to review a single page from a fourth-grade-level textbook. Group A was given the piece of paper itself to study, while Group B was shown a movie of the page, and Group C viewed it on a television screen. Twenty minutes later, subjects were tested on their retention of the material. The group that studied the paper copy averaged a retention rate of 85 percent. Those who saw it on the movie screen averaged 25 to 30 percent, and those who read it on the TV monitor had a retention and comprehension rate of *3 to 5 percent*.[31]

This last study points to the reason for television's apparent suppression of left-brain mental processes: the technology of the device itself. The images appearing on a TV screen (or computer monitor) are generated by a cathode-ray tube that emits radiant light, rather than the reflected or ambient light that brings us the rest of our visual experience. Television is the only radiant-light source we use for information; we seldom stare at light bulbs or the sun. In all other instances, our visual experience is the result of light from a radiant source reflecting off the objects we "see" and entering the brain through the retina in the eye. This difference is significant because the qualities of radiant light and ambient light are quite opposed: whereas ambient light has a broad spectrum of variation, radiant light is uniform. Ambient light also contains an infinite variety of information, while the radiant light emanating from any cathode-ray tube contains absolutely none. Perhaps most importantly, ambient light does not in and of itself have any particular effect on our nervous system, whereas radiant light has a potent activating and deactivating influence on many neurological processes.

Finally, television drastically reduces the visual field compared with any other visual experience, even reading. Research has confirmed that the eye movements associated with reading—including frequent momentary glances off of the page—create a great deal of neurological stimulus.

What all this meant to researcher Woodburn Heron and others is that because television engages only a very small portion of the brain's visual system, because the colors that make up the images and the accompanying sounds are far less complex than those in the natural environment, and because the rest of the body doesn't participate in the experience, watching TV creates a condition similar to that known as sensory deprivation. To test his insight, Heron monitored the brain waves of four adult test subjects while they underwent a ninety-six-hour period of sensory deprivation, and then compared those EEG recordings with another set taken while the subjects watched television. Heron's striking and paradoxical finding was that despite TV's high sensory output, only a few minutes of viewing had a dulling effect on the brain equal to that of sensory deprivation.[32] When we combine Heron et al.'s research with research psychologist Magdalena Vernon's statement in *Perception through Experience* that "indefinite prolongation of exposure to perceptual deprivation might result in a long-term impairment of cognitive ability and emotional stability, especially in young children," we can begin to see the basis for Emery's rejection of television as an educational medium.[33]

Whether or not one chooses to accept the scientific connection between television viewing and sensory deprivation, common sense alone dictates that there is something to it. Anyone who has ever observed children sitting in front of a TV has noticed how quickly they appear to be hypnotized.

And what are the neurological effects of video games? In a recent study, the Japanese brain-mapping expert Ryuta Kawashima used the latest brain-scanning technology to measure brain-activity levels in hundreds of teenagers playing Nintendo. He compared the scans with those of another group of teens doing a simple, repetitive arithmetical exercise. Later, Kawashima repeated the test using magnetic resonance imaging. Like Emery, Kawashima was stunned by the results, which were the same for both procedures. Because video games are highly stimulating and require fast reactions by the players, he assumed that the scans of the game players would compare favorably with the arithmetic group. Quite to the contrary, the results revealed that playing Nintendo stimulated activity only in the lower, more primitive parts of the brain associated with vision and movement, while the simple math stimulated both the left and right hemispheres of the neocortex—the areas most associated with learning, memory, and emotion. These results speak not only to the effects of video games on children's cognitive growth but also to their previously discussed social and emotional effects. It is primarily the right hemisphere of the neocortex that regulates our emotional arousal, and the Nintendo experiment clearly shows that video games have a suppressive neurological effect on it.[34]

At the end of her report, Merrelyn Emery was careful to note that some children are more vulnerable to the negative effects of TV than others, depending on a complex mixture of other environmental factors, including, of course, the amount of television they watch. And at this point, I think it is safe to extend the same statement to video games and other technologies as well.

Where does all of this leave us? Not only is the tidal wave of high-tech games and entertainment negatively influencing the quality of children's thinking and feeling (to an extent yet to be fully measured, and perhaps impossible to measure), but it is also potentially impairing their ability to have any thoughts at all. Unless we act soon to reverse these trends, inner wildness will be in grave danger, and we will be left with a generation of young people forced to grope their way half in the dark through adolescence and early adulthood, with neither flashlight nor map to help guide them.

EIGHT

ADULTHOOD ARRESTED

Adulthood is the capacity to make successful and successive
connections to an unpredictable and changing world.
—Cheryl Merser, *Grown-Ups:*
A Generation in Search of Adulthood

I learned this, at least, by my experiment; that if one
advances confidently in the direction of his dreams,
and endeavors to live the life he has imagined, he will
meet with a success unexpected in common hours.
—Henry David Thoreau, *Journal*

There exists no more repulsive and desolate a creature
in the world than the man who has evaded his genius.
—Friedrich Nietzsche, *Untimely Meditations*

LIKE CHILDHOOD, adolescence is a cultural construct. Somewhat
paradoxically, it is a younger one; childhood, as we have seen, began evolving into its present form centuries ago, while adolescence
is still a kid by comparison. Derived from the Latin *adolescere*,
meaning "to mature," the term did not come into widespread use in
English until the publication of psychologist G. Stanley Hall's seminal book *Adolescence* in 1904.

At the risk of oversimplifying matters, adolescence can be seen
as a stepchild of the Industrial Revolution. There were complex sociological and economic reasons for tacking another phase onto a
child's developmental timetable. As the factory system gradually
replaced household industries and skilled-trade apprenticeships and
forced young workers into menial industrial jobs, they were effectively cut off from traditional sources of mentoring and pathways
into meaningful adult life. As more and more fathers were absorbed

into factory labor, two thousand years of patriarchal authority began to break down. Already teens were facing the modern dilemma of navigating into adulthood with more options but less structure and guidance than previous generations had experienced.[1]

As we have seen, the exponential population growth in the nation's cities caused by industrialization and immigration aroused the concern of educational and social reformers, who led successive movements to extend compulsory schooling, reduce child labor, and create supervised youth recreation centers and programs. When the federal government mandated compulsory school attendance until age sixteen, at the end of the Great Depression, the deal was sealed: packing all of the nation's teenagers into warehouses otherwise known as high schools made adolescence a universal phenomenon. By midcentury, the middle-class norm of a sheltered, extended childhood was equally universal,[2] and the acquisition of higher and higher levels of formal education became the main goal of the teen and early adult years.

Meanwhile psychology, then in its infancy as a science and very much influenced by Darwin's theory, was beginning to look at childhood from an evolutionary standpoint. It was G. Stanley Hall who first insisted that adolescence was a biological life stage, and likewise it was his book that established the idea firmly in the public mind. Hall, a staunch New England Protestant who spent a year in a theological seminary at his mother's urging before changing hats and becoming the first American to earn a PhD in psychology, defined adolescence as "the dawn of puberty ... soon followed by a stormy period of great agitation, when the very worst and best impulses in the human should struggle against each other for its possession, and when there is peculiar proneness to be either very good or very bad."[3] Interestingly, one of the central chapters in Hall's book is on juvenile crime and delinquency, in which he presents voluminous statistics from around the world to show that the great majority of criminals are first convicted when they are adolescents.[4] Here he strikes a now-familiar note: "Juvenile crime thus shows the great difficulty which youth finds in making adjustments to the social surroundings.... In passing from home to the new conditions of industrial life with its severer code, control is increasingly difficult."[5]

The problem, as Hall saw it, is that puberty awakens a young person's deepest urges and passions; however, in many the "power of self-control" is "latent and undeveloped," and "its necessity must be slowly learned."[6] To make matters worse, "Vice and crime ... open such wide fields of originality and differentiation of human varieties, that it is no wonder that the feral traits of primal man often seem so attractive to children and even to women, compared to the more monotonous, tamed, and toned down humdrum life of good citizenship."[7]

And then he proposed the solution:

> Indeed it seems very clear that much of the art of living consists in self-control, the development of which in the individual is the unconscious but perhaps primary purpose of family, church, state, laws, customs, and most social institutions, and that the progress of the world and the advance of personal liberty is just in proportion as the power of self-control has been developed in the community at large.[8]

Modern children are growing up too fast, he argued, and teenagers need more time in specially designed, adult-monitored environments in order to develop the self-control that would save them —and a frightened society—from lives of vice and crime. With those sentiments, Hall added his voice to the hue and cry for institutions where adolescent energies could be sublimated through education, sports, and other age-appropriate activities, and where young people would be shielded from adult pressures and temptations. Work, he believed, exposed them prematurely to the stresses and corruptions of the adult world.[9] In true Darwinian fashion, Hall concluded, "At any rate, for those prophetic souls interested in the future of our race and desirous of advancing it ... it will come by increased development of the adolescent stage, which is the bud of promise for the race."[10]

My reason for spending so much time on the thoughts and words of Stanley Hall is that as the founder of the *American Journal of Psychology*—still one of the most influential publications in the field today—and as a prominent university president, he became to child psychology what Horace Mann was to education. Hall's views, more than any others, would go on to provide the "scientific" underpinnings for future social policy regarding American youth. The origins of adolescence are a complicated matter, but suffice it to say that it is here to stay as the stage of life, beginning with puberty and ending an indeterminate number of years later, that has been set aside for young persons to make their final preparations for landing in adulthood.

After a century of study, discussion, and social planning, adolescence is now as thoroughly homogenized as the earlier stages of life, so the steps of childhood are more or less the same for everyone in the country. Kids enter preschool at age three, elementary school at six, followed by middle school (with the parameters varying slightly by region), until they graduate from high school at seventeen or eighteen. At this point, those who already haven't been shut out of the game by institutionalized racism and classism either head directly into the workforce or pursue further education in the hope of establishing higher-status careers. This leads us to the question at hand: if society has so smoothly paved the way from birth to adulthood, why do so many of today's adolescents end up like airliners circling the airport on autopilot, with more and more of them running out of fuel before they figure out how to break free from the holding patterns their lives have become?

Let's take another peek back in time. Every generation of children has to wrestle with the social, political, and economic constraints of its historical period. Today's problems happen to be high rates of family instability, disconnection from the adult world, pressure to achieve academically, activities organized strictly by age, and —partly as a result of all these, the issue at hand—delayed flights to adulthood.[11] One point of thinking retrospectively is to remind ourselves that contrary to what we may have been taught, things haven't always been this way. Certain changes across our lifetimes occur so incrementally that they tend to slip beneath our notice. Here I think of the old analogy of the chef placing the lobster in a pot of cold water on the stove over a low flame. The chef doesn't need to put a lid on the pot because the poor lobster won't try to escape— it never knows it is being cooked because the temperature rises so gradually. Many of us can relate to this idea when, for instance, we reflect on the years we spent treading water in high-school classrooms, waiting for something to happen that never did.

Let's return to the time before the teen years were called *ado-*

lescence, prior to the careful engineering of childhood. In *Huck's Raft*, Stephen Mintz contrasts the modern-day pattern with the life of Herman Melville, born in 1819. By the time Melville was twelve, his middle-class father had gone bankrupt, gone insane, and then died, at which point young Herman had to quit school and go to work in his uncle's bank. That job was followed by work as a store clerk, a farmworker, a teacher, and a cabin boy on a whaling ship —the inspiration for one of the greatest works in Western literature—all before the age of twenty.[12]

Prior to the invention of adolescence, Melville's story was more the rule than the exception. Most postpubescent individuals were left to make rapid and unpredictable transitions into the adult world, sometimes by choice, sometimes by necessity. Consider that fifteen-year-old Benjamin Franklin, the son of a candle maker, helped his older brother found the first independent newspaper in the American colonies; or that Admiral David Farragut captained a combat vessel during the War of 1812 when he was only twelve; or that Alexander the Great assumed command of the Macedonian army at the age of sixteen and set out to conquer the world at twenty. And there would surely be similar accounts starring young women if biology and tradition had not forced them directly into motherhood —an adult role if ever there was one. Closer to home, consider that my grandfather, and possibly yours as well, crossed the Atlantic alone when he was eleven to seek a better life in America. As recently as 1920, only one out of six American teenagers had graduated from high school; the rest began assuming adult roles of one kind or another when they completed eighth grade.

The supreme irony of Hall's book is that it contains over fifty pages of examples, like the above, of famous individuals who accomplished tremendous feats at young ages because their teen years weren't put on hold with the kinds of compulsory, preparatory, adult-structured activity that he ultimately advocated. Hall was so blinded by the common Calvinist fear of inner wildness that he failed to apprehend the huge downside of domesticating adolescence and making it the same for everyone.

Hall couldn't see that for many young people predictability and routine would make the trip to adulthood harder, not easier. He couldn't understand that predictability and routine often come at the expense of a young person's inner drive, whether we call it inner wildness, *élan vital,* or the daimon—a word that, after, all, literally means "unpredictable." As we heard from Hillman in chapter 5, the daimon "is out of step with time, finding all sorts of faults, gaps, and knots in the flow of life—and it prefers them." Or, as May put it, the presence of the daimon is felt as "the grasp of fate upon us."

This is not to say that the present state of affairs is ill intentioned. It's only natural that we as a society endeavor to prepare the way for our young people. Just as we didn't want to see them fall and skin their knees when they were learning to toddle and run, we don't want to see them bruise their egos as they begin to head off on their own. And so we have tried to regularize the transition and do everything in our power to help kids become successful adults. But we have to ask ourselves, as Hall neglected to do: at what cost? If we don't trust young people's ability to intuit the right goals for themselves and allow them to experiment with their own ways of reaching them, we increase the likelihood that they will miss the call of their daimon and instead be led down false paths by the push and pull of peer pressure, parental and societal expectations, and the latest popular trends.

Child psychologist, parent educator, and popular writer Eda LeShan pondered the same question in the late 1960s as the movement to protect children and enhance every facet of their development was coming into full swing. She had this to say in *The Conspiracy against Childhood:*

> One of the important aspects of growth is an acceptance of the necessity, the inevitability of error and failure. Genuine growth is impossible unless we are willing to risk failure— and we *will* fail, many times. But the alternative is to never be truly alive at all. Despite the fact that every discovery, every invention, every work of art, has been created out of the inner courage, the capacity to accept the possibility of failure, we seem to be forcing our children into a position where failure is intolerable and to be avoided at all costs.[13]

LeShan, looking back over the twentieth-century changes in society's views toward children and childhood, much as I have tried to do in this book, went on to sum them up as the search for a blue-print, some way of manipulating the manner in which they grow in order to produce the ideal child. She writes:

> In our attempts over the past half-century to learn new and better ways to raise our children, we have tended to overlook or underestimate the profound and precious qualities in each child that need to "be as they grow." Because we thought that we might discover some "good" or "perfect" ways to raise our children, we have often been frightened when our children, each so new and special, so truly unpredictable, do not fit our calculations or expectations, but instead insist on defying our formulas![14]

I quote LeShan at some length because she was one of the lone voices of her generation calling society's attention to the emerging threats to children's inner wildness. The 1960s, however, were not the first time someone noticed young people's existential problem of being overguided and overcontrolled by the adult status quo. Listen to social critic Randolph Bourne in 1911, at the very onset of the formation of the concept of adolescence:

> We are not to start life with a code of its laws in our pocket, with its principles of activity already learned by heart, but we are to discover those principles as we go, by conscientious experiment. Even those laws that seem incontrovertible we are to test for ourselves, to see whether they are thoroughly vital to our own experience and our own genius. We are animals, and our education in life is, after all, only different in degree, and not in kind from that of a monkey who learns the trick of opening his cage. To get out of the cage, the monkey must find and open a somewhat complicated latch. How does he set about it? He blunders around for a long time, without method or purpose, but with the waste of an enormous amount of energy. At length he accidentally strikes the right catch, and the door flies open. Our procedure in youth is little different. We feel a vague desire to expand, to get out of our cage, and liberate our dimly felt powers. We blunder around for a time, until we accidentally put ourselves in a situation

where some capacity is touched, some latent energy liber-
ated, and the direction set for us, along which we only have
to move to be free and successful.[15]

I find it fascinating how well Bourne's words, from the perspective of a young person—he was twenty-five when he wrote *Youth
and Life*—complement LeShan's from the vantage point of a parent, despite their being two generations apart. In Bourne's thinking
we can clearly hear the voice of the daimon when he speaks of acci-
dents, blundering, and dimly felt powers. And in LeShan's we can
sense the wisdom of a mother who doesn't have her needs and wants
mixed up with her child's daimon. Totally unknown to each other,
both are in utter agreement that what adolescents do *not* need, if
they are to respond authentically to the urgings of their inner wildness, is to have everything laid out for them in advance. Another
ramification of institutionalizing adolescence that Hall didn't fore-
see was that homogenizing the passage to adulthood would lead society to homogenize its expectations of the younger generation as
well. Bourne, a contemporary of Hall's, on the other hand, did. Perhaps because he was a hunchback, Bourne was acutely aware of the
strong tug of conventionality on a young person's inner wildness.
"Society, as we have seen," he warned, "is one vast conspiracy for
carving one into the kind of statue it likes, and placing it in the most
convenient niche it has."[16] "This treason to oneself," he continued,
"is perhaps the greatest mistake of youth, the one unpardonable
sin."[17]

The daimon's job is to prevent that treason, and it is inner wildness that enables the daimon to do it. However, as we will see, the
work of reaching adulthood is only growing more problematic because our culture's efforts to socially engineer the transition are
leaving the daimon with no role to play. Again, this doesn't mean
that young people don't need help from adults along the way; they
often do. But that support needs to be timely, measured, and never
forced. What young people need most of all from adults is acknowledgment for who they actually are, rather than comparisons with
some cultural image of who they're supposed to be—comparisons
the advertising industry exploits mercilessly as it sells superficial
badges of identity in the form of clothing, cars, computers, phy-
siques, and experiences.[18]

• • •

To answer the question of why so many young people are struggling to establish meaningful adult lives, we must unravel a multifaceted paradox. Sociologically speaking, one isn't considered a full-fledged adult in modern Western society until one has reached five "markers" in life: leaving home, finishing school, starting work, getting married, and having children. Meanwhile, at the same time that the path leading to the threshold of adulthood has become increasingly standardized, the condition of the route beyond the doorway is turning in the opposite direction. According to sociologists Richard Settersten and Frank Furstenberg, two of the lead researchers in the aforementioned University of Pennsylvania's "Transitions to Adulthood" study (see the introduction), which incorporated massive quantities of U.S. census data from 1900 to 2000, the timing and sequencing of reaching the traditional adulthood markers are rapidly becoming less predictable and more "prolonged, diverse, and disordered."[19] In fact, the ages at which young people are reaching the markers has risen so dramatically over the course of the last generation that some sociologists are questioning the accuracy of this method of defining adulthood.[20]

It is essential to recognize for our immediate purposes that because the old, patriarchal customs governing the adulthood markers no longer apply, adolescents are not bound as their predecessors were to the ready-made frameworks provided by traditional social structures. More than ever before, young people are free to find their own ways into the adult world. Of course, I am speaking extremely generally here, because our culture still has a long way to go to eliminate racial and gender bias; and early and frequent childbearing has been inexorably linked to the lack of access to economic and educational resources since the dawn of civilization. Nevertheless, relative to the past, most adolescents today can look forward to a far greater range of options than ever before. Or as sociologist James Côté writes in *Arrested Adulthood*, "I believe that now, more than any other time in history, the possibilities for self-development are enormous ... as each traditional marker declines, taking with it old barriers and taboos."[21]

Côté proposes that we scrap the outmoded, external definition of adulthood entirely and adopt an internal one instead. He writes that to avoid getting lost in today's "culturally destructured" society, young people must be self-directing and self-determining individuals. For Côté, the kind of psychological integration that Carl Jung called "individuation" has become the true measure of adulthood, not the assumption of social roles such as worker, spouse, parent, and so on.

It would appear that young people are in complete agreement. When a group of 140 American twenty-one- to twenty-eight-year-olds was recently asked to identify what they considered the signs of attaining maturity, they listed the acceptance of responsibility for one's self, financial independence, and independent decision-making as the top three signs, with becoming a parent listed as number six and marriage as eleven.[22]

At the heart of the paradox, however, lies a huge "if": young people can take advantage of the current open-ended nature of adulthood only *if* they have as much self-knowledge as they have knowledge of the world, and *if* they are assertive, playful, creative, and perhaps above all persistent. Yet, as we have seen in the preceding chapters, many of our extant institutions are steering them in the opposite direction, toward passivity, conformity, ambivalence, and a lack of determination.

Côté's current assessment is that some adolescents are taking advantage of the loosening of external constraints and striving successfully to develop to their full potential; however, the majority are "passively allowing themselves to be manipulated by the profit-based mass structures that have arisen in the place of traditional cultural institutions." Like futurist and economist Jeremy Rifkin, who writes that our entire culture is being commodified,[23] Côté increasingly sees the purveyors of mass culture stepping in and filling the void as our cultural destructuring continues.[24] The problem has already become so severe, with many young people failing to find their place in the adult world, that Côté believes we are now in the process of unwittingly adding yet another stage to the end of childhood, one in which the trappings and mannerisms of adult life mask an underlying immaturity and lack of purpose. He calls this stage "youthhood." His fear is that many people will be content to stay mired there because they will still be able to consume and entertain themselves to their hearts' content, leading dampened lives of quiet desperation in a kind of Brave New World that asks little of them.[25] The sharp and sudden rise in antidepressant usage in both adolescent and adult populations certainly lends credence to these concerns.

Unfortunately, Côté's analysis of the problem lacks hard sociological data to reinforce its urgency, and it is equally unfortunate that the "Transitions to Adulthood" study maintains a largely neutral stance in its interpretation of the voluminous body of data it collected. According to the study's authors, the sudden and pronounced extension of the ages at which young people are reaching traditional adulthood markers can be explained by simple trends such as an increase in the number of students pursuing higher education and for longer periods of time and relaxed societal attitudes toward birth control and nonmarital cohabitation.

I beg to differ. Young people are getting stuck because they have been forced to live thoroughly domesticated childhoods. They are arriving at the increasingly fuzzy border between adolescence and adulthood without enough practice in making choices and doing things for themselves. So many decisions have been made on their behalf and so much has been done for them that they have not developed a secure sense of self-direction and competence. They were programmed to perform for external rewards, which squelched their creativity and suppressed the eagerness for novelty and challenge with which we are all born. We then expect them to flip a switch, as it were, and suddenly become autonomous adults capable of establishing orderly lives in an ever more chaotic and confusing world. But it just doesn't work that way. The self-confidence, maturity, and self-awareness that being an adult requires cannot be manufactured out of whole cloth. These are not inborn traits. They are characteristics that young people develop over time—if and when they are given the opportunity to exercise them.

Alexandra Robbins and Abby Wilner, the authors of *Quarterlife Crisis: The Unique Challenges of Life in Your Twenties*, also question the idea that today's widespread delay in coming of age is a simple matter of shifting demographics. They bemoan the absence of in-depth sociological and psychological studies confirming what they have found to be the ground reality: a majority of today's young adults are struggling mightily to achieve the kind of psychological adulthood Côté is talking about. Robbins and Wilner, both professionals in their "twentysomethings," as they refer to their transitional decade—Robbins is a journalist, and Wilner a

Web-site administrator—base their insights on a combination of their own experiences and interviews with more than one hundred of their twentysomething peers. Here is their conclusion:

> So while the midlife crisis revolves around a doomed sense of stagnancy, of a life set on pause while the rest of the world rattles on, the quarterlife crisis is a response to overwhelming instability, constant change, too many choices, and a panicked sense of helplessness. Just as the monotony of a lifestyle stuck in idle can drive a person to question himself intently, so, too, can the uncertainty of a life thrust into chaos. The transition from childhood to adulthood—from school to the world beyond—comes as a jolt for which many of today's twentysomethings simply are not prepared. The resulting overwhelming senses of helplessness and cluelessness, of indecision and apprehension, make up the real and common experience we call the quarterlife crisis.[26]

The authors argue that a "quarterlife crisis" can be far more daunting than a midlife crisis because the latter idea is widely accepted and there are plenty of books, films, and support groups to help people through these changes. Most people entering their twenties, on the other hand, don't realize that "the whirlwind of new responsibilities, new liberties, and new choices can be entirely overwhelming for someone who has just emerged from the shelter of twenty years of schooling."[27] Many quarterlife-crisis sufferers feel that they are the only ones having a hard time with this transition, which makes them reluctant to talk about it with anyone and leads to widespread isolation and a sense of hopelessness. As a result, according to Robbins and Wilner's research, there is a high rate of mental and emotional disorders among twentysomethings, including addiction, anxiety, depression, and many other kinds of problems.[28]

Because the cartography showing the way to the adult world is so out of date, and because access to guides and mentors has been largely cut off, young people in search of adulthood sorely need each other for support. They need to establish communities in which they can forge a new set of shared norms and goals that are relevant to today's rapidly changing world. Unfortunately, at a time when they need each other most, they are becoming increasingly distant from one another.

The roots of this alienation can be found in the cumulative isolation of contemporary childhood. At home kids are connecting less and less with each other because so much of their play is mediated by adults, technology, or the entertainment industry. In this regard I see an enormous change between my childhood and today's every time I return to Washington, D.C., to visit friends and family. One of my favorite things to do while I'm there is to take a long, slow walk around my old neighborhood and let the memories come flooding back. Every time, I am struck by how few children are playing outdoors. I see the signs of children—toys and sports equipment on the porch, bikes in the yard, and so on—but rarely do I encounter an actual child. The kids are all inside, watching TV, playing video games, surfing the Net, doing their homework, or practicing musical instruments.

As children grow older, the nature of their interpersonal communication changes as well. Like so much else, much of it is now mediated electronically, and the quality of that communication tends to be more superficial and less intimate. When kids do get together, the conformity that is part and parcel of the youth culture created by the modern marketplace leaves them with a feeling of what David Riesman calls being "alone in a crowd."[29] They connect by sharing paid-for, prepackaged experiences instead of touching each other's minds and hearts, and as a result their relationships tend to be shallow and distant as well.

Isolation also comes from spending twelve or more years in classrooms that are growing more and more competitive and task-driven, and less and less cooperative and interactive. The time and space that school once granted to forming and sustaining real friendships have largely been purged from the school day, and, as the pressure to meet external performance standards continues to ramp up, teachers seldom have any leeway to attend to their students' social needs and development.

When you add all of this isolation up, you get the very phenomenon upon which Robbins and Wilner are reporting: a generation of young people who urgently need each other's support and yet who don't know how to reach out for it. The subject of connectedness, or lack thereof, brings us back to Jung's model of healthy psychological development, the ultimate goal of which, again, is individuation. Reaching the goal involves a paradox of its own: one can achieve the kind of inner growth that leads to individuation—understanding our emotional selves, opening up an awareness of our unconscious patterns, becoming comfortable with intimacy, developing a sense of our purpose in being alive—only in the context of other people. Jung's reasoning is thus: "As the individual is not just a single, separate being, but by his very existence presupposes a collective relationship, it follows that the process of individuation must lead to more intense and broader collective relationships and not to isolation."[30] Or, harkening back to Deci and Ryan's Self-Determination Theory, the answer is for young people to be able to be both autonomous and relational at the same time. The trouble, however, is that individuation is not a given. It is highly vulnerable to the cultural tendency, so articulately described by Bourne, to level everyone down to the same standards. And it cannot be accomplished, wrote Jung, "by keeping to the path prescribed by collective norms." In fact, he wrote, "The more a man is shaped by the collective norm, the greater is his individual immorality." To this he added that any serious check to our individuality stunts our psychological growth, and it then follows that any social group consisting of stunted individuals "cannot be a healthy and viable institution"[31]—the very situation to which Robbins and Wilner are trying to alert us nearly a century after those words were written.

The quarterlife crisis is, in essence, a form of "identity crisis," a term coined by the great twentieth-century psychologist Erik Erikson, from whom we will hear more in a moment. While a state of identity confusion is now considered a standard feature of adolescence, in reality it is entirely an artifact of contemporary American culture. It is not a given. As we just saw, life for teenagers in this country looked very different in the nineteenth century, and it continues to look different in many other cultures today.

David Riesman's classic 1950 study of what he called "social character" points to the origins of many of the stereotypical characteristics of the modern-day American teenager: the raging hormones, the pendulum swings from conformity to rebellion, the susceptibility to peer pressure, and so on. According to Riesman, three primary character types have evolved over time, as a result of the interaction between the individual and the surrounding society. In all early cultures, the "tradition-directed character" was shaped entirely by tradition, ritual, and religion. These external sources of authority accomplished the task of controlling behavior and transmitting the society's norms and values to its younger members in a seamless and automatic way. Those who didn't fit the mold were drawn into special roles like shaman or sorcerer.

When, for whatever reason, the grip of a society's traditions begins to loosen, there is a tendency for the family to step into the gap, thus giving rise to the "inner-directed character." Fathers and mothers now become the absolute authority, and the rules and expectations are laid out for children in hard and fast terms. The younger generation reflexively internalizes the cues of parents and other adult authority figures, and thus can be counted on to conform to those standards without questioning them. Inner-directed people require little in the way of social control because, as the term implies, their sense of direction comes from inside, having been implanted early in life by their elders.

In most industrial societies, however, the authority of the family has itself gradually broken down, in which case the "other-directed character" comes to the fore. Other-directed individuals tend to look outside of themselves for validation and direction, rendering them particularly sensitive to signals from peers and the mass media. This, according to Riesman, leaves them especially vulnerable to manipulation and makes real happiness and personal fulfillment virtually impossible. The other-directed character confuses goodness with approval and has trouble defining his or her own goals and standards.

To make matters worse, other-directed *parents* depend on the reciprocal approval of their children. They lack the parenting confidence that inner-directed parents enjoyed, and their lack of self-assurance becomes magnified when they turn to contemporaries, advice books, and the mass media for guidance. With that comes the tendency to latch on to the latest child-rearing scheme, but what gets passed on to the child, much more than the content of the technique, is a kind of diffuse anxiety.[32]

It's another double-edged sword: our culture has reached the stage in its evolution where the individual is no longer tightly bound by tradition or family and is finally free to define him- or herself, yet that very freedom makes it extremely hard to do so. Most adolescents today are entirely other-directed, which makes it very difficult to hear the voice of their daimon calling to them from within.

But Riesman doesn't leave us without a way out. According to his model, there are three ways in which people can adapt to the conditions of an other-directed society: adjustment (conformity), anomie (deviance), and autonomy. While most adults try to cope with the demands of growing up by either mindlessly conforming or rebelling, young people still have the opportunity to become autonomous individuals who shape their own character through conscious selection of the right role models and experiences. It is possible for them to adjust to society's behavioral norms without sacrificing the freedom to choose whether and when to conform[33]— if, I would add, they have already had sufficient practice in making their own life choices and accepting the consequences that follow.

For Riesman, becoming autonomous involves transcending the circumstances of our birth and finding our own way to the forms of work, play, and relationships that will enable us to explore hidden parts of ourselves. It involves creating new alternatives, which, in turn, involves reconceptualizing work and play so that both become activities in which we can invest our emotional and creative energies in ways that bring us a sense of meaning and purpose. To do so, he writes, calls for a high degree of awareness of one's feelings, one's potential, and one's limitations and for a completion of the task of detaching oneself from the "shadowy entanglements" of today's other-directed culture—whose demands "always appear so reasonable."[34]

The bottom line for Riesman is that, although the dominant culture will always oppose real autonomy, only an autonomous person is capable of true freedom—everyone else will eventually end up conforming in one way or another. And the battle for that freedom is won by continually struggling to establish our own identities, no matter how great the odds.

Erikson called the transition between childhood and adulthood —which he, like Hall, thought necessary in the modern era—a "psychosocial moratorium." Actually, Erikson held, every culture institutionalizes some kind of moratorium for its young people, whether it's a rite of passage, an apprenticeship, or higher education.

Unlike Hall, however, he sees so-called juvenile delinquency not as a failure of adolescent self-control but rather as an attempt to create one's own rite of passage when no other options seem to exist.[35] Likewise, mythologist and author Michael Meade calls teenage risk taking and antisocial behavior forms of "self-initiation."[36]

For Erikson, the purpose of a time-out before young people irreversibly enter adulthood is to give them the opportunity to construct a coherent whole out of all the various pieces of their identity that they have been gathering throughout childhood. He saw the formation of identity as a step-by-step process, with children going through a kind of miniature crisis before graduating from one phase of growing up to the next. It is important to note that Erikson used the term "crisis" to denote not an emergency or a catastrophe but a turning point, a transitional period in which the child's rising capabilities are accompanied by greater vulnerability. For instance, as a toddler's mobility improves, the increased speed of motion also means a higher risk of injury.

Without going fully into Erikson's complex, Freudian model, we can appreciate his point that the outcome of whatever identity crisis an adolescent might encounter lies in how he or she fared with earlier crises. In other words, to the extent that young people are unable to develop a basic sense of trust, both in themselves and in the outside world, when they are small children; or to exercise their own autonomous will by saying "No!" and "Mine!" *ad infinitum*; or to engage in real play and real accomplishment during their school years; or to establish positive connections with models and mentors as they grew older, the holes in their identity will become roadblocks of larger proportions when they reach adolescence.[37]

And so for Erikson, whose ideas stemmed from his therapeutic work with young people with identity issues of pathological proportions, the stereotypical kinds of dysfunctional teenage behavior that we consider "normal" today are not normal at all. Rather, they are signs—switching back to my own idiom—that serious damage has been done to their inner wildness during their journey through childhood:

> Youth after youth, bewildered by the incapacity to assume a role forced on him by the inexorable standardization of American adolescence, runs away in one form or another,

dropping out of school, leaving jobs, staying out all night, or withdrawing into bizarre and inaccessible moods. Once "delinquent," his greatest need and often his only salvation is the refusal on the part of older friends, advisers, and judiciary personnel to type him further by pat diagnoses and social judgments which ignore the special dynamic conditions of adolescence.[38]

Thus Erikson stood squarely against the standardized adolescence that Hall and others worked so hard to establish; in fact, he saw it as a root cause of young people's identity confusion. Again, however, he did recognize that the rapidly changing face of a modern technological society has made both a secure identity and the necessary time set aside to establish it prerequisites for a satisfying transition to adult life.

So Hall has gotten his wish: the "increased development of the adolescent stage." American society indeed provides young people with an ever-lengthening moratorium before they have to make adult commitments; in fact, we are already in the process of adding yet another official extension to the existing moratorium, according to psychologist Jeffery Arnett, one that he has termed "emerging adulthood." Arnett, in a book by that title, argues that the time has come to recognize the span between the traditional end of adolescence and full adulthood, which stretches from the late teens to the midtwenties, as yet another pit stop on the track to maturity. Today, writes Arnett, it is emerging adulthood that has become the phase properly dedicated to "identity exploration," the period of instability and of feeling in transition formally associated with adolescence, a period that is pregnant with possibilities.[39]

Rapidly increasing numbers of adolescents are choosing to spend their emerging adulthoods in college, the "institutionalized identity moratorium," as Côté calls it, and the place where young people can purchase identities based on academic credentials.[40] Unfortunately, there is a hidden pitfall here: as more and more adolescents travel this route to adulthood, the value of a college degree drops. College is, in many ways, becoming an extension of high school, not a true institution of higher learning where children mentally mature into adults.

At the same time, college costs are spiraling out of sight, which means that graduates are facing fierce competition for well-paying jobs at a time when their lives are already heavily mortgaged by student loans. The burden of debt that many graduates now carry forces them to accept the first job that comes along after graduation, instead of searching for the life work their daimon would otherwise guide them to do. Many of the entry-level jobs that once offered a road toward economic independence no longer exist; nor does the traditional occupational ladder, which in the past young people could gradually climb just by sticking with their careers. Instead, young people are often expected to do the jobs with the least value, prestige, and pay, and they are looked upon as undeserving of jobs with significant status because they are regarded as less responsible and capable than they once were. Stuck in unstable jobs and living situations, many are unable to earn enough to live independently and maintain the lifestyle they need to lead to be considered fully functioning adults.[41]

Côté reminds us, too, of "the forgotten half"—the nearly 50 percent of American youth who don't graduate from college and whose incomes have dropped by 20 to 30 percent in the last two decades. Being locked into a low socioeconomic status doesn't necessarily deny one access to psychological adulthood, but it certainly reduces the available options and makes the process more difficult.[42]

Escaping the maze that adolescence has become requires a rare ability to be both autonomous and relational. To find their way out of the confusion and on to the life course of continuing growth and change that our high-tech world demands, young people need to be able to sift through multiple alternatives in an open-ended, informational way, so that they can, as Randolph Bourne so eloquently put it, steer clear of the forces—parental expectations, peer pressure, media stereotypes—that will otherwise "warp, and conventionalize, and harden" them. Yet they just don't know how; they don't know who they are or what they want to reach for. If they do somehow manage to chance upon the exit from the maze, they often wander out onto the path of least resistance, into a life ruled by circumstance and impulse, procrastination and avoidance.

Consider the story of a former student of mine. I briefly introduced Isaac in chapter 3, though not by name: he was a member of the class that raised almost $10,000 to travel to Puerto Rico to do relief work. It was Isaac, then thirteen, who entirely on his own initiative phoned all of the local media outlets to tell them about the project. His calls resulted in several TV and print stories, which led to substantial contributions from a number of anonymous donors.

After graduating from our school, Isaac tried public high school, and, while he didn't find the coursework particularly difficult, he quickly decided the academic routine wasn't for him. He chose to homeschool instead, and because both of his parents worked full-time, he was essentially homeschooling himself. Isaac pursued a variety of interests independently, and when he was fifteen he helped organize and raise funds for a small group of young people to attend an international conference of democratic schools in New Zealand. He bought a round-the-world ticket for himself and continued traveling for several months before returning home. When he was sixteen, he arranged an internship at a national clearinghouse for alternative-education resources. That year the organization was slated to host the next annual meeting of the international conference Isaac had attended the year before, and so, utilizing the adult-level Web-design skills he had honed during his time at home, he soon established himself as one of the primary organizers of a weeklong gathering that would ultimately draw over six hundred people from twenty-two countries around the world. The conference was unanimously praised as the best in the organization's eleven-year history.

The following year, Isaac became the organization's full-time office coordinator at its headquarters on Long Island. The director of the organization, a veteran educator in his sixties, was a powerful mentor, and Isaac quickly became his right-hand man. Isaac's duties included managing the Web site and the substantial sales from the online store, fielding worldwide requests for information, and helping to establish an annual national education conference, the purpose of which would be to serve as one of the organization's principal revenue sources. By his third year as conference director, he had promoted the meeting so successfully that it brought in more than $25,000, thus erasing the organization's perennial deficit.

Along the way, Isaac was also accepted by the college of his choice. He tried it out, but again found that formal academic study was not what stirred his soul. Presently, at the ripe old age of nineteen, he is helping to found an alternative high school in Albany and is one of three full-time members of the teaching staff. The school, which is in its first year, is thriving.

The trouble with reifying another extension of childhood, such as emerging adulthood, is that it normalizes the postponement of growing up and turns the Gabies and Pauls and Elinors and Isaacs of our culture into marginalized exceptions. It makes us lose sight of the fact that it is still entirely possible for children to reach puberty with their inner wildness intact. Those who "survive" arrive fully equipped to make thorough and exciting use of their adolescent years before confidently steering themselves to the adult lives they are meant to lead.

It is important to note that Gaby, Paul, Elinor, and Isaac did not come from privileged backgrounds. Affluence is not what enabled them to take full advantage of their adolescent "moratoriums" in order to explore, expand, and deepen themselves. They kept their balance and remained on course toward what Thoreau calls "the lives they have imagined" because they had already established an inner template for self-direction and self-discovery.

How did they do this? There are no secret ingredients. From the beginning, they simply had parents who trusted their ability to make responsible choices and who understood the importance of allowing their children to follow their own inner guidance and learn from their mistakes along the way. I should add that, when they were born, their mothers did not relinquish control of the birthing process to the medical system. Their moms and dads made sure that nothing disturbed the bonding process in the hours and days following birth.

Likewise, when it came time for school, their parents didn't just reflexively hand them over to a monolithic institution that might have little regard for kids as unique individuals. On the contrary, their parents found an educational environment that respected their children's right to be themselves, empowered them to direct their own learning and solve their own problems, nourished their imagination and creativity, and was staffed by teachers who cared deeply about them and were happy to serve as mentors and models. At home, their parents didn't overindulge them with entertainment in the form of elaborate toys, electronic games, and commercialized play; nor did they clutter their lives with extracurricular activities.

When Gaby, Paul, Elinor, and Isaac did take music lessons or play organized sports, it was genuinely their choice, not a parental directive or subtle manipulation. And, I might add, they always performed their share of household tasks.

In middle school, all four children engaged in internships and apprenticeships in which they did real work and got a real preview of the adult world. And in high school their parents assumed that these teenagers were mature enough to dictate the conditions of their education. As we have seen, Gaby and Paul chose to go to public school, where they successfully sifted through the contents of that massive, unbending structure to find the people and information they needed to pursue their interests and goals. Elinor, who found public school too large and impersonal, located a small boarding school with a good art program and a strong sense of community. Isaac, as we have just seen, was able to create his own educational program with the full support of his parents.

Because these engaged, autonomous young people are already so secure in their identities—so well on their way to being individuated—it is unlikely that they will succumb to the ever-present temptation to shy away from grown-up challenges and commitments in favor of the easy road to a subsistence based on ready-made pleasure and the fulfillment of only minimal social expectations. This is not to say they won't fall down and skin their knees from time to time. They will encounter obstacles, but when they do, they will be able to marshal their inner resources and seek whatever outward assistance they might need to figure out a way over, around, or underneath them.

Perhaps giving lost young people a larger bubble within which to find themselves *is* the answer for those whose inner wildness has been wounded so terribly that they still lack an adequate sense of self and direction even when they have entered their twenties. I would be the last to argue that such youngsters are exhibiting some sort of developmental abnormality. But if there were ever a case in which it is far wiser to focus on prevention than on triage, this is it. For as the examples of kids like Gaby, Paul, Elinor, and Isaac make so indelibly clear, children whose inner wildness remains vital won't face a major crisis of identity at twenty-five, won't collapse under the weight of conventional expectations and student debt, and won't grow deaf to the inner voice urging them toward the fulfillment of their own unique destinies.

And that is why I am issuing this urgent plea to all of us who say we care about children: to come to the defense of their right to a full and undomesticated childhood, so they can boldly answer the call of their daimon and lead lives of unquenchable distinction.

NINE

SAVING INNER WILDNESS

Our salvation lies in all of us—men, women
and children—recovering the reciprocity,
power, and wildness of our earthly nature.
—Chellis Glendinning, *My Name Is Chellis
and I'm in Recovery from Western Civilization*

I HAVE COVERED A LOT of ground in this book, traveling from
birth to adulthood with stops along the way to delve into history, parenting, biology, psychology, education, sociology, philosophy, literature, and occasionally my students' or my own personal
stories. When I first showed the outline of this book to an editor, she
was excited by my thesis and shared my concern about the plight
of young people today. But the breadth of the book's scope worried
her. Lacking formal training in all but one of the areas I proposed
exploring, did I have the requisite credentials for such a complex
project?

But that's the point, I argued. The fact that I am not a special-
ist is exactly what makes me the right person for the job. Experts
in their fields have already written about individual aspects of the
problem, and I am grateful to them: the effects of mechanized births
on babies, of overly permissive or overly controlling parenting on
children, of factory education on students, of identity confusion on
adolescents, of media addiction on everyone. All are aware in some
way or another that childhood is changing—and not for the better—but to date no one has fitted all the pieces together into one
coherent whole. Meanwhile, I have been working with children of
every imaginable kind on the ground level for thirty-five years, and
I have witnessed firsthand many of the changes that have occurred
in childhood over that time. I have seen with my own eyes their effects on kids, and I have seen many of the causes as well.

Another editor saw the value of my unusual perspective, and it is thanks to her that you are reading these words. Again, my goal throughout has been to assemble the entire puzzle, to examine as thoroughly as possible the far-ranging alterations to American childhood, their origins and development, and, most important, how they are affecting the tender inner selves of our children. If we don't ask these hard questions, our efforts to change things for the better are often reduced to putting Band-Aids on compound fractures and dabbling in the latest popular trends.

Inner wildness is endangered, but it need not become extinct. In fact, as I look around me today, I see much that inspires cautious optimism. For instance, more and more reports questioning children's bulging backpacks and overstuffed schedules appear in the popular media every day. And, as I mentioned in the introduction, concerned parents and politicians in numerous states are joining forces to challenge the current administration's woefully misguided, if not downright cynical, educational policies. Other parents are waking up to the fact that allowing their kids to while away the hours in front of a menagerie of video screens is not good for them and are encouraging them to pursue a hobby or to play outdoors instead. Thankfully, our national system of free public libraries is still alive and well, and every region has its own parks and nature-education centers, many of which are also free. And there still exists a healthy nationwide network of overnight, wilderness-based summer camps, most of which have scholarship programs for families who can't afford the fees.

Despite the slide of childhood down the slope of domestication, there remains an ample supply of opportunities for unmanaged learning, play, work, and adventure—and when those opportunities can't be found, it is always possible to create new ones. That is the beauty of undomesticated experience: it is largely self-generated, and except, perhaps, in the case of international travel, it rarely depends upon sophisticated technology. Young Isaac's trip around the world cost him little more than his airfare because of the web of relationships he had formed before he left home. He rarely had to buy his dinner while he was away, and he never saw the inside of a hotel room.

Let's review the chief nemeses of inner wildness briefly and in the most basic terms: fear causes a need to control, and control causes domestication. Any serious discussion of what we can do to prevent further damage to childhood—and reverse some of the existing damage—must first address this equation. Following this logic, the fear that sets the landslide in motion is based primarily on a *perception* of danger. I emphasize the word "perception" because it is the critical variable. This brings us to a parallel equation: fear is an emotion, and emotions are not rational. The perception of danger packs just as powerful a wallop as actual danger itself. Some years ago I spent a day with a group of students on an out-door "high-ropes" course. Created by a not-for-profit organization known as Project Adventure, the high ropes consist of a series of aerial obstacle courses, called "elements," set twenty to forty feet up in trees. One of the less difficult elements in the course that we "played" on consisted of a narrow steel cable stretched between two trees approximately thirty feet apart. At first glance, it appeared to be relatively easy to walk from one tree to the other because there was a waist-high rope handrail on either side of the cable and we were all wearing safety harnesses that were connected by another rope to an experienced staff person on the ground.

However, just to make things a little more interesting, the course designer had stretched the handrails in such a way that they gradually dropped lower and lower until, at the midpoint of the span, they were too low to reach while standing up. Then they criss-crossed and slowly inched back up as you progressed to the other end. This meant there were several feet in the middle where there was nothing to hold on to, so continuing forward required a great act of faith in one's balance (and perhaps in guardian angels). I should point out that we had been led through a painstaking safety orientation session before we began this adventure with a capital *A*. The instructors had told us that the steel clip linking the safety rope to the harness was strong enough to lift six airplanes, and that we shouldn't push ourselves beyond our personal limits. There was no shame—they repeated this several times—in asking to be lowered before we had finished traversing an element.

Truly, crossing the street is more dangerous than messing about on a ropes course. Thanks to the harness, belay rope, and a multi-tude of protocols, the actual danger is almost nil. But I can assure you that when you are walking a tightrope between two towering white pines at the point at which there is no longer anything to hold on to, the perceived danger is astronomical. It no longer matters how many planes the carabineer can lift or how many safety harnesses you're wearing. Taking that next step requires all the courage you have ever mustered.

And so it is with the culture of fear I described in the first chapter. The perceived danger, especially from the point of view of the majority of parents who are trying to raise young children today, is exponentially higher than the actual danger. However, as we saw with the Halloween-candy myth, the perception frightens parents enough that they shift into control mode and hold their kids close to them. The same perception then permeates every parental decision, with parents living in daily fear of their kids' falling ill, getting hurt, being abducted or abused, failing in school, becoming delinquent teenagers, and ultimately becoming unsuccessful adults.

As I mentioned early on, the pattern of control is set in motion the very instant we enter the world. The widespread perception that birth is a risky and potentially dangerous proposition has led to a total technological takeover of the process, the combined effects of which are significant barriers to the bonding that nature intends from the moment we emerge from the womb. Ironically, although the United States leads the way in the development of high-tech safety devices and procedures, our infant and maternal mortality rates stubbornly continue to rank us on a par with many third-world countries. Again, it's all about perception. Most of us have come to believe that childbirth is fraught with peril and that a carefully controlled hospital birth promises greater safety, so the overwhelming majority of pregnant women unquestioningly submit to a series of standardized, medicalized interventions, even though these drugs and procedures often compromise the baby's developmental needs.[1] I'm referring to the IVs for administering fluids and anesthetics to the mother, the invasive monitors that measure the baby's vital signs during labor and delivery, and the numerous postnatal medications and procedures that separate the baby from the mom—and this is during a "normal" birth. We must keep in mind that in 2004 nearly 1.2 million Caesarean sections—29.1 percent of all births—were performed in the United States, according to the National Center for Health Statistics, a *38 percent increase* since

1997.[2] C-sections are major surgery, and babies born by this route are exposed to the maximum number of invasive hospital interventions.

The good news is that perceptions occur inside our minds, which ultimately are controlled by no one but ourselves. This means we can potentially change our perceptions at any time. We need only suspend our assumptions long enough to rethink them. The bad news is that most of us are creatures of habit, and over time we develop habitual ways of thinking that get harder and harder to change as we grow older. Becoming "set in our ways" is the folksy expression for this very human tendency. When you stir fear into the mix, altering our perceptions grows exponentially more difficult. Recall for a moment the implications of the triune brain theory: fear triggers the dominance of the primitive reptilian brain, which is quite incapable of rational thought. The primary concerns of the reptilian brain are survival, safety, and physical comfort. The "fight or flight" reflex is centered here. Given that we are constantly bombarded by messages of fear regarding the world political situation, terrorism, the environment, our children's health and welfare, the status of our schools, and so on into the night, it is not hard to understand why we're in the fix we're in.

It is theoretically possible for us to change our perceptions in an instant, but doing so involves transcending the myriad levels of reinforcement for the image of the world as a dangerous place. If we are to be truly in control of our own thought process, our neocortex must be in command, which means that we must feel a sufficient degree of sovereignty over our circumstances. We must create a neutral space between us and our current perceptions—a kind of mental adolescence, if you will—within which we can experiment with new ways of perceiving both children and childhood.

I do recognize that it may not be possible for all parents to protect their children's inner wildness. Ours is a nation still deeply divided by race and class, and far too many parents lack the resources necessary to live in neighborhoods where it is safe for their kids to play outside or to seek other educational options if the local schools are not meeting their personal needs. As Jonathan Kozol reveals in *The Shame of the Nation*, the gains that were made in urban schools during and immediately following the civil rights movement have largely been reversed. Racial and socioeconomic segregation have once again become the order of the day; and in fact, Kozol argues, the situation has gotten so drastic that the education system in this country is now an apartheid institution, where the physical conditions in minority schools are frequently atrocious and the teaching methods demeaning and robotic.[3]

Happily, however, undomesticated activities are generally elemental: they involve doing less, not more. They don't depend upon expensive, hard-to-access resources. It is absolutely possible to restore the novelty, the independence, the adventure, the wonder, the innocence, the physicality, the solitude—the juice—to childhood without any special circumstances. It's an inside job really, requiring the trust and the courage to take the next step forward when there is no handrail to hold on to. Once we have done it, and discovered that everything is still quite okay, we can gradually develop a confidence that will make the restoration process easier and easier.

Let's backtrack through childhood and look at some of the specific things we can do to protect, nurture, and restore our children's inner wildness.

Thanks to the past four decades of the natural-childbirth movement, pregnant women currently have access to a nationwide system of alternatives to medicalized hospital births. Though the laws regulating midwifery vary from state to state, every region has a cadre of experienced midwives who attend births in their clients' homes or in freestanding birthing centers. When their clients experience serious complications during pregnancy or labor, most of those midwives can also tend to births in the hospital, where the hospital's technology and medical procedures may be needed to ensure a safe and healthy outcome. Once in the hospital, however, a midwife will do everything in her power to minimize interventions and support the bonding process in the days and weeks following the birth.

The primary difference between midwives and obstetricians is that midwives are trained to view pregnancy and birth as an instinctive and normal process, with occasional exceptions. Obstetricians, however, are conditioned, both by their medical training and by the constant threat of malpractice lawsuits, to be crisis managers, always on the lookout for worst-case scenarios. Therefore, midwives are far more apt to interact with women as individuals and allow the birth process to run its natural course, while the overwhelming majority of obstetricians tend to treat their patients as a statistic and attempt to control every aspect of the experience. Additionally, there is now a widespread network of doulas, nonmedical birth assistants who offer a wide variety of services to pregnant women and their families before, during, and after birth. Their support helps mothers to feel safe and relaxed, greatly reducing the need for disruptive interventions.

Of course, a positive birth and postnatal period that leaves parents feeling empowered and results in a secure bond between infant, mother, and father is only that, a positive start. It doesn't mean that all is lost if the outcome was less than ideal, because in time the lost ground can be made up. But I can say from my own professional experience with hundreds of families that the parents who remained in charge of the process are far less likely to be anxious and fall into the extreme of permissiveness or authoritarianism.

In any event, two decades' worth of parenting adventures now lie ahead. The ongoing task of nurturing children's inner wildness is an inside job on the parents' part, too. It is especially incumbent upon parents, given the sadly domesticated state of American culture, to pay careful attention to their own inner wildness, because, as Eda LeShan wrote, "The conspiracy against childhood is really a conspiracy against ourselves. We cannot help our children to discover and nurture their inner selves unless we are able first of all to do this as adults, as parents, and as teachers—as persons."[4]

Thus, my inclination as a school director trying to support struggling children is very often to ask the parents how *they* are doing. I will frequently advise them that the best way for them to help their kids is to help themselves first. If *their* lives are lacking in joy or meaning, if *they* are too stressed out to maintain a satisfying connection with their spouse or child, and if *they* can find a way to change things for the better, then their kids will automatically reap the benefits. We are models for our children, and they will inevitably pattern their lives after our example. Thus, it is imperative that we attempt to lead lives that nurture our own inner wildness.

But what if our parents, for whatever reasons, were unable to model for us how to live autonomously and creatively? What if they didn't know how to raise us in ways that nurtured our inner wildness? These questions most certainly applied to me, and perhaps they apply to a great many of you. Family patterns can be extremely hard to leave behind because there is such a strong pull either to repeat the pattern or to do the polar opposite, which seldom ends up any better. Herein resides the real work and perhaps the biggest challenge of parenting, which is an incredible learning experience if we are fully willing to embrace the task.

The bottom line is that when parents are sufficiently informed, aware, and open to learning and personal growth, it is indeed possible for them to buffer their homes against the seductions and manipulations of a society based on conformity and mass consumption. And it is possible for them to raise their children safely and successfully without robbing them of their independence and their right to seek their own destiny.

The first practical, grassroots thing parents can do to nourish their kids' inner wildness is to turn off the boob tube and read to them. Better still, especially when they are young, tell them stories, either simple fairy tales or original ones that you make up as you go along. You can also sing to them instead, or teach them nursery rhymes, or tell them old family stories about their ancestors. At the ages of five and six, my eldest daughter developed a fascination with Jesus, and sometimes at bedtime she would ask me to tell her stories about his life.

When my children were young, my wife and I were both already leading busy, heavily committed lives, so bedtime was often the only reliable time for reading and storytelling. We therefore did everything in our power to make it a sacrosanct ritual and never to rush it. It is so important to repeat that favorite book four times, or to leave time for a conversation about whatever that night's interlude may have evoked.

The benefits of reading to children, I think, are obvious, but I will spell them out just the same. First and foremost, it is a wonderful way of sustaining the loving bond between parent and child. Second, it is the best way I know to help instill a love of reading; indeed, it is primarily how my own daughters learned to read. As four- and five-year-olds, they began memorizing verbatim their favorite books. Then they somehow began to recognize the patterns within the text, and before long they were reading independently. My wife and I never turned our nighttime sessions into reading lessons, because that would have spoiled the fun; the girls just gradually figured it out on their own. Third, reading is one of the best antidotes to television and other electronic media. When kids watch TV or movies, all of the imagery is provided for them, and if they watch too much of it, the image-making center in the brain starts to shut down. Reading to kids, on the other hand, especially books without a lot of pictures, constantly stimulates their imaginations.

The content of what we read to our kids is a critical factor. It should go without saying that we should read to them only material they are excited about hearing, but at the same time it is important to keep in mind that because they love us and want so much to please us, they are likely to enjoy almost anything we offer. In my experience, both as a parent and a teacher who has been reading aloud to kids longer than I care to remember, you can't go wrong with fairy tales and ancient Greek, Roman, and Native American myths. The biggest reason I favor fairy tales and myths is that they are the container for the traditions upon which Western civilization is built, and as such they are a rich source of sustenance for inner wildness. Moreover, they were carefully constructed by their creators to help young people make sense of the often confusing and frightening world around them.

According to Rollo May, myths have three vital functions: to give us a sense of personal identity, to make possible a feeling of community, and to help us deal with the mystery of creation.[5] Myth unites the conscious and unconscious, the past and present, the individual and society, and, as May wrote in *The Cry for Myth*, it "refers to the quintessence of human experience, the meaning and significance of human life."[6] Or, as the twentieth-century classicist Gilbert Highet wrote, a bit more poetically:

> Myths deal with the greatest of all problems, the problems which do not change because men and women do not change. They deal with love, with war, with sin, with tyranny, with courage, with fate: and all in some way or another deal with the relation of man to those divine powers which are sometimes to be cruel, and sometimes, alas, to be just.[7]

A century earlier, Friedrich Nietzsche also issued a strong argument for the positive role played by myth. "Without myth every culture loses the healthy natural power of its creativity," he wrote, and "myth alone saves all the powers of the imagination and of the Apollonian dream from their aimless wanderings."[8]

Nietzsche, whose life spanned the height of the Industrial Revolution, was alarmed, even then, by the effects that modern science and technology were beginning to have on inner wildness. May later picked up on that identical concern in the 1950s and '60s and made it one of the centerpieces of his explorations in psychology, arguing that by his era America had completely lost touch with the kinds of deep mythology that help give us direction and clues as to our purpose in life. He echoed David Riesman and others in pointing out that the breakdown of tradition means that it is incumbent on the individual today to assemble his or her own personal set of values, and that myths are an eternally trustworthy repository of good information.[9]

The psychologist Bruno Bettelheim's extraordinary work with autistic children made him acutely aware of the modern tendency toward existential confusion and disconnectedness. It was Bettelheim who discovered the value of fairy tales as a therapeutic tool, a practice that led him to state in the 1970s:

> Just because his life is often bewildering to him, the child needs even more to be given the chance to understand this complex world with which he must learn to cope. To be able to do so, the child must be able to make some coherent sense out of the turmoil of his feelings. He needs ideas on how to bring his inner house into order, and on that basis be able to create order in his life. He needs—and this hardly requires emphasis at this moment in our history—a moral education which subtly, and by implication only, conveys to him the advantages of moral behavior, not through abstract ethical concepts but through that which seems tangibly right and therefore meaningful to him. The child finds this kind of meaning through fairy tales.[10]

Bettelheim saw fairy tales as a particularly effective source of nourishment and healing for inner wildness because they deal especially with the universal human problems that preoccupy children's minds: separation anxiety, sibling rivalry, interpersonal conflicts, being on one's own, and coming to terms with both the positive and negative sides of one's personality. "The more I tried to understand why these stories are so successful at enriching the inner life of the child," he wrote in *The Uses of Enchantment: The Meaning and Importance of Fairy Tales*, "the more I realized that these tales, in a much deeper sense than any other reading material, start where the child really is in his psychological and emotional being."[11] Bettelheim became an ardent advocate for a revival of the classic fairy tales because of the ways they resonate with children's magical way of thinking and help them to accept their unconscious wishes, urges, and fantasies. If they don't go through this process, he believed, kids either develop a rigid personality that inclines them to try to control and suppress everything or become overwhelmed and feel out of control.[12]

The beauty of fairy tales is that they always include solutions to the struggles against adversity that life inevitably presents us. And the fact that fantasy is their medium and that the characters are archetypal figures allows children to externalize what's going on in their minds. For instance, they can project wishful thinking onto a good fairy, destructive impulses onto an evil witch, fears onto a voracious wolf, and jealousy onto an animal that pecks out the eyes of its rivals. The animals in the stories, according to Bettelheim, represent our own instinctive, animal nature, and the constant tension between the light and dark sides of humanity in the stories mirrors the conflicting urges that exist within all children and helps them to make peace with those urges.[13]

The best-selling author Jim Trelease is a contemporary advocate for reading aloud to children. After establishing himself as an award-winning artist and journalist, Trelease began making weekly volunteer visits to the schools in his community to talk with students about art and journalism as careers. Before long he noticed that most of the students he got to know didn't like to read very much, but the ones who did nearly always came from classrooms where the teachers read aloud every day. Those observations, combined with his experience of reading to his own kids at home, inspired him to write *The Read-Aloud Handbook*, which remained on the *New York Times* bestseller list for seventeen weeks and is now in its fifth edition.[14] The *Handbook* is an excellent resource for parents and teachers; the first half contains an in-depth explanation of the benefits of reading aloud to kids, and the second half is an annotated bibliography of more than a thousand of the best English-language children's books. Trelease's book was so influential that in 1985 the U.S. Department of Education's Commission on Reading called reading aloud to children the single most important activity one can do to raise a successful reader.

If parents and teachers faithfully read aloud to their kids, and if parents model reading at home by spending time with good books of their own, then, as my experience has shown, it is virtually guaranteed that those children will develop into competent, independent, joyful readers. Reading then feeds inner wildness in yet another way, by being an important source of autonomy for kids. As Riesman put it so succinctly, "To be alone with a good book is to be alone in a new way."[15]

Another basic thing parents can do to protect their kids' inner wildness is to get them out into nature as frequently as possible. Psychologist Chellis Glendinning believes the essence of our humanity is withering because modern society has so thoroughly alienated itself from nature, a separation that began as soon as the early agriculturalists started fencing themselves in and the natural world out. The first step toward recovery is simply to unenclose ourselves, to get outside under the open sky and let ourselves see the colors, feel the wind, and smell the grass. If the best you can do is the city park, so be it. Begin there. If you can get out into the forest or the desert, so much the better. The important thing is that we physically reunite ourselves with nature in any way possible, so that our inborn sense of connectedness begins to reestablish itself.[16]

As I said at the outset, there is an intimate relationship between inner and outer forms of wildness, and even the most basic interactions with the natural world can be a way for children to venture out from under the layered quilt of domestication that childhood is fast becoming. When I take students out to our school's 250 acres of wilderness land twenty-five miles from Albany, within minutes I can see them begin to shed their urban and suburban skins and come alive. Their eyes glisten with wonder. Their bodies become more relaxed, their movements more fluid. The kids who have trouble regulating their impulses grow calmer, more focused. Sometimes we have a project in mind: maple-sugaring, building a debris shelter, or identifying trees and wildflowers. But most of the time I just turn them loose to explore the brook, climb a tree, start a campfire, or toy with the possibility of getting lost in the forest. On the drive back to school at the end of the day, the change is tangible in every child. We don't do it nearly enough.

I'm reminded of a recent late-summer morning when eight-year-old Aden came charging down from his home up the street to tell me all about the month-long cross-country tour from which he'd returned the night before. Aden's father is a teacher at my school, and he and his wife had bought a used camper van for the trip, which they now intended to resell for approximately what they had paid for it. In it they covered over eight thousand miles of America's majesty, spending time in a number of national parks out west. It was their encounters with grizzly bears, elk, and coyotes that Aden was in the biggest hurry to tell me about. The words came rushing out so fast that I had to slow him down several times so I could understand everything. One of his favorite tales was about how one of the geysers in Yellowstone erupted, off schedule, just as he and his younger sister were approaching it.

Aden's family is barely getting by on a very modest income, and yet they were able to put together an adventure that none of them is likely to forget. Aden is currently researching an itinerary for another tour, and the plan to sell the camper has been put on hold. Thanks to a mother and father who understand children's need to be connected to the natural world, Aden and his sister will not end up suffering from what futurist and journalist Richard Louv calls "nature deficit disorder." Although Louv is playing off the term attention deficit disorder, humor is not his intent. He believes there is a strong link between the fact that nearly eight million American children suffer from some kind of mental disorder and that the overwhelming majority of kids in our highly urbanized and technologized culture have very little day-to-day interaction with nature.[17]

In her work with adults, Glendinning has found that the next step toward recovery is to travel inside ourselves and relearn how to achieve nonordinary states of consciousness, as indigenous peoples did and still do with ease and regularity.[18] Thankfully, kids have it much easier than most adults because they have ready access to nonordinary states through fantasy and the imagination, adventure, free play, dance, poetry, music, art, and even idle daydreaming—unless, of course, we continue to allow modernity to shutter these doors and windows of the soul.

Finally, there is the question of what to do about the many-headed hydra known as electronic media, an issue not only for parents but for everyone who cares about children. While I have been forthcoming about my bias toward freedom and self-direction throughout this book, here is one instance where I believe it is absolutely appropriate and necessary for both parents and society to intervene on children's behalf and place firm limits on how much access kids have to electronic media. I say this because, just like the many-headed hydra—Hercules would cut one head off the monster only to find two in its place—the electronic media have a cancerous, devouring quality that overwhelms the inner wildness of children who for whatever reason have a strong need to be stimulated or distracted. This is a battle for their souls that they simply cannot win by themselves. As I tried to show in chapter 7, TV, video games, the Internet, and so on, are collectively such a seductive, addictive medium, and the content is increasingly so violent and pornographic, that they are causing major physical and psychological damage to our nation's young people.

According to Victor Strasburger and Edward Donnerstein, whose findings on the impact of electronic media I discussed earlier, today's electronic media represent a genuine public health threat. Strasburger and Donnerstein's report ends with a comprehensive set of recommendations that addresses all responsible parties. Regarding the role of parents, the trouble begins with the majority of moms and dads who neglect to monitor with consistency or regularity the media their children are exposed to. Not only do parents frequently underestimate the number of hours their offspring spend viewing, but they also underreport the amount of problematic programming. Their advice to parents on this score is this: limit your children's overall media use to no more than one or two hours per day, monitor media content, and watch and discuss television programs with them.

Strasburger and Donnerstein go on to urge mental health professionals to appreciate the relatively new cultural influence of electronic media on their young patients, and in the process to educate parents and advocate for improved, healthier media and lower exposure to them. Pediatricians who treat children or adolescents should make taking an inventory of their media consumption standard practice, especially when doctors see patients with a history of aggressive behavior or learning difficulties.

Schools have a role to play too. Strasburger and Donnerstein point out that, although the United States was the first country in the world to have television, it is one of the few Western nations that lack a comprehensive, school-based media education program. For instance, Australia mandates media education for every student from kindergarten through grade 12; Ontario, Canada, does the same for middle and high-school students; and England, Scotland, and South Africa all have far more formal programs than the United States does to inform students about the adverse effects of electronic media.

The United States is also unique in its lack of any forceful public policy regarding television. Moreover, the entertainment industry has a historic ability to find loopholes in the minimal limits the government does set on media violence, and so Strasburger and Donnerstein call on Congress and the Federal Communications Commission to put more enforcement teeth into its rules. They also urge the Food and Drug Administration to place much tighter restrictions on the advertising of alcohol and tobacco, which both industries are also highly adept at skirting around. Additionally, they call on parents and mental health professionals to aggressively lobby their legislators to take action in both critical arenas.

Ultimately, write Strasburger and Donnerstein:

What is needed is a virtual sea-change in attitude, from one of crass commercialism to one of respectful paternalism for the unique psychology and needs of young people. The American public is quick to criticize teenagers for their early sexual activity, drug-taking, or violent behavior; yet these youngsters are learning important behavioral cues from the media that surround them. . . . Children and teenagers comprise a captive audience for entertainment producers, but they also represent the next and only source of adults in American society. As such, they deserve far better than what they are being exposed to now.[19]

• • •

On the educational front, it is entirely possible for parents to monitor the quality of their children's experience and to involve themselves in whatever way necessary to ensure that their kids aren't forced to surrender their innate curiosity and thirst for knowledge and competence. Parents don't have to challenge the educational system all at once, though we should never lose sight of the fact that if enough parents ever do so in a united fashion, the situation will begin to change in a hurry. They can consider starting small, which is what author and attorney Sara Bennett and her husband did when they took up the issue of homework with the private school their children were attending in Brooklyn, New York.

In *The Case against Homework*, Bennett and Nancy Kalish relate how the homework burden Bennett's kids carried home each afternoon was adding so much stress to family life that she and her husband began researching the available literature on the educational value of homework. Armed with substantial evidence that homework does not stimulate genuine learning, especially before the high school years, the Bennetts began pressuring the school to reduce the load. The school initially pooh-poohed their objections with the statement that the school's reputation for rigor depended on lots of homework, and that the other parents demanded and expected it. Undeterred, the Bennetts kept pushing the issue until the school's parents' association finally placed it on the agenda of their monthly meeting.

When the Bennetts began lobbying other parents to attend the meeting, they quickly discovered that they were far from alone in their concerns. Parent after parent spoke passionately in the packed house about how homework was killing their children's love of learning, and how their kids were dropping outside activities and fighting with their parents at home. While all of this was going on, the Bennetts' eighth-grade son, who was president of the middle-school student council, organized his peers to sign a petition requesting a student forum to discuss homework, which took place several days later. In the end, the Bennetts didn't come away with everything they wanted, but the school did agree to abolish vacation homework, drastically reduce the amount assigned on weekends, and lighten the weeknight load substantially.[20]

On the teaching side, it is still possible to buffer classrooms against the production demands of an assembly-line system of education. While it is increasingly becoming an act of personal courage to do so, teachers can relax controls and introduce choice and democracy to their nine-to-three mini-societies. They can move beyond what Wendy Grolnick calls the "receptacle model" of education, whereby their job is to keep their students plugged in and fill them up with mostly meaningless information, and instead serve as mentors and role models.[21] I have even seen it happen in a centralized urban high school with nearly three thousand students, the one my daughters attended in Albany. In the case of Lily, my eldest, perhaps the strongest influences on her decision to become a high-school history teacher were two of her history instructors at Albany High. In spite of the large class sizes and other impediments to a healthy education, these two master teachers were able to make the subject, which had always been a strong interest of Lily's, meaningful and alive. They taught their classes in a relaxed, noncontrolling way that modeled a love of history rather than an expertise in classroom management, and in the process they inspired her to do the same.

My younger daughter, Sarah, had a similar experience at Albany High, where, as a senior, she entered the school's Career Explorations Program. Interested in children and teaching, she spent her mornings in a college-style seminar that explored educational theory and her afternoons as a teacher's assistant in a variety of classrooms around the city. Sarah was impressed by one elementary special-education teacher in particular, and found that she enjoyed working with special-needs kids the most. At this writing Sarah is in college completing her certification to work in that field.

If teachers find themselves hopelessly roadblocked when they try to teach creatively, they should consider doing what Josh Hornick and Ken Danford did in Amherst, Massachusetts, when the regional middle school where they were both working rebuffed their efforts to implement team teaching and an interdisciplinary curriculum. Hornick and Danford quit their jobs in order to found North Star, a highly innovative and successful learning center for teenagers that nourishes inner wildness on every level. There, both of these determined teachers conduct regular classes in areas of student interest, but their primary role is to serve as mentors to center members, as well as to help them to connect with additional mentors in the community at large, so that they will have ample access to the adult modeling that is sorely missing from contemporary society.

According to Stephen Hamilton, codirector of the Family Life Development Center at Cornell University, the way in which schools isolate youth from the adult world and from their communities is the single greatest cause of the failure of our educational system to help young people make successful and satisfying transitions into adulthood.[22] Hamilton writes that the systemic absence of internship and apprenticeship opportunities, like the one my daughter was fortunate to have access to, is becoming an increasingly significant barrier to finding work that is meaningful and that enables young people, especially those who do not go on to college, to achieve financial independence. Because of the shift in the fundamental nature of the economy, students who do not graduate from college are increasingly stuck in a kind of no-man's-land. Society forces them to obtain an education, but then severely limits the supply of jobs for which that education qualifies them.[23]

The answer, for Hamilton, is to reconstruct the apprenticeship model that used to exist in this country. He based his recommendations on a year spent studying the educational system of what was then West Germany, whereby high school students who are not on the college track spend the last three years of their compulsory education participating in apprenticeship programs in vocations that interest them.[24] Hamilton noticed a striking difference between the fate of American and German adolescents as they wrestle with establishing their identities as adults. He found that far fewer Germans got stuck in the kind of limbo that has become so prevalent in this country because the combination of their apprenticeship experience and close relationships with mentors familiarizes them with adult responsibilities and roles, giving them a clear view of adult opportunities and the pathways leading to them.[25]

The downside of the West German system is that it rigidly sorts children in elementary school according to academic performance, with only the high achievers accepted into the college track, thereby reinforcing social-class bias. What is needed in this country, argues Hamilton, is an apprenticeship system that differs from the old American and current West German system in two fundamental ways: it should begin as early as the middle-school years, enabling young teens to explore career options through apprenticeships, and it should be flexible and extend beyond narrow vocational training. Hamilton's model would include a wide range of opportunities for children to interface with the adult world, such as community-service projects and internship options that don't lock a young person into a specific career track but provide them with the mentoring and other kinds of growth experiences that will help them read their inner maps to adulthood.[26] The Metropolitan Career and Technical Center that I profiled in chapter 2 is an excellent prototype of what Hamilton is describing.

My only addition to Hamilton's ideas would be to emphasize much more strongly that all young people, not just those who don't attend college, stand to benefit hugely from early and frequent contact with the adult world. While no widespread school-based apprenticeship and internship system exists in our country, there are still a number of readily available ways for young people to locate these types of experiential learning opportunities. For instance, every state has a branch office of the Department of Labor's Bureau of Apprenticeship and Training, which administers nearly thirty-seven thousand apprenticeship programs around the country.[27] The reference sections of most public libraries also contain comprehensive guides and directories that list and describe thousands of national and international internship and apprenticeship opportunities; among them are Ferguson's *Guide to Apprenticeship Programs*, the *National Directory of Internships*, and Peterson's *Internship Bible*. Finally, of course, an Internet search will turn up a plethora of interesting possibilities.

Not only has modernity cut off teachers and other unrelated adults from serving as mentors and guides to our young people, it has made it increasingly hard for parents to do so as well. For all of the reasons cited above, there is a growing gap between many adolescents and their parents. At a time when young people need more parental guidance and acknowledgment, the family discourse often gets bogged down in conflicts that belonged to an earlier period: household chores, homework, diet, personal hygiene, and so on. The truly important issues, such as insecurity, sexuality, friendship, drugs and alcohol, and future goals and aspirations remain undiscussed, and teens turn to the media and to peers for information and support. This issue of familial alienation led family-systems therapist Yehuda Fine, who has made adolescent issues the focus of his thirty-five-year career, to spend the last several years crisscrossing the country to hold a series of workshops with large groups of high-school students by day and their parents by night. Thus did he gather the data for *The Real Deal: For Parents Only— the Top 75 Questions Teens Want Answered Today.*

Fine's mission is to build bridges between teenagers and their beleaguered moms and dads. He has ample compassion for parents who are trying to bring up kids in a stressed-out world in which over 25 percent of American children are being raised by a single parent and in which the average family communicates with each other for less than eight minutes per day. He begins his workshops by listening to young people talk about the sensitive issues many of them feel they can't talk about with their parents. Later, he relays to the parents disturbing facts like these:

- 100 percent of their kids have a friend who has a drug or alcohol problem.
- 100 percent have a friend who has been depressed.
- 100 percent know someone who is regularly having sex.
- 90 percent or more have a friend who has thought about suicide.
- 75 percent want to get married eventually, but only 20 percent think they will have a fulfilling marriage.
- More than 50 percent think they might get divorced.
- And most disturbing of all, only 15 percent think they can turn to their parents for support in a crisis, while 85 percent wish they could talk more openly with their parents about all of these issues.[28]

Fine's advice to parents is 100 percent in keeping with my earlier statement that the experiences that support children and their inner wildness tend to be elemental and uncomplicated. He simply urges us to talk to our children often, and to make sure that no topic—sex, alcohol, depression, violence—is off-limits. Our kids want to know what we think, as long as we don't lecture them to death. Whatever information we don't share with them they will wind up getting from peers, the media, or the local drug dealer.

Children also want to be involved in family matters and problems, writes Fine, so make sure to include them in important discussions. And above all, never be afraid to admit you were wrong or to apologize. The worst error any of us can make is trying to be the perfect parent. When we act like parents who can do no wrong, we give our teens the message that they can't approach us for help because there's no way they can measure up to our standards. We blow the chance to teach them how to face adversity and learn from their mistakes. Children growing up in families in which they can't admit their failures become extremely vulnerable to the very outside influences from which they may need parental safeguards.

In order to rescue childhood from the onslaught of modernity, we have to create a world in which young people are free to be their autonomous selves, to explore, experiment, and learn from their own experience. At the same time, this has to be a world in which they enjoy enduring, nurturing, mutually honest relationships with adults—parents and otherwise—who can lend them the necessary support as they attempt to navigate their personal pathways to adulthood. They also need equally honest and enduring relationships with their peers, because, while inner wildness draws sustenance from solitude, isolation and alienation drain its energy and force it to retreat.

Young people today have an unprecedented opportunity to explore and express their unique reasons for being on this earth, and yet they can't do it if their inner wildness is in tatters. Yes, their ultimate challenge is to find their own way and to allow their personal daimon to guide them. But they need a kind of help that must be sensitively offered, a measured form of assistance that doesn't discount their ability to figure life out for themselves. Perhaps more than anything, they need us to patrol the perimeters of childhood and defend them from the invasive tendrils of control.

Inner wildness is like a wildflower in a meadow, which needs the basic requirements for growth—adequate soil, plenty of sunlight, the right measure of rain, and sufficient space in which to grow. It does not need the constant, diligent attention of a gardener. What a wildflower mainly needs is protection from tractor wheels, sickle mowers, and greedy real-estate developers. Like the wildflower, inner wildness is amazingly resilient. Unless it goes entirely unnourished and unprotected, its built-in resistance to adverse conditions will see it through tough times. If necessary, it will hide until the environment becomes more favorable, and then it will reemerge and quickly make up for lost time. This is the miracle of childhood, one that I have witnessed daily for the last three and a half decades.

The thought I want to leave you with is this: it is absolutely possible, despite the many obstacles and complications, for us to reestablish childhood as an undomesticated period of fertile growth and exploration, the time set aside for children to construct whole, authentic selves that are imbued with the spirit and determination of their inner wildness. It is not too late to prevent childhood from disappearing, but it is imperative that we act now.

ACKNOWLEDGMENTS

I would like to thank Bunty Ketcham for being such an important second mother to me and for encouraging and supporting me just the way my mom would have done were she still around. Also to Bunty for providing me with a much needed writer's retreat at Skerries, her glorious summer "camp" in the Adirondack Mountains of upstate New York. Likewise to Rosalie Bianchi and Paul Juncker for providing me with another amazing retreat in New Mexico's Zuni Mountains and for taking such good care of me while I was there. To Dave Harrison, Renee Iannacone, Jacob Lettrick, and Ed Stolar for scouting out relevant leads for my research and for their invaluable editorial feedback. To the wonderful librarians at the New York State Library for cheerfully finding all the books I needed. To Helene Atwan at Beacon Press for deciding to take another chance on me; to my editor, Christine Cipriani, for adding a feminine perspective and helping me to focus my message; and to Christine's assistant, Cristina Rodriguez, for stepping into the breach at crunch time. To the staff at the Albany Free School and all the members of the greater Free School community for their encouragement and for their backup during the final push to complete the book. To my agent, Jill Grinberg, for believing in me and helping me keep my cool under pressure. To Kadea Metara for teaching me to trust myself. To my sister Samantha Wallace for her support on every level. To all of the incredible kids who have been my teachers over the years and on whose behalf I undertook this project. To my own two extraordinary daughters, Lily and Sarah, for their respect and wise counsel. And finally to my wife, Betsy, who midwifed this book into being. It wasn't an easy birth.

NOTES

INTRODUCTION

1. Natalie Angier, "A Strange Malady Called Boyhood," *New York Times*, July 24, 1994.

2. Ralph Nader, *Children First: A Parent's Guide to Fighting Corporate Predators* (Washington, DC: Corporate Accountability Research Group, 1996), ix.

3. Joseph Chilton Pearce, *Evolution's End: Claiming the Potential of Our Intelligence* (New York: HarperCollins, 1992), 110–11.

4. Ibid., 115–17.

5. www.childbirth.org/section/CSFAQ.html.

6. Berry Brazelton, *Infants and Mothers* (New York: Dell, 1989), 3.

7. Neil Postman, *The Disappearance of Childhood* (New York: Delacorte Press, 1982), 136.

8. Richard Settersten Jr., Frank Furstenberg Jr., and Rubin Rumbaut, eds., *On the Frontier of Adulthood: Theory, Research, and Public Policy* (Chicago: University of Chicago Press, 2005).

9. James Côté, *Arrested Adulthood* (New York: New York University Press, 2000), 180.

10. Stephen Mintz, *Huck's Raft: A History of American Childhood* (Cambridge, MA: Harvard University Press, 2004), 380.

11. Côté, *Arrested Adulthood*, 3.

12. Maxine Schnall, *Limits: A Search for New Values* (New York: Clarkson N. Potter Publishers, 1981), 23.

13. National Home Education Research Institute, www.nheri.org.

14. Mintz, *Huck's Raft*, 383.

ONE: THE TAMING OF THE CHILD

1. Peter Stearns, *Anxious Parents: A History of Modern American Childrearing* (New York: New York University Press, 2003), 18–20.

2. Robert Bly, *Sibling Society* (New York: Addison-Wesley, 1996), 33.

3. Christopher Lasch, *The Culture of Narcissism* (New York: Norton, 1978), 164.

4. Stearns, *Anxious Parents*, 37.

5. Ibid., 40.

6. Stephen Mintz, *Huck's Raft: A History of American Childhood* (Cambridge, MA: Harvard University Press, 2004), 1.

7. Lloyd deMause et al., *The History of Childhood* (New York: Psychohistory Press, 1974), 77.

8. J. H. Plumb, "The Great Change in Children," *Horizon* 12 (Winter 1971): 7.

9. Barry Glassner, *The Culture of Fear* (New York: Basic Books, 1999), 93.

10. Joel Best and Gerald Horiuchi, "The Razor Blade in the Apple: The Social Construction of Urban Legends," *Social Problems* 32:488–99.

11. Ibid.

12. Joel Best, *Threatened Children: Rhetoric and Concern about Child-Victims* (Chicago: University of Chicago Press, 1990), 132.

13. Paul Shepard, *Nature and Madness* (San Francisco: Sierra Club Books, 1982), 35.

14. David Elkind, *The Hurried Child* (Boston: Addison-Wesley, 1981), xi.

15. Foster Cline, *Parenting with Love and Logic* (Colorado Springs: Pinon Press, 1990), 23.

16. Mintz, *Huck's Raft*, 347.

17. Wendy Grolnick, *The Psychology of Parental Control: How Well-Meant Parenting Backfires* (Mahwah, NJ: Lawrence E. Erlbaum Associates, 2003), 111.

18. Ibid., 111.

19. Elkind, *The Hurried Child*, 28.

20. Grolnick, *The Psychology of Parental Control*, 82.

21. Ibid., 15.

22. Diana Baumrind, "Parental Disciplinary Patterns and Social Competence in Children," *Youth and Society* 9, no. 3 (1978): 239–76.

23. Grolnick, *The Psychology of Parental Control*, 9.

24. Edward Deci and Richard Ryan, *Intrinsic Motivation and Self-Determination in Human Behavior* (New York: Plenum, 1985), 122.

25. Ibid., 33.

26. Ibid., 11.

27. Grolnick, *The Psychology of Parental Control*, 57.

28. James Garbarino, "The Impact of Anticipated Reward upon Cross-age Tutoring," *Journal of Personality and Social Psychology* 32 (1975): 421–28.

29. Eva Pomerantz and Missa Eaton, "Developmental Differences in Children's Conception of Parental Control," *Merrill-Palmer Quarterly* 46, no. 1:140.

30. Grolnick, *The Psychology of Parental Control*, 40.

31. Ibid., 47.

32. Deci and Ryan, *Intrinsic Motivation and Self-Determination*, 130.

33. Ibid.,138.

34. Elkind, *The Hurried Child*, xi.

35. William Sears and Martha Sears, *The Attachment Parenting Book: A Commonsense Guide to Understanding and Nurturing Your Baby* (New York: Little, Brown, 2001).

36. John Bowlby, "Developmental Psychiatry Comes of Age," *American Journal of Psychiatry* 135, no. 1 (January 1988): 1–9.

37. Deci and Ryan, *Intrinsic Motivation and Self-Determination*, 43.

TWO: INTO THE CORRAL

1. Peter Stearns, *Anxious Parents: A History of Modern American Childrearing* (New York: New York University Press, 2003), 83.

2. National Commission on Excellence in Education, *A Nation at Risk* (Cambridge, MA: USA Research, 1984).

3. "What's Behind Naughtiness?" *Parents*, June 1935, 26.

4. Ellen Key, *The Century of the Child* (New York: Putnam, 1909).

5. Albert Einstein, university diary.

6. Edward Thorndike, *Animal Intelligence* (New York: Hafner, 1911), 16.

7. Ibid., 284.

8. Stephen Mintz, *Huck's Raft: A History of American Childhood* (Cambridge, MA: Harvard University Press, 2004), 11.

9. Bernard Wishy, *The Child and the Republic: The Dawn of American Child Nurture* (Philadelphia: University of Pennsylvania Press, 1968), 11.

10. Paul Shepard, *Nature and Madness* (San Francisco: Sierra Club Books, 1982), 87.

11. Lloyd deMause et al., *The History of Childhood* (New York: Psychohistory Press, 1974), 364.

12. Mintz, *Huck's Raft*, 10–12.

13. Ron Miller, *What Are Schools For?*(Brandon, VT: Holistic Education Press, 1997), 19.

14. Michael Katz, *The Irony of Early School Reform* (Cambridge, MA: Harvard University Press, 1968), 41.

15. Horace Mann, *Massachusetts Teacher* 2 (May 1849): 139.

16. Neil McCluskey, *Public Schools and Moral Education: The Influence of Mann, Harris, and Dewey* (New York: Columbia University Press, 1958), 38.

17. After Napoleon's stunning defeat of the Prussian army in 1806, the

philosopher Johann Fichte responded to the collapse of German morale in French-occupied Berlin by exhorting the Prussian government to reorganize the country's compulsory education system in order "to mold the Germans into a corporate body, which shall be stimulated and animated in all the members by a common interest. . . . So there is nothing left for us but to apply the new system to every German without exception, so that it is not the education of a single class but the education of the nation. . . . Then, in order to define more clearly the new education which I propose, I should reply that the very recognition of, and reliance upon, free will in the pupil is the first mistake of the old system and the clear confession of its impotence and futility. . . . The new education must consist essentially in this, that it completely destroys freedom of the will in the soil it undertakes to cultivate. . . . If you want to influence man at all, you must do more than merely talk to him; you must fashion him, and fashion him in such a way that he simply cannot will otherwise than what you wish him to will." Johann Fichte, *Addresses to the German Nation* (New York: Harper and Row, 1968), 13–18. In 1810 King Frederick William III enacted Fichte's recommendations, and soon thereafter Prussia helped to defeat Napoleon and regained its position as a dominant power in Europe.

18. Ron Miller, "A Brief History of Alternative Education," in *Almanac of Education Choices* (New York: Macmillan Publishing, 1998), 7.

19. John Gatto, *The Underground History of American Education* (New York: Oxford Village Press, 2001), 144.

20. Katz, *The Irony of Early School Reform*, 121.

21. Howard Zinn, *A People's History of the United States* (New York: HarperCollins, 2001), 263.

22. Ibid.

23. Gatto, *The Underground History of American Education*, 38.

24. Katz, *The Irony of Early School Reform*, 3.

25. Ibid., 214.

26. Gatto, *The Underground History of American Education*, 43.

27. Paul MacLean, *The Triune Brain in Evolution* (New York: Plenum Press, 1990), 9.

28. Ibid., 15–18.

29. Leslie Hart, *Human Brain and Human Learning* (New York: Brain Age Publishers, 1983), 108.

30. Elkind, *The Hurried Child*, 55.

31. Hart, *Human Brain and Human Learning*, 110.

32. Elkind, *The Hurried Child*, 158.

33. Hart, *Human Brain and Human Learning*, 110–11.

34. Humberto R. Maturana and Francisco J. Varela, *The Tree of Knowl-*

edge: The Biological Roots of Human Understanding, trans. Robert Paolucci (Boston: Shambhala Publications, 1987), 22.

35. Ibid., 245.

36. Ibid., 26.

37. Humberto Maturana, *Autopoiesis and Cognition* (Boston: D. Reidel Publishing, 1980), 79.

38. Fritjof Capra, *The Web of Life* (New York: Doubleday, 1996), 97.

39. Ibid., 28.

40. John Briggs and F. David Peat, *Seven Life Lessons of Chaos* (New York: HarperCollins, 1999), 57.

41. Ibid., 57.

42. Erich Jantsch, *The Self-Organizing Universe: Scientific and Human Implications of the Emerging Paradigm of Evolution* (Elmsford, NY: Pergamon Press, 1980), 7.

43. Joseph Chilton Pearce and Michael Mendizza, *Magical Parent, Magical Child* (Nevada City, CA: Touch the Future Press, 2001), 27.

44. Joseph Chilton Pearce, *Evolution's End* (San Francisco: HarperCollins, 1992), 20.

45. Edward Deci and Richard Ryan, *Intrinsic Motivation and Self-Determination in Human Behavior* (New York: Plenum, 1985), 266.

46. See my *How to Grow a School: Starting and Sustaining Schools That Work* (New York: Oxford Village Press, 2006) for accounts of eighteen different schools that foster self-determination.

47. Leo Tolstoy, *Diary* (New York: Doubleday, 1927), 157.

48. Mercogliano, *How to Grow a School,* 28.

49. Ernest Crosby, *Tolstoy as a Schoolmaster* (London: Simple Life Press, 1904), 8.

50. William Symonds, "Meet the Met: A School Success Story," *Business Week,* June 16, 2006.

51. David Colfax and Micki Colfax, *Homeschooling for Excellence* (New York: Warner Books, 1988), 4–5.

52. Ibid., 97.

THREE: NO WORK AND NO PLAY

1. Maria Montessori, *The Absorbent Mind* (Madras: Kalakshetra Publications, 1967), 85.

2. Ibid., 93.

3. A. S. Neill, *Summerhill: A Radical Approach to Child Rearing* (New York: Hart Publishing, 1960), 59.

4. Ibid., 59–60.

5. Peter Stearns, *Anxious Parents: A History of Modern American Child Rearing* (New York: New York University Press, 2003), 127.

6. Ibid., 133–34.

7. Ibid., 128.

8. Ibid.

9. Ibid., 245.

10. William Wilson, *The City Beautiful Movement* (Baltimore: Johns Hopkins University Press, 1989), 82.

11. Jane Addams, *The Spirit of Youth and the City Streets* (New York: Macmillan, 1918), 14–15.

12. Ibid., 107.

13. Wilson, *The City Beautiful Movement*, 82.

14. Ibid., 91.

15. Dom Cavallo, "Social Reform and the Movement to Organize Children's Play during the Progressive Era," *History of Childhood Quarterly* 3, no. 4 (1976): 509–22.

16. Richard Kraus, *Recreation and Leisure in Modern Society* (Santa Monica, CA: Goodyear, 1978), 182.

17. Stearns, *Anxious Parents*, 2.

18. Ibid., 97.

19. Brian Sutton-Smith, *Toys as Culture* (New York: Gardner Press, 1986), 246.

20. Stearns, *Anxious Parents*, 206.

21. Committee on the Health and Safety Implications of Child Labor, National Research Council and Institute of Medicine, *Protecting Youth at Work: Health, Safety and Development of Working Children and Adolescents in the United States* (Washington, DC: National Academies Press, 1998), 3.

22. Ibid.

23. Ibid., 2.

24. Stephen Hamilton, *The Future of Youth and Work* (New York: Free Press, 1990), 3.

25. Cindy Rodriguez, "Teens with Wads of Cash Flex Spending Muscle," *Boston Globe*, February 20, 2002.

26. Ibid., xvii.

27. Ibid., xi.

28. Ibid., 297.

29. Ibid., 149.

30. Ibid., 158.

FOUR: REAL PLAY

1. Edward Deci and Richard Ryan, *Intrinsic Motivation and Self-Determination in Human Behavior* (New York: Plenum, 1985), 122.

2. Richard Evans, *Jean Piaget: The Man and His Ideas* (New York: Dutton, 1973), 101–28.

3. Margaret Boden, *Jean Piaget* (New York: Viking Press, 1979), 9–12.

4. Jean Piaget, *Play, Dreams and Imitation in Childhood* (New York: Norton, 1951), 90.

5. Ibid., 156.

6. Brian Sutton-Smith, "Piaget on Play: A Critique," *Psychological Review* 73, no. 1 (1966): 104–10.

7. Piaget, *Play, Dreams and Imitation in Childhood*, 149.

8. Ibid.

9. Ibid., 154.

10. Ibid., 148.

11. Ibid., 171.

12. Dorothy Singer and Jerome Singer, *The House of Make-Believe: Children's Play and the Developing Imagination* (Cambridge, MA: Harvard University Press, 1990), 199–200.

13. Ibid., 200–201.

14. Wendy Grolnick, *The Psychology of Parental Control: How Well-Meant Parenting Backfires* (Mahwah, NJ: Lawrence E. Erlbaum Associates, 2003), 57.

15. Shlomo Ariel, *Children's Imaginative Play: A Visit to Wonderland* (Westport, CT: Praeger Publishing, 2002), 7.

16. Ibid., 33–34.

17. Ibid., 44–52.

18. Singer and Singer, *The House of Make-Believe*, 69.

19. Ariel, *Children's Imaginative Play*, 55.

20. Stephen Davis and John Fantuzzo, "The Effects of Adult and Peer Social Initiations on the Social Behavior of Withdrawn and Aggressive Maltreated Preschool Children," *Journal of Family Violence* 4, no. 3 (September 1989): 227–48. Also John Fantuzzo et al., "Peer Mediated Treatment of Socially Withdrawn Maltreated Preschool Children: Cultivating Natural Community Resources," *Journal of Clinical Child and Adolescent Psychology* 34, no. 2 (2005): 320–25.

21. Johann Huizinga, *Homo Ludens* (London: Routledge, 1949), 46–210.

22. Edith Cobb, *The Ecology of Imagination in Childhood* (New York: Columbia University Press, 1977), 27.

23. Ibid.

24. Ibid., 109.

25. Ibid., 15.

26. Ibid., 111.

27. Teresa Amabile, *Creativity in Context* (Boulder, CO: Westview Press, 1996), 90.

28. Ibid., 7–8.

29. In P. Schilpp, *Albert Einstein: Philosopher-Scientist* (Evanston, IL: Library of Living Philosophers, 1949), 18–19.

30. Beth Hennessey and Teresa Amabile, *Creativity and Learning* (Washington, DC: National Education Association, 1987), 5.

31. Amabile, *Creativity in Context*, 35–38.

32. Ibid., 110.

33. Ibid., 95–96.

34. Hennessey and Amabile, *Creativity and Learning*, 10–11.

35. Ibid., 12–14.

36. Ibid., 22–23.

37. Ibid., 26.

38. Johann Huizinga, *Homo Ludens* (London: Routledge, 1949), 206.

39. Sheila Flaxman, "Play: An Endangered Species," *Education Week*, February 16, 2000.

40. In Mark Gerzon, *A Childhood for Every Child: The Politics of Parenthood* (New York: Outerbridge and Lazard, 1973), 125.

41. Brian Sutton-Smith, *Toys as Culture* (New York: Gardner Press, 1986). Roland Barthes, *Mythologies* (New York: Wang and Hill, 1972), 54–55.

42. UNESCO, "The Child and Play" (Paris, 1980), 11.

43. Mary Ann Pulaski, "Toys and Imaginative Play," in Jerome Singer, ed., *The Child's World of Make-Believe* (New York: Academic Press, 1973), 74–103.

44. Singer and Singer, *The House of Make-Believe*, 85.

45. Sutton-Smith, *Toys as Culture*, 244.

46. Ibid., 246–53.

47. Ibid., 252.

48. Ibid., 75.

49. Grolnick, *The Psychology of Parental Control*, 142.

50. Ibid., 37.

51. Huizinga, *Homo Ludens*, 206.

52. Ibid., 8.

53. Ibid., 211.

54. Brian Sutton-Smith, *A History of Children's Play* (Philadelphia: University of Pennsylvania Press, 1981), 293.

55. Ibid., 296.

56. Ibid., 288.

FIVE: THE WILDNESS WITHIN

1. Henry David Thoreau, *Journal* (Princeton, NJ: Princeton University Press, 1981), August 30, 1856.

2. Wilhelm Reich, *Children of the Future* (New York: Farrar, Straus, Giroux, 1983), 7.

3. Eric Warmington and Philip Rouse, ed., *Great Dialogues of Plato* (New York: New American Library, 1956), 415–22.

4. Ibid., 445.

5. Rollo May, *The Cry for Myth* (New York: Norton, 1991), 17.

6. Ibid., 124–27.

7. James Hillman, *The Soul's Code* (New York: Random House, 1996), 39.

8. Ibid., 83.

9. Benedetto Vitiello et al., "National Estimates of Antidepressant Medication Use among U.S. Children, 1997–2002," *Journal of the American Academy of Child and Adolescent Psychiatry* 45, no. 3 (March 2006): 271–79.

10. Thomas Delate et al., "Trends in the Use of Antidepressants in a National Sample of Commercially Insured Pediatric Patients, 1998 to 2002," *Psychiatric Services,* no. 55 (April 2004): 387–91.

SIX: THE IMPORTANCE OF SOLITUDE

1. Terry Tempest Williams, *Red* (New York: Pantheon Books, 2001), 6.

2. Ibid., 17.

3. John Gatto, *Dumbing Us Down: The Hidden Curriculum of Compulsory Schooling* (Philadelphia: New Society Publishers, 1992), 29.

4. Michael Shapiro, "Against the Current: Barry Lopez on Writing about Nature and the Nature of Writing," *The Sun,* no. 366 (June 2006): 9.

5. Annie Dillard, *An American Childhood* (New York: Harper and Row, 1987), 148–49.

6. Edward Teale, *The Thoughts of Thoreau* (New York: Dodd, Mead, 1962), 133.

7. Henry David Thoreau, *Walden; or, Life in the Woods* (Mount Vernon, NY: Peter Pauper Press, 1967), 89.

8. Ibid., viii.

9. Ron Miller, *What Are Schools For?*(Brandon, VT: Holistic Education Press, 1997), 88.

10. Teale, *The Thoughts of Thoreau,* 239.

11. Richard Lebeaux, *Young Man Thoreau* (Amherst, MA: University of Massachusetts Press, 1977), 109–10.

12. Gary Paul Nabhan and Stephen Trimble, *The Geography of Childhood: Why Children Need Wild Places* (Boston: Beacon Press, 1994), 113.

13. Ibid., 88.

14. Ibid., 89–91.

15. Ibid., 23.

16. Ibid., 12.

17. David Quammen, *Wild Thoughts from Wild Places* (New York: Scribner, 1998), 102–3.

18. Ibid., 108.

SEVEN: CHILDHOOD LOST

1. Miller McPherson, Lynn Smith-Lovin, and Matthew Brashears, "Social Isolation in America: Changes in Core Discussion Networks over Two Decades," *American Sociological Review* (June 2006).

2. The Crimes against Children Research Center, "Online Victimization: A Report on the Nation's Youth" (June 2000), www.unh.edu/ccrc/pdf/Victimization_Online_Survey.pdf.

3. Marshall McLuhan, *Understanding Media: The Extensions of Man* (Cambridge, MA: MIT Press, 1994), 7–17.

4. Neil Postman, *The Disappearance of Childhood* (New York: Delacorte Press, 1982), 77.

5. Ibid., 28–95.

6. Ibid., 97.

7. Emory Woodard, "Media in the Home 2000" (University of Pennsylvania, Annenberg Public Policy Report, 2000).

8. Donald Roberts, "Media and Youth: Access, Exposure, and Privatization," special issue, *Journal of Adolescent Health* (2000, 27): 8–14.

9. Frank Bocca, "New Media Technology and Youth: Trends in the Evolution of New Media," special issue, *Journal of Adolescent Health* (2000, 27): 22–29.

10. Woodard, "Media in the Home 2000."

11. Victor Strasburger and Edward Donnerstein, "Children, Adolescents, and the Media: Issues and Solutions," *Pediatrics* 103, no. 1 (January 1999): 29–39.

12. Susan Villani, "Impact of Media on Children and Adolescents: A 10-Year Review of the Research," *Journal of Child and Adolescent Psychiatry* 40, no. 4 (April 2001): 392–401.

13. Strasburger and Donnerstein, "Children, Adolescents, and the Media."

14. Villani, "Impact of Media on Children and Adolescents."

15. Strasburger and Donnerstein, "Children, Adolescents, and the Media."

16. Rebecca Collins et al., "Watching Sex on Television Predicts Adolescent Initiation of Sexual Behavior," *Pediatrics* 114, no. 3 (September 2004): 280–89.

17. Strasburger and Donnerstein, "Children, Adolescents, and the Media."

18. Committee on Communications, "Children, Adolescents, and Advertising," *Pediatrics* 95, no. 2 (February 1995): 295–97.

19. Susan Linn, *Consuming Kids: The Hostile Takeover of Childhood* (New York: New Press, 2004), 1.

20. Ibid., 158.

21. Ibid., 127–29.

22. Ibid., 127.

23. Nicholas Carnagey et al., "The Effect of Video Game Violence on Physiological Desensitization to Real-Life Violence," *Journal of Experimental Social Psychology* (March 2006).

24. Villani, "Impact of Media on Children and Adolescents."

25. Craig Anderson, "An Update on the Effects of Playing Violent Video Games," *Journal of Adolescence* 27 (October 2003): 113–22.

26. Eric Uhlman and Jane Swanson, "Exposure to Violent Video Games Increases Automatic Aggressiveness," *Journal of Adolescence* 27 (October 2003): 41–52.

27. Carnagey et al., "The Effect of Video Game Violence."

28. Deborah Johnson, "Raise Parents' Awareness of Risks, Benefits of Cyberspace," *AAP News* (February 2003): 61–68.

29. Frank Duffy, "Dyslexia: Regional Differences in Brain Electrical Activity by Topographic Mapping," *Annals of Neurology* 7 (1980).

30. Martin Pawley, *The Private Future* (London: Thames and Hudson, 1973).

31. From an interview with Joseph Chilton Pearce in the *Journal of Family Life*, vol. 5, no. 1:37.

32. Woodburn Heron et al., "Visual Disturbances after Prolonged Perceptual Isolation," *Canadian Journal of Psychology* 10 (1956): 13.

33. Magdalena Vernon, *Perception through Experience* (London: Methuen and Company, 1970), 116.

34. Tracy McVeigh, "Computer Games Stunt Teen Brains," *London Observer*, August 19, 2001.

EIGHT: ADULTHOOD ARRESTED

1. Stephen Mintz, *Huck's Raft: A History of American Childhood* (Cambridge, MA: Harvard University Press, 2004), 132.

2. Ibid., 187.

3. G. Stanley Hall, *Adolescence* (New York: Appleton, 1905), 407.

4. Ibid., 328.

5. Ibid., 333–34.

6. Ibid., 339.

7. Ibid., 342.

8. Ibid., 339.

9. Mintz, *Huck's Raft*, 187.

10. Ibid., 50.

11. Ibid., vii.

12. Ibid., 75.

13. Eda LeShan, *The Conspiracy against Childhood* (New York: Atheneum, 1968), 336–37.

14. Ibid., 340.

15. Randolph Bourne, *Youth and Life* (Boston: Houghton Mifflin, 1911), 233–34.

16. Ibid., 286–87.

17. Ibid., 256.

18. Robert Kegan, *In Over Our Heads: The Mental Demands of Modern Life* (Cambridge, MA: Harvard University Press 1994), 42.

19. Richard Settersten Jr., Frank Furstenberg Jr., and Rubin Rumbaud, *On the Frontier of Adulthood: Theory, Research, and Public Policy* (Chicago: University of Chicago Press, 2005), 5.

20. Ibid., 225.

21. James Côté, *Arrested Adulthood* (New York: New York University Press, 2000), 36.

22. Settersten, Furstenberg, and Rumbaud, *On the Frontier of Adulthood*, 230–31.

23. Jeremy Rifkin, *The Age of Access* (New York: Tarcher/Putnam, 2000), 4–10.

24. Ibid., 5–6.

25. Ibid., 180.

26. Alexandra Robbins and Abby Wilner, *Quarterlife Crisis: The Unique Challenges of Life in Your Twenties* (New York: Tarcher/Putnam, 2001), 3–4.

27. Ibid., 4.

28. Ibid., 6.

29. David Riesman, *The Lonely Crowd* (New Haven, CT: Yale University Press, 1950), 373.

30. Sir Herbert Read, ed., *The Collected Works of C. G. Jung*, vol. 6 (London: Routledge & Keegan Paul), 448–50.

31. Ibid.

32. Riesman, *The Lonely Crowd*, 1–69.

33. Ibid., 192.

34. Ibid., 302.

35. Erik Erikson, *Identity: Youth and Crisis* (New York: Norton, 1968), 157.

36. From a conversation with the author, November 1994.

37. Erikson, *Identity*, 91–135.

38. Ibid., 132.

39. Jeffrey Arnett, *Emerging Adulthood* (Oxford: Oxford University Press, 2004), 8.

40. Côté, *Arrested Adulthood*, 179.

41. Anton Allahar and James Côté, *Richer and Poorer: The Structure of Social Inequality in Canada* (Toronto: Lorimer Press, 1998), 107–10.

42. Seth Schwartz et al., "Identity and Agency in Emerging Adulthood," *Youth and Society* 37, no. 2 (2005): 201–29.

NINE: SAVING INNER WILDNESS

1. In 1940 56 percent of American births occurred inside the hospital, a figure that rose to over 99 percent in 1999 (*National Vital Statistics Report*, Centers for Disease Control, November 23, 2004), p. 6.

2. See www.consensus.nih.gov/2006/cesareanprogramabstractcomplete .pdf.

3. Jonathan Kozol, *The Shame of the Nation* (New York: Crown Publishing, 2005), 8–20.

4. Eda LeShan, *The Conspiracy against Childhood* (New York: Atheneum, 1968), 346–47.

5. Rollo May, *The Cry for Myth* (New York: Norton, 1991), 30.

6. Ibid., 26.

7. Gilbert Highet, *The Classical Tradition: Greek and Roman Influences on Western Literature* (Oxford: Oxford University Press, 1965), 540.

8. Friedrich Nietzsche, *The Birth of Tragedy and the Genealogy of Morals* (New York: Doubleday, 1990), 135.

9. May, *The Cry for Myth*, 16.

10. Bruno Bettelheim, *The Uses of Enchantment: The Meaning and Importance of Fairy Tales* (New York: Knopf, 1976), 5.

11. Ibid., 6.

12. Ibid., 6–7.

13. Ibid., 66–79.

14. Jim Trelease, *The Read-Aloud Handbook* (New York: Penguin, 2001).

15. David Riesman, *The Lonely Crowd* (New Haven, CT: Yale University Press, 1950), 99.

16. Chellis Glendinning, *My Name Is Chellis and I'm in Recovery from Western Civilization* (Boston: Shambhala Publications, 1994), 179.

17. Richard Louv, *Last Child in the Woods* (Chapel Hill, NC: Algonquin Books), 99–101.

18. Glendinning, *My Name Is Chellis,* 185.

19. Victor Strasburger and Edward Donnerstein, "Children, Adolescents, and the Media: Issues and Solutions," *Pediatrics,* January 1999, 102–55.

20. Sara Bennett and Nancy Kalish, *The Case against Homework* (New York: Crown Publishers, 2006), 224–27.

21. Wendy Grolnick, *The Psychology of Parental Control: How Well-Meant Parenting Backfires* (Mahwah, NJ: Lawrence E. Erlbaum Associates, 2003), 133.

22. Stephen Hamilton, *Apprenticeship for Adulthood* (New York: Free Press, 1990), 121.

23. Ibid., 4.

24. Stephen Hamilton, *The Interaction of Family, Community, and Work in the Socialization of Youth* (New York: William T. Grant Foundation Commission, 1988), 33.

25. Hamilton, *Apprenticeship for Adulthood,* 4.

26. Ibid., 17.

27. Go to www.doleta.gov/OA/bat.cfm.

28. Yehuda Fine, *The Real Deal: For Parents Only—the Top 75 Questions Teens Want Answered Today* (Bloomington, IN: Unlimited Publishing), 5.

INDEX

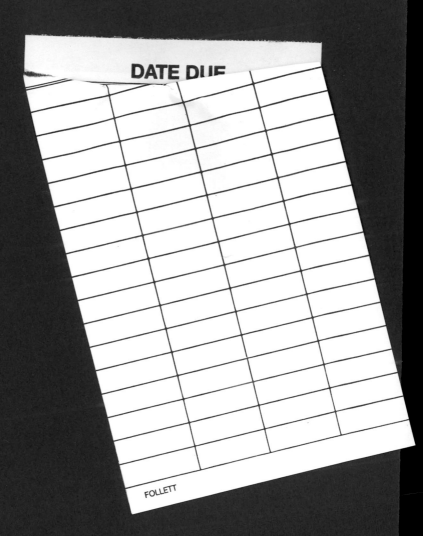

DATE DUE

FOLLETT